THE RISE AND DECLINE OF THE ASIAN CENTURY

To all the women of my life,
but most especially
to the loving memory of my mother
and
to my favourite sister,

Sandy...

(And to an esteemed but anonymous friend
whose wisdom guided this work from afar.)

The Rise and Decline of the Asian Century

False Starts on the Path to the Global Millennium

CHRISTOPHER LINGLE
Visiting Associate Professor of Economics
Weatherhead School of Management
Case Western Reserve University

Routledge
Taylor & Francis Group

LONDON AND NEW YORK

First published 1997 by Sirocco Publishing

Reissued 2018 by Routledge
2 Park Square, Milton Park, Abingdon, Oxon, OX14 4RN
711 Third Avenue, New York, NY 10017, USA

Routledge is an imprint of the Taylor & Francis Group, an informa business

Publisher's Note
The publisher has gone to great lengths to ensure the quality of this reprint but points out that some imperfections in the original copies may be apparent.

Disclaimer
The publisher has made every effort to trace copyright holders and welcomes correspondence from those they have been unable to contact.

A Library of Congress record exists under LC control number: 98168429

ISBN 13: 978-1-138-36021-1 (hbk)
ISBN 13: 978-0-429-43324-5 (ebk)

Contents

Acknowledgments

Many people had a hand in whatever might be good about this book. However, they are not responsible in any way for remaining errors or oversights. For the remaining detritus or hubris, *mea culpa*.

I am grateful to my former colleagues in the Department of Economics of Emory University for their support during my appointment as Visiting Scholar from 1995-96. In particular, I would like to thank Paul Rubin and Peter Aranson for their generous assistance.

Similarly, my colleagues at Case Western Reserve University served willingly as sounding boards for the views expressed here. I owe special thanks to Bill Peirce for his role in my invitation to serve as Visiting Associate Professor of Economics in the Weatherhead School of Management. Bob Baird graciously accepted the thankless task of reading over an early draft that required the use of gallons of red ink.

Troy and Harry Beecham also provided valuable insights and encouragement during early drafts of the manuscript.

Of those who aided me, Teresa Wyszomierski was no doubt the heaviest lifter in bringing these words to print. She spent endless hours poring over different drafts, revising revisions, clarifying unclear thoughts, unblocking my writer's block, and suggesting changes in structure and content. She deserves credit and my deepest thanks for going above and beyond the duty of a friend.

Preface

Throughout my career, I have been interested in the interplay between economics and politics. To this end, I became a keen student of numerous economic and political institutions during my tenure at universities in different parts of the world. Having left the United States in 1978 for a one-year stint abroad, I was drawn to exotic environs while I continued my investigations. Instead of taking a temporary sojourn, I became an international nomad and expatriate.

I found myself sharing experiences with people whose basic institutions were undergoing dramatic changes. For example, I was in Turkey during and after martial law; in Italy during the terror of the Red Brigade; in England during the 'Winter of Discontent' that led to the 'Thatcher Revolution;' in Post-Franco Spain as it first stumbled and then fully embraced democracy; in Poland when the Solidarity movement had just begun; in South Africa as apartheid began to crumble; in China during the first student protests that led to the Tiananmen Square demonstrations; and in Europe when the Iron Curtain was lifted and the Berlin Wall dismantled. All these experiences had a definite impact on the ideas expressed in this book. (Despite the fortuitous timing of my comings and goings, I accept neither credit nor blame for any of those events!)

My efforts here reflect an attempt to put order in the place of what appears to be chaos amidst East Asia's rapid dash toward economic development. Many will think it a fool's errand to search for general observations about this vast and diverse region. In large part, I undertook this formidable task in response to the encouragement of the many people who were intrigued by my contrary and counter-intuitive views on East Asia's economies.

Although much has been written about the East Asian economies, there are many gaps in the interpretation of their past and future. One neglected area is the importance of the role played by institutions and institutional change on the dynamics of economic growth and development. In hopes of correcting this deficiency, this book seeks to identify and examine those institutions that have had and will have an impact upon economic activities in East Asia.

An important message that I wish to convey to the Asian context is the applicability of one of the most significant lessons of modern economics. That is, international trade is not a negative-sum game as portrayed by some populists who assert that countries will incur losses from liberalized trade that exceed the benefits to their respective communities. Nor is trade a zero-sum game whereby gains to some are offset by the losses experienced by others, as has been intimated by Lester Thurow. The successes of the emerging East Asian economies will *not* cause net losses for mature economies. Granted there will be some losers on the micro level; but on balance the standard of living of most workers and consumers will improve with the expansion of international trade in all affected countries.

It is widely recognized that growth in East Asia arose from the 'marketization' of the region's economies. Those countries that have enjoyed material gain have done so by deregulating their economies or by eliminating central planning. These steps are essentially an adaptation of many of the successful institutions of the mature Western economies.

This being the case, the persistence of high-paced growth in East Asia's 'miracle' economies will depend upon the degree to which institutional innovation and evolution continue in the region. Indeed, all the East Asian countries will face rapidly changing challenges that will require equally rapid and flexible institutional responses.

The emergent worldwide economic order discussed here is in the context of an impending 'Global Millennium.' This new order of expanding international trade relations has been facilitated by the confluence of increased capital mobility and access to information. Economic success in this coming era will require further separation between economic and political spheres, greater tolerance of institutional innovation, and increased transparency and accountability of existing economic and political structures. These conditions are as important for the mature Western economies as they are for developing economies, in Asia or elsewhere.

In particular, governments are the most static of those institutions that impact on our lives. If we are to succeed in achieving our respective life purposes, institutions of government must become more fluid and less intrusive.

The idea of an 'Asian Century' is a seductive myth based upon simplistic reasoning and misleading extrapolations of past performance. Unfortunately, the inherent conservatism and inflexibility of East Asia's economic and political institutions will interfere with processes necessary for sustaining the high growth rates that might have led to the region's global dominance.

1 Introduction: Getting lost along the 'Asian way'?

Just when it seemed safe to go into the bookstore, yet another book about the Asian-Pacific economies stares you in the face. Indeed, the indisputably brisk pace of economic development in Asia has spawned a veritable growth industry for publishers and authors. However, this book promises to offer a decidedly different viewpoint that challenges the orthodoxy about developments in that region. This may seem to be a preposterous claim in light of the recent record of high-powered growth in most of the economies of East Asia.[1] However, there are reasons to believe that long-run trends may reverse the fortunes of these ostensible economic powerhouses.

Beginning in the early 1990s, the flood of references to an impending 'Asian Century' has prompted various responses. On the one hand, a mountain of statistical and anecdotal evidence has been offered to support the popular notion of steadily rising fortunes in East Asia. (Comparative statistics of real GDP growth for East Asian economies and some of the Western industrialized economies appears in Table 1.1 and is discussed in the next chapter.) On the other hand, an equally voluminous number of publications has heralded the demise and imminent collapse of the economies and the culture of the West. With little protest and perhaps even less introspection about these claims, a new refrain has proclaimed the end of the 'American Century' and its replacement by the 'Asian Century.'

Basic statistical analysis indicates that as a gauge of future trends, undue emphasis has probably been placed on East Asia's relatively recent economic gains. Indeed, predictions of an 'Asian Century,' along with all its associated threats and opportunities for the rest of the world, simply may not come true. In the first instance, it is implausible that East Asia could, over such a brief span of time, develop the requisite combination of military, moral, political, and economic wherewithal necessary for global leadership. On the one hand, there is a supposition that mutual economic interests will keep the region pacified. Unfortunately, this assumption ignores the cultural diversities and ethnic divisions that have contributed to historical mistrust among neighbors in the region. On the other hand, the economic logic behind the presumption of an 'Asian Century' is highly contentious.

Table 1.1
Real GDP growth

Per cent change; data are annual averages

	1950-59	1960-69	1970-79	1980-89	1990-95
OECD average	..	5.2	0.9	5.8	1.9
United States	4.0	4.3	3.2	2.7	1.8
Germany	..	4.4	3.1	1.8	2.5
UK	2.6	3.2	2.4	2.4	1.0
China	..	..	..	9.3	10.2
Hong Kong	..	..	9.2	7.3	5.1
Korea	4.3	7.6	9.6	7.8	7.8
Indonesia	..	3.0	7.6	5.7	7.1
Japan	..	10.1	5.2	3.8	2.1
Malaysia	..	..	8.1	5.7	8.9
Philippines	7.1	4.8	6.1	1.9	2.3
Singapore	..	8.9	11.1	7.4	8.6
Taiwan	..	..	9.8	8.1	6.4
Thailand	4.7	8.3	7.3	7.0	8.9

Source: International Monetary Fund (and selected national statistical services)

While it may be difficult to avoid encountering a new book on the emerging economies of Asia, it is virtually impossible to find one that is anything other than optimistic.[2] Indeed, it might be an understatement to say that optimism about the prospects for Asian economies has been infectious. On the one hand, there is the breathlessly bullish sketch in the well-worn 'megatrend' format of John Naisbitt.[3] On the other hand, there is the reasoned and informed optimism of Jim Rohwer.[4] The Naisbitt book is suitable for beginners and maybe undergraduates, while the elegant writing style and depth of knowledge exhibited in the Rohwer book commend it to a more learned audience. In between, numerous other volumes follow the overall theme of the relentless advance of the economies of Asia.[5]

In fairness, most authors who speak to this issue do identify some possible shortcomings. However, it is often almost as an afterthought, or to provide an impression of balance. To date, no other book has offered a systematic challenge to the conventional wisdom of an ascendant 'Asian Century.' It should be noted, however, that while this book will point out many of the problems associated with the region's political or economic institutions, there is no claim that these maladies are unique to East Asia. Corruption, authoritarian regimes, political nepotism, inefficiency, and the disregard for the environment can be found in all parts of the world. However, there are some unique combinations of these problems in East Asia that should not be obscured by overly-optimistic projections of economic opportunities there.

There are several pertinent reasons for promoting an integrated set of counterarguments to the rosy scenario of continued, progressive economic development in Asia. Trained economists instinctively seek to test the propositions and conclusions of other observers against their own reasoning faculties. Alarm bells should immediately go off whenever forecasts are based upon casual empiricism or crude extrapolations from the recent remarkable record for much of the region. Equally troubling is the implicit blind faith that suggests that asset prices in the region (e.g., real estate values and commercial rents) can go up forever. It should not be forgotten that the inexorable and frenzied price rises for land in Tokyo during the 1980s eventually collapsed like speculative bubbles elsewhere. Similarly, stock markets in East Asia have exhibited a considerable amount of volatility that should generate serious questions about their integrity and their long-term viability.

Yet the goal of this questioning process must provide something of merit beyond the formal, intellectual exchange. Discussion of the recent and future development of East Asian economies can surely be enriched with a bit of cool water being sprinkled onto some of the overheated rhetoric. However, the consensus is so heavily weighted in favor of the optimists that many other observers might err against their better judgment. Granted, the optimists do acknowledge the existence of some uncertainties and problems with investments or other operations in the region. Yet none offer a comprehensive accounting of these issues, and therefore there is an incomplete evaluation of the risk factors inherent in the region. It may be true that high rates of return are often available under situations where there are great risks. Unfortunately, the popular perception of sustainable, robust economic growth in East Asia has resulted in a distorted picture of the risk/return profile.

A more sober reckoning of prospects for investments and commercial operations in Asia can do no harm. If the critical assessment offered here is overstated, it will be swept away in the advancing tide of Asia's economies. However, if such a pause in the frenetic pace is warranted, it might lead to fewer losses in the search for what has come to be portrayed as almost a 'sure thing.' For my own part, I would advise my pension fund managers, and the corporations in which they invest, to be a bit more cautious in committing my retirement money in East Asia's emerging markets.

Interestingly, the most seductive arguments supporting the optimistic expectations for East Asia's development raise thorny issues relating to the presumed capacity of these economies to sustain recent growth rates. In this con-

3

nection, it is certainly worth pondering the volatility of the emergent economies of China, India, Indonesia, Malaysia, and the Philippines or even Burma-Myanmar, Cambodia, Laos, and Vietnam. Similarly, there are intriguing questions worth exploring about the likely path of those Asian countries that are further along in their economic life cycle, such as Hong Kong, Japan, Singapore, South Korea, and Taiwan.

The unbridled optimism behind the projections for East Asia may be the result of a misplaced emphasis on observations over a limited and recent period of time. Admittedly, some economies in the region have achieved rapid economic growth with a reasonably even distribution of income for three decades or more. However, it is possible to cite numerous instances in history where institutional arrangements with fundamentally fatal flaws produced extended periods of favorable results. For example, the Spanish economy under Generalissimo Franco recorded some of the highest growth rates in the world during the 1950s and 1960s. Similarly, the economies of South African apartheid and Soviet communism generated high growth rates until their inherent weaknesses hastened their demise. Even the North Korean economy has 'worked' over the past several decades.

At the same time, the pessimistic interpretation of Asia's recent past and economic prospects can be the source of considerable skepticism on its own. In any event, a strong economic record does not guarantee that any single country or region can provide political or moral leadership. Furthermore, it does not necessarily follow that a locally successful economic model can serve as a universally applicable paradigm for prosperity.

An effective critique of the economic arguments behind the 'Asian Century' must address the disturbing aspects of the 'growth without grace' occurring in parts of Asia. Booming growth does not insure widely shared improvements in living standards or the quality of life. Uneven economic development can create or exacerbate disparities in regional income distribution that may strain the social fabric. Other negative side effects of high-paced economic growth have been apparent in much of the region. Corruption, rising costs, crowding, and pollution all have the potential for derailing the 'Asian Century,' either individually or collectively.[6]

Even the most casual visitor to most parts of this booming region will find disturbing evidence of the heavy environmental costs that are often associated with high rates of economic growth. However, this story is a bit more complicated and will be thoroughly analyzed later. In addition, strains upon inadequate infrastructure in congested urban areas threaten to become a nightmare as promises for improvement have borne little fruit. Progress to date on many of the much-needed infrastructural projects has been painfully slow because many ventures have yet to break ground, while those underway are quickly becoming obsolete. Corruption and rising crime are reaching epidemic pro-

4

portions, partly because of the moral void created by authoritarian and social-ist regimes. Fortunately, these vices are more susceptible to exposure and cor-rection, due to the increased transparency associated with democratic reforms in some countries like Japan and Korea. There are also numerous sources of regional instability stemming from conflicting claims over the sovereignty of offshore islands and some disputed borders. As manifestations of internecine rivalry and nationalism, these disputes are no less threatening than former clashes of ideology that have mostly been put to rest with the retreat of com-munism from the region.

If the fulcrum of global affairs is to shift from the West to the East, there must be forces at work that go beyond what may prove to be little more than a momentary spate of economic dynamism. The phenomenon that is expected to move the center of economic gravity eastward is 'Asian values.' That it is im-possible to identify a consistent set of 'Asian values' is but one aspect of the implausibility that Asia will coalesce into a homogeneous region to lead the rest of the world. Obviously, countries within certain sub-regions may share cultures and underlying values, and there are overlappings from religious or ethnic migration. Nonetheless, East Asian cultural traditions are considerably different from those in Central and South Asia. Whatever its role in the un-clear development of the 'Asian Century,' cultural diversity ranks high among the many factors that ultimately place a limit upon prospects for Asian Pacific economic superiority.

The critical issue is whether or not the institutions underlying these impres-sive economic results provide a permanent basis for growth that can survive business cycles and external shocks. For all the flaws of Western capitalism, the resilience, adaptability, and durability of its supporting institutions have allowed it to withstand the test of time, as well as the ideological assaults ar-rayed against it for several centuries. There are compelling reasons to believe that the institutions that are credited with the rise of East Asia lack the flexi-bility and stamina necessary to weather storms brewed by a global economy that will be connected electronically and driven by intensive competition.

Several venerable Asian institutions share the dubious distinction of exert-ing pressures that might stifle the driving forces of economic development. Like a number of their Latin American counterparts, many East Asian econo-mies are characterized by some fairly typical institutionalized seeds of de-struction, e.g., corruption and crony capitalism. However, many Asian econo-mies are uniquely distinguished by an institutional bias against individualism. Asian cultures that inculcate conformity at the expense of initiative restrain the enterprising spirit that underpins the innovative process necessary for sus-tained economic growth. Schumpeter's process of 'creative destruction,' whereby obsolete technologies are replaced by superior innovations, is

5

thwarted in East Asia due to the absence of several necessary layers of commercial and managerial activity.

Justified as an antidote against the spread of communism, authoritarianism became the dominant political arrangement in most of East Asia after World War II. In the post-Cold War world, freedom of thought and expression will be essential for encouraging the native entrepreneurial actions necessary for continued economic advance. Socially and politically oppressive actions taken by authoritarian regimes in East Asia are an anachronism, along with economic protectionism. The authoritarian approach, although effective in the past in terms of mobilizing and focusing productive inputs, will prove self-defeating in the new global economy.

In light of these innate weaknesses of the Asian 'miracle' economies, it is reasonable to challenge the assertion that the next century will be dominated by Asian influences.[7] It is also reasonable to question whether the rest of the world would be better off if it were to conform to so-called 'Asian values.'

Some clarifications and a few disclaimers might be in order here. In the first instance, although the arguments developed here are decidedly contrarian and bearish about the future, there is no intention to devalue the great benefits enjoyed by those Asians fortunate enough to participate in the recent bursts of economic growth. Neither is there a suggestion that an economic collapse in the region is imminent or unavoidable. Perhaps most importantly, the pointed criticisms offered here of the policies or traditions of the region must not be interpreted as being grounded in a presumption of cultural superiority. Indeed, much of the analysis offered here is based upon an assumption of the existence of universal values that are not the exclusive province of certain ethnic groups.

In sum, the case to be presented here will establish that it may be premature, or misguided and possibly dangerous, to accept that there will be a seismic shift in the locus of economic power to Asia. While an important World Bank report on East Asia concluded that good economic policies and prudent leadership lay behind the achievements of its 'miracle' economies,[8] the institutional arrangements of these countries are unlikely to foster a sustainable equilibrium. The overriding thesis presented here is that the cultural and political institutions associated with the East Asian economies will contribute to the unraveling of the promise of the 'Asian Century.'

Looking ahead to the Global Millennium

Whatever the values that might be said to constitute an 'Asian Model,' these will be subjected to the challenges and stresses of modernization. Winners in the post-industrial international economic order of the next millennium will be those countries where cultural and political institutions readily adapt to rapidly

6

changing conditions.[9] The essence of growth is change, and conservative regimes that doggedly fight to preserve the status quo will retard economic growth, thereby precluding improved living standards for their citizens. There are two basic schools of thought concerning the future interaction of cultures brought about by the internationalization of commerce. One camp views this interaction as an antagonistic clash of civilizations that will require the imposition of some form of cultural protectionism.[10] The alternative view advocates extensive freedom for cultural institutions to evolve, so that they can better serve people in response to changing social and economic demands. It is presumed here that the second course of action offers a better bet for securing long-term prosperity, even if it causes some short-term dislocations.

Therefore, it is inappropriate to lament the passing of an 'American Century' or to applaud the coming of an 'Asian Century.' What is unfolding is best described as a 'Global Millennium' that has begun in response to a steady momentum toward increased economic interdependence, and the development of a worldwide capital market. In turn, survival and success in the open and highly competitive Global Millennium will require flexible, efficient institutions and innovative, risk-taking entrepreneurs. Rigid authoritarian regimes in East Asia will therefore find it increasingly difficult to maintain their competitive advantage, or to continue their high pace of growth.

In this setting, only those regimes that promote and protect individual freedom by abstaining from collectivist repression will nurture the entrepreneurial spark essential for economic growth. Economic advance is impossible when the human spirit is imprisoned by rigid rules and inefficient institutions. True expressions of entrepreneurship can only be cultivated in an environment of extensive individual freedom. Because it fosters the intellectual development needed for invention, individual freedom is both a means and an important social end. Having said that, it is often argued that the rights of the individual should not be treated as absolute. But then neither should 'community welfare' be accorded supremacy, especially if its primary goal is to perpetuate the political status quo.

Present or past economic successes are not always reliable indicators of future performance. Despite the political concern attached to trade deficits between East Asian economies and some of the advanced industrialized economies of the West, most economists accept that different saving and consumption patterns allow such imbalances to be sustained over long periods of time. By themselves, trade surpluses do not merit praise, nor should trade deficits inspire damnation. Countries that experience deficits in their trade balances are not always harmed, nor are those that run surpluses necessarily blessed. Of more significant concern to long-term, global patterns of growth are 'intellectual deficits,' where ideas and innovations might only flow from West to East, as free-thinkers migrate from East to West.

7

Organization of the text

The first task is to examine how the notion of an emerging 'Asian Century' originated. To this end, Chapter One offers a brief historical account of the transition in thinking about the potential for economic growth in East Asia. These changes in perception can be traced to observers both within and without the Asia Pacific region. Interestingly, the surge in Asian self-confidence has been matched by a wave of Western self-deprecation and despair. However, one of the basic propositions of the thesis presented here is that the modernizing process will not be a zero-sum game, where gains by one group necessarily come at the expense of others.

In Chapter Two, issues relating to the imaging and conceptualization about Asia are discussed. Of notable interest in this regard are a variety East Asian institutional arrangements. For example, Asian variations on democracy and a set of uniquely 'Asian values' are often said to underlie the impressive economic growth record of the Asian 'miracle' economies. This chapter provides the background necessary for evaluating whether or not the performance of East Asian economies can be attributed to a distinctive model for development and, if a model does exist, if it might be exportable to other developing regions of the world.

Chapter Three raises questions concerning the alleged cause and effect relationships between East Asia's institutional structures and economic growth in the region. In the first instance, the notion of Asia as a homogeneous and monolithic unit is challenged. Second, it is suggested that the social, political and economic institutions that are said to have contributed to the region's growth do not provide a sound basis for the continuation of East Asia's record-breaking increases in output.

In the 1980s, any author writing about East Asia who wished to be taken seriously would devote at least one chapter to Japan. However, changing conditions in the 1990s now require that such attention be paid to China instead. And so it is that China is the focus of Chapter Five.

The next three chapters explore a paradox implicit in some Asian cultural and political institutions. Although these institutions may have contributed to short-run gains in East Asian economic growth, there are reasons to believe that they undermine long-run growth potential. Chapter Six weighs the economic and political costs against the presumed benefits of East Asian institutional arrangements. Chapter Seven looks at sources of geopolitical uncertainty that might disrupt the economic momentum of the region. Chapter Eight provides a counter-intuitive yet compelling argument concerning the environmental degradation so prevalent in the region. Contrary to the popular view of many environmentalists, the free market is not the cause of the problem. It appears that pollution arises instead from the collective nature of political and social institutions in East Asia. It is suggested that market-based policies can effectively address environmental concerns while allowing higher standards of living through economic growth.

In the end, the strongest challenge to the popular view of Asian-Pacific ascendancy in world affairs lies in real uncertainty about the region's economic future. Chapter Nine examines the genesis of this widespread euphoria about the region, and then explores specific problems with economic growth that should be anticipated. One pressing question concerns the consequences of East Asian 'miracle' economies adopting Japan's approach to development. If they follow suit, it is reasonable to ask at what point might these other economies experience the sort of extended recession that has wracked the Japanese economy for most of the 1990s.

Chapter Ten provides a recap of the problems that can be expected to arise from the economic policies and institutions common to East Asia. These are considered in the context of the emerging world economic order prompted by the globalization of capital markets and propelled by aggressive and pervasive competition.

In my youth, I found it important to stake out a position and defend it. Part of this compulsion was based upon a belief that I was privy to some 'truth' that ought to be pointed out to others. It is now clear to me that the important thing is not whether there is some right or wrong view, but that there needs to be open debate over important issues. It is from that understanding that I offer the views expressed in this book.

Notes

1   For the purposes of the discussion here, the list of countries in East Asia includes Brunei, Burma-Myanmar, Cambodia, China, Hong Kong, Indonesia, Japan, Laos, Malaysia, the Philippines, Singapore, South Korea, Taiwan, Thailand, and Vietnam.

2   As the book went to print, a critique appeared that shadows some of the issues discussed here. See, 'A Reality Check for Asia', *Business Week*, 2 December 1996.

3   *Megatrends Asia: The Eight Asian Megatrends that are Changing the World*, London: Nicholas Brealey, 1995.

4   *Asia Rising: Why America Will Prosper as Asia's Economies Boom*, New York: Simon & Schuster, 1995.

5   For example, J. Abegglen, *Sea Change: Pacific Asia as the New World Industrial Center*, New York: Free Press, 1994; M. Borthwick (et al.), *Pacific Century: The Emergence of Modern Pacific Asia*, Boulder: Westview Press, 1992; J. Fallows, *Looking at the Sun: The Rise of the*

New East Asian Economic and Political System, New York: Pantheon Books, 1994; E. Fingleton, *Blindside: Why Japan is Still on Track to Overtake the U.S. by the Year 2000,* Boston: Houghton Mifflin, 1995; F. Gibney, *The Pacific Century: America and Asia in a Changing World,* New York: C. Scribner's Sons, 1992; and S. Winchester, *Pacific Rising: The Emergence of a New World Culture,* New York: Prentice Hall, 1991.

6   In the annual survey by Hong Kong-based Political and Economic Risk Consultancy, Ltd. (PERC), 8 of 12 East Asian countries studied scored worse in 1996 than a year ago, while only 3 countries showed an improvement (India, Japan and Singapore). At the top of the corruption graph was China, followed by (in order) Vietnam, Indonesia, the Philippines, India, Thailand, Taiwan, South Korea, Malaysia, Hong Kong, Japan and Singapore.

7   Hong Kong, Singapore, South Korea, and Taiwan are often referred to as the 'four tigers.' Other emerging economies in the region that are joining the ranks of high growth economies include China, Indonesia, Malaysia, the Philippines, and Thailand.

8   *The East Asian Miracle: Economic Growth and Public Policy,* Oxford: Oxford University Press, 1993.

9   For a broad view on the economic analysis of institutions, see D. North, *Institutions, Institutional Change, and Economic Performance,* New York: Cambridge University Press, 1990.

10   Samuel Huntington expressed this thesis in 'The Clash of Civilizations?' *Foreign Affairs* (1993, Vol. 72, No. 3). His views have been expanded in a recent book, *The Clash of Civilizations and the Remaking of World Order,* New York: Simon & Schuster, 1996.

2 Making sense of the 'Asian Century'

Like any expansive catch-phrase, reference to a pending 'Asian Century' holds different meanings for different people. Some of this interpretive diversity is evident in selective references to an 'Asian Century,' an 'Asian-Pacific Century,' an 'Asian-Pacific Age,' a 'Pacific Century,' or a 'Pacific Era.' These allusions also oscillate between inclusive or exclusive definitions that focus upon some combination of geographic, economic, or strategic concerns. In the extreme, almost all of these are exclusive. Discussion is often limited to East Asia, and as such, often excludes Oceania (the Pacific Islands, Australia, and New Zealand), Siberian Russia, and North Korea. Similarly, although the references often include North America, the relevant countries of Latin America are often neglected.

This geographic focus is somewhat understandable because most of the interest in the region has been prompted by the recent impressive economic advances of a growing number of countries in East Asia. After being liberated from decades or centuries of economic repression and varying periods of stagnation, East Asian governments and their citizens appear captivated by a near-obsessive concern with the creation of wealth. In turn, foreign merchandisers have focused their attention on the industrialized and newly industrializing economies of the region because rising living standards in the region hold the promise of hundreds of millions of new middle-class consumers. At the same time, economic nationalism like Malaysia's *Bumiputra* policy and Indonesia's *Pribumi* policy has been coincidental with rapid gains in national income.[1] Further stoking the excitement is the high degree of heterogeneity of East Asian economies, as well as diverse endowments of natural resources, that are expected to allow exceptional opportunities for complementary production within the region. This prospect is already being realized through the ongoing expansion of intra-regional trade linkages and capital flows. For the most part, a sense of euphoria has accompanied the 'marketization' of the region's formerly socialist economies of the region, and has been heightened by signs of commitment to expanded regional cooperation.

All of this promise seemed reasonable because many of the mature, industrialized economies of the West were experiencing a slowdown, while the high-performing Asian economies were surging ahead. This forward momentum allowed East Asian economies either to cast off their lesser developed status, or to experience the initial stages of economic takeoff. As a group, these high-growth economies (China, Hong Kong, Indonesia, Japan, Malaysia, Singapore, South Korea, Taiwan, and Thailand) recorded an average of 5.5 percent per capita income growth during the period 1960 to 1990. This was about double the rate of growth of the mature high-income industrialized economies of the West (see Table 1.1). Meanwhile, developing economies elsewhere in the world were lagging behind, with 70 percent of them growing at a rate below the average of the industrialized economies. As a result, many observers predict that, first, the Japanese, and then the Chinese, economies will surpass the US early in the next century.

Pure commercial interests are not the only aspects associated with the 'Asian Century.' On the one hand, the notion of an institutionalized Pacific Basin Community derives from the organizational membership open to those countries that lie along the Pacific shores. For example, the Asian-Pacific Economic Cooperation forum (APEC) includes North American Free Trade Agreement (NAFTA) partners, the Association of Southeast Asian Nations (ASEAN), as well as some South American and East Asian countries that border the Pacific.[2] A less inclusive grouping is the East Asian Economic Caucus (EAEC), that seems to have been designed to limit American hegemony over the region. On the other hand, the notions of the 'Pacific Basin' or the 'Pacific Rim' or the 'Asian-Pacific' provide a purely geographic description of the region. In still other arrangements, strategic political concerns overlap, and are perhaps inseparable from, economic interests as in the case of the ASEAN Regional Forum (ARF).[3]

Romancing the 'Asian Century'

Defining the region that is supposed to dominate the 'Asian Century' is not as easy as it may appear. Early declarations of the 'Asian Century' pointed to a transition from European colonial domination to a coming century of independence. Later references emphasize a shift in economic superiority from West to East. At the same time, many Western observers began to retreat from the politically incorrect assertion of the cultural superiority of the West so that external criticism of Asia would not appear to be racially or culturally moti-

12

vated. This evolution is the result of a change in the motivating factors underlying the concept.

From a 'negative' viewpoint, the political ends motivating these various conceptualizations extend either from a 'yellow peril' scenario or a sense of cultural self-flagellation among opinion makers in the West, to a mixture of hubris, opportunism, and nationalism among Asians. From a 'positive' viewpoint, economists and politicians envision the emergence of the 'Asian Century' as a moment of great opportunity for both developing and developed economies around the world.

The concept of an integrated Pacific Basin was rejuvenated in wake of the successes of the European Common Market during the 1960s and early 1970s. The demise in the 1980s and 1990s of central and autarchic economic policies among many of the East Asian economies has provided yet another reason for optimism. Although the notion of pan-Asian unity is credible, many of the inherently divisive forces and circumstances that exist in East Asia are blithely overlooked.

Numerous impediments will hinder the formation of a Pacific alliance along the complex lines of the Atlantic community. The most obvious hurdles are the region's geographic dispersion, diversity of languages, cultures and religions, and the widely heterogeneous nature of, and disparities in, economic development. In part, the differences in economic development stem from diversity in natural resource endowments and the state of technological advance. Before the 1990s, widespread reliance upon centralized economic planning and the absence of private property rights created even greater obstacles to economic growth. Fortunately, the marketization of the nominally socialist economies of Asia has reduced the significance of this specific impediment to growth. Certainly, the wide embrace of international trade and the privatization of economic activities has prompted more enthusiasm about regional prospects. On the whole, the expectation is that as the resources of the region are utilized more efficiently, the opportunities for profits and rising incomes will be spread more widely.

Regardless of the difficulties, there is an appealing economic logic in the development of closer relations among the countries that lie along the Pacific Rim. This view has been enthusiastically embraced by many American and other Western analysts. As for Asians, the triumph of Asian nationalism over European imperialism initially provided some basis and focus for mutual interests. However, after falling prey to Japanese attempts to exploit these sentiments and to consolidate the region under the East Asia Co-Prosperity Sphere, it is not surprising that many Asians are wary of any scheme that could be subverted into a vehicle for domination by a single member.

Despite all the diversity in background and content behind the concept, the 'Asian Century' has come to signify the indisputable rise of Pacific Asia as the new center of gravity for world commerce and international affairs. In order to understand the bases of the contemporary understanding behind this concept, it is useful to examine the historical evolution of several alternative interpretations.

The long march West: Where West becomes East

In the 19th century, Napoleon Bonaparte predicted that the attention of the world would shift away from Europe toward the youthful, resource-rich nations to the West. Later, American President Theodore Roosevelt commented that the shift would continue as the world's attention marched toward the western US and the Pacific. This sentiment has been shared by a long line of American statesmen who believed that the logical field of expansion for American power and influence was to be found in the Pacific. In this historical context, Roosevelt's reference to a 'Pacific Era' was merely an articulation of the new compass bearing for American ascendancy, rather than a prognostication of the rising fortunes and eventual dominance of Asian-Pacific economies. In particular, the US acquisition of the Philippines after the Spanish-American War increasingly shifted the attention of Washington away from the Western hemisphere.

American expansionism was often coupled with a presumption of Western cultural dominance over non-Europeans, with Asians in particular viewed as doomed to perpetual suffering under economic stagnation and despotism. For example, the German philosopher Hegel saw no possibility for the development of individuals within Asian cultures. Similarly, Weber, the German sociologist and political economist, anticipated stagnation arising out of the apparent incompatibility between Asians' sense of religious and economic rationality, because Confucian values were seen as antithetical to the dynamic motivation necessary for capitalistic endeavors. Specifically, the distrust of merchants and disdain for formalized legal structures meant that economic achievement was considered to be of secondary importance. Because their traditional cultures were interpreted as the source of various endogenous barriers to economic, social, and political enlightenment, historical fact and theoretical analysis pointed to an unenviable plight for most Asians.

View from the 1950s: Economic stagnation and grinding poverty

These dour expectations seemed to be justified by the situation in Asia immediately after the second World War. Nonetheless, the early gloom for the region at the start of the post-World War II period gave way to a variety of evolving themes that altered Western perceptions about the position of Asia in the wider world. For most of the 1950s, Western attentions reflected a preoccupation with the perceived threat of communist expansion in the region. The vulnerability of many Asian political institutions was heightened by resurgent and insurgent nationalism leading toward de-colonialization and the loss of empire by European powers. In addition, the susceptibility of Asia's war-ravaged economies to a 'communist fix' made Western-assisted reconstruction a moral and practical necessity. In sum, much more concern was directed toward avoiding the fall of Asian dominoes, rather than pondering the rise of Asian dynamos.[4]

Western interaction with Asian institutional arrangements seldom resulted in a clear understanding of the potentials for success and failure in the region. Ironically, Burma-Myanmar began the post-World War II period with the highest standard of living and the greatest potential due to its rich stock of natural resources. One of the most striking misreadings was the expectation at the beginning of the 1950s that there was little hope for Japan to be successful due to its implausible approach to economic development. By the end of the decade, while the American economy grew at about 2.5 percent per annum, Japan's economy recorded 9 percent per annum. At the same time, Japan's population enjoyed equally impressive improvements in longevity as well as sharp increases in education. Despite these achievements, most Westerners assumed that progress would not be sustained over the next decade, much less that it would continue for the next 30 years into the 1990s. After all, it was widely believed that the principle advantage of most Asian economies was the abundance of relatively cheap, if not especially skilled, labor.

View from the 1960s: Initial signs of an economic takeoff

By the 1960s, Japan's pace of economic recovery matched or exceeded that of West Germany's, and both had made considerable progress in the democratization of their respective political institutions. From 1960 until the mid-1980s, Japan's economy grew at about six percent per annum, a pace two-thirds faster than the American economy and double the rate in Western Europe. However, Eurocentrism in Western thinking meant that relatively little attention was focused on events in Asia. In all events, the combined GDPs of the economies along the rim of the Pacific (excluding China) constituted only about eight percent of total world output, or about one-third that of the North Atlantic Basin.

By the middle of the 1960s, India had established its credentials as the 'world's largest democracy,' even if this distinction was blurred by the government's counterproductive flirtations with centralized economic planning. In the midst of these developments, Westerners began to be exposed to a definite sense of optimism arising out of the assorted works of futurologists, economists, Asianists, philosophers, and journalists. Perhaps less significantly, In-

15

dian gurus, sitar music, and Oriental philosophies exercised deep, if fleeting, influences upon Western youth culture during this period.

Obviously all was not well in Asia, but then it never had been. Continuing disengagement of the West from mainland China made it easy to ignore the troubling signs of economic collapse and social catastrophe occurring in that country. At last there were encouraging signs of an economic takeoff in what were to become East Asia's newly industrialized countries (NICs): Hong Kong, Singapore, South Korea, and Taiwan. Western opinion was favorably disposed toward the successful development of these economies, since their performance was seen to validate the Western economic model, even if their political arrangements did not meet the standards of Western democracy.

Meanwhile, the West had begun to develop a conventional view of Japan that would soon change. Most commentators seemed content to explain Japan's success in terms of its 'cheap' labor, low levels of defense spending, and the boost given to its economy by the presence of the occupation troops. In any event, there was not much cause to disagree since most of Japan's competitive advantage was in labor-intensive industries with low value-added products.

View from the 1970s: Shifting from Main Street to Wall Street

The 1970s were marked by some major shifts in Western understanding of Asian institutions, coupled with the development of serious efforts at regional economic integration. The continuing and remarkable economic growth rates in East Asia required a re-evaluation of the chorus of doom about that region's prospects. A new search was on to determine the source of the economic accomplishment of these otherwise tradition-bound communities.

Max Weber's contention in the late nineteenth century that Confucianism would retard the modernization of much of Asia seemed to have been turned on its head. It therefore became widely believed that the political elements of neo-Confucianism and a commitment to collectivist government were the source of East Asian dynamism. This newly found respect for Confucian tenets portrayed East Asian cultures as being able to retain their distinctive identity, and to exercise some control over their destiny in the face of industrial progress and modernization. In sharp contrast to its more traditional version, neo-Confucianism tends toward a distinct political ideology. Many of Asia's current authoritarian rulers and paternalistic bureaucrats legitimate their rule by deferring to neo-Confucianism through selective adherence to the original belief structure. A sense of political order in a neo-Confucian world cannot possibly evolve as a spontaneous outcome of the expressed preferences of individual citizens, because it requires the judicious involvement of 'virtuous' political rulers. Religious agnosticism in much of Asia supports the neo-

16

Confucian insistence that governments take an active hand in managing the instability of the world. Similarly, extensive market interventions by the state are justified on the basis of a rejection of the notion of a self-regulating economy.

This modern interpretation of Confucianism includes elements of nationalism, along with paternalistic authoritarianism, to justify the preeminence of the community over the rights of the individual. As such, community consensus is placed ahead of individual initiatives. Consequently, while the Western democracy relies upon the agent-principal relationship between governments and citizens, democracy based upon neo-Confucianism advocates a one-way conversation between the ruler and the ruled. Once these basic relationships become entrenched, popular inertia and logistical impediments discourage the establishment of rival authority structures. Uncontested dominance led to a self-confident, albeit immature, political leadership in the region that was able to impose a sense of stability and control over the polity. When combined with the high rates of economic growth, there was a strong impression that East Asian rulers were responsible for a new and superior approach to economic development.[5]

In the meantime, Japanese industrialists embarked on a course that defined the path of economic growth followed to this day. An overall favorable and somewhat envious impression began to form in the minds of Western observers and trading partners. Reports of a high saving rate, 'lifetime employment,' a dedication to quality production, and the expanding market shares for Japanese products engendered awe and consternation among Japan's trading partners. It certainly caught the attention of their competitors and a number of scholars.[6]

At this time, an influential work by an American professor, Daniel Bell, led to a popular fascination with the concept of an information society. By taking early steps in addressing the post-industrial society, Japan's manufacturing structure was inalterably modernized and its path to success was set. Their advances in the application of information systems and industrial production helped to create the impression that Asians were broadly open to modernity. These attitudes helped form the commitment to quality and excellence that many other East Asian economies followed under Japan's tutelage.

The 1970s were also distinguished by the generally successful formation of numerous regional associations among Asian countries designed to serve mutual strategic or economic interests. One of the most exclusive of these arrangements, ASEAN, focused on an immediate if somewhat narrow interest. Its formation in 1967 reflected the need for a buttress against communist encroachment in other parts of Indo-China. Wider security interests also began to catch the attention of Japanese scholars, diplomats, and politicians. Perhaps it was at this point that a revived sense of the community of Pacific countries

17

began to take shape among thinkers in Japan. The proliferation of other regional organizations will be discussed in the next section on the development of Asian thought on the 'Asian Century.'

Following its ill-fated interventions in Vietnam, there was some anxiety that American disengagement might seriously diminish its Asian presence. However, Japan wished to continue its free ride under the American defense umbrella in a manner that was also consistent with their nominally pacifistic, or at least non-interventionist, foreign policies. Following this line of thought, various thinkers offered blueprints for expanding linkages with Japan's neighbors, both near and far. In 1978, Japanese Prime Minister Ohira established a study group to look into the issue of Pacific Basin cooperation. However, an early initiative behind this movement involved a Pacific free trade area or PAFTA that included only the five major regional economies: Australia, Canada, Japan, New Zealand, and the United States. These suggested institutional arrangements were based on insights derived by the late 1960s regarding the growing importance of Japan to global economic affairs. Of special concern to Japan was the effect that stresses and problems in global financial and trading systems would have on its growth and trading activities. Later proposals were made for the establishment of an Organization for Pacific Trade, Aid, and Development (OPTAD). However, that framework was stillborn.

By the end of the 1970s, it had become clear that Japan's economic activity had shifted away from the sectors of its early successes, to industries such as consumer electronics, shipbuilding, and steel production. Although the presumed labor cost advantages had disappeared, Japanese durable goods began to flood the markets of industrialized countries.

View from the 1980s: New fire in an old dragon

By the 1980s, the narrow attention focused upon Japan expanded to take note of the impressive economic developments elsewhere in the region.[7] What were thought to be temporary trade surpluses began to take on a sense of permanence. Given that saving rates in many of the developed Western economies were low or declining, the Asian propensity to save became the object of approval and an area of scholarly interest.[8] As evidence of the benefits of Deng's reforms in China became apparent, the image of ascendant Asian economic supremacy was given a renewed boost. With the disappearance of the stultifying effects of Maoist dogma, the lure of a 'billion consumers' on the mainland was more than enough to fix the minds of eager Western business interests who sought to enter this rapidly opening market. In short order, China shifted from an isolated and economically self sufficient economy to take its place among the top ten exporting countries in the world.

Indeed, a sort of 'Sinomania' has developed in the US that supplants the quasi-isolationism induced by the bitter experience of the Vietnamese War. Amidst the corporate rush to stake out commercial market shares, China scholars stood poised to market their expertise in response to an increasingly breathless enthusiasm for all things Chinese. Meanwhile, the decline of economic fortunes in Europe characterized as 'Eurosclerosis' yet again prompted second thoughts about the viability of the liberal capitalism of the West.

By the 1980s, East Asian 'Tiger' economies (Japan followed by Hong Kong, Singapore, South Korea, and Taiwan) experienced extraordinary growth whereby their per capita GDPs doubled and then redoubled in increasingly shorter time spans. In the early 1990s, there were regular reports of near double digit growth in China, Indonesia, Malaysia, Thailand, and most the Tiger economies. While industrialized economies of North America and Europe recorded average annual GDP growth of 3 percent from 1980 to 1990, the measure for Asian-Pacific economies was 8.4 percent over the same period. The growth rates for Latin America (1.3 percent) and the Middle East combined with Africa (2.9 percent) lagged even further behind those of dynamic East Asia.

Gazing ahead from the 1990s: Waiting for Guangzhou or Japan as number two?

The optimistic outlook for the region got another boost in the early 1990s from the economic marketization and, to a lesser degree, political democratization of an increased number of East Asian countries. The former communist countries of Burma-Myanmar, Cambodia, Laos, and Vietnam are struggling to join their neighbors on a higher growth path by opening up their economies. For reasons dictated by their own domestic dynamics, the Philippines, South Korea, Taiwan, and Thailand have disposed of their dictators or juntas to embrace democracy more fully.

At the same time, several highly publicized meetings of APEC provided a platform for conveying the growing importance of the synergy between the Pacific Rim and countries with a trading focus upon the Asian Pacific and North American markets. By this time, a clear consensus had formed around the seemingly undeniable economic prowess of East Asia. The persistence of Japan's trade surpluses with its industrialized trading partners and the relentless rise of the yen, combined with the rapidly rising fortunes of other countries in the region, bolstered this impression. This generally favorable review has evidently been propagated by certain media tendencies. As so often happens, due to their lack of analytical skills in the area of economics, members of the media often only repeat what they have heard others say. Such superficial coverage actually plays well to a general public that seldom requires full information about such issues. However, the veneer of legitimacy conferred by the media may cause investors to rely unduly on such spurious knowledge. Indeed, many business interests have promoted the image of the 'Asian Century' in order to shape public policy in a manner conducive to trade opportunities for themselves. In addition, this sort of hysteria colors the advice provided by investment analysts.

A good example of this can be found in the declarations of Mr Barton Biggs of Morgan Stanley, who asserted that he was 'maximum bullish' on China after only a brief visit in late 1993. A few weeks later, he acknowledged his limited understanding about China as he subsequently withdrew a significant portion of Morgan Stanley's equity holdings there. As a result, Hong Kong's stock market went into a tailspin. This sort of general ignorance about Asia among Westerners helps sustain the momentum behind visions of an 'Asian Century.' As indicated in the preface, books on the supremacy of East Asian economic models, and by implication the inferiority of Western liberal capitalism, have also stoked enthusiasm for the region.

An important influence on the historical evolution of the 'Asian Century' is the apparently increasing dominance of the 'Overseas Chinese,' i.e., ethnic Chinese living outside mainland China. Numerous authors have portrayed this geographically diffuse and politically dispersed entity as a force that rivals even the industrial behemoths of Japan. In this sense, an 'Offshore China' exists which has access to business networks, vast amounts of financial capital, and managerial expertise. Equally important, this group exercises substantial control over access to the world's largest potential consumer market and the cheapest pool of labor.

With each passing year of the 1990s, China's economic strength seemed to grow, while Japan's economy continued to be mired ever further in recession. As such, whatever developments may overtake Japan as the dominant economy of the region, China can be expected to fill the void with assistance from the offshore Chinese.

Other countries in the region have also begun to show great promise. With its reform program firmly on track, eventually even India will mount a serious challenge as the dominant force in the region. In addition, reforms undertaken by erstwhile communist regimes in Burma-Myanmar, Cambodia, Laos, and Vietnam, provide a sense of optimism and urgency for the widening economic advance throughout East Asia.

Maturing of the West: Self-doubts and praise for the East

Western regard for East Asia has always reflected a mixture of awe, praise, and skepticism. In any case, these reactions have always tended to be intense, regardless of whether the focus was upon the threats or the opportunities emanating from Asia. Marco Polo's accounts provided images of an exotic and alluring culture, but then as now, the allusions to economic opportunities were the real source of interest.

During the 1990s, the sense of optimism about the transformations occurring in Asia began to mirror a growing pessimism and sense of decline in the West. Meanwhile, magisterial works by various philosophers supporting this view found considerable resonance among Western intellectuals eager for self-critical analysis. A thread from these earlier works can be found in the important contributions of Kennedy and Olson.[9] Olson applies economic reasoning to provide a general theory of the factors that underlie the decline of nations. In sum, he suggests that rising national income allows interest groups to gain strength and influence over the political agenda. The result is a form of economic sclerosis that undermines a country's long-run growth potential. Kennedy's thesis is a bit more precise in pointing to 'imperial overreach' and military adventurism as the bases for the erosion of power. However, the military-industrial complex is but one type of interest group in Olson's analysis. Nevertheless, the high-growth East Asian economies have benefited from the absence of such interest group pressures, while many Western countries suffered from a 'demosclerosis' that sapped their economic vitality.[10] It remains to be seen if Asian countries will be able to shield their modernization process from such influences.

Strategic concerns have also prompted increased interest in Pacific Asia. The end of the bipolar world allowed Asian powers a more prominent place in world affairs. Naturally, Asian military ascendancy over the past century has played a significant role in altering Western attitudes toward Asia. First, there was the ignominious defeat of a European power by an Asian upstart in the Russo-Japanese war. Similarly, the initial military supremacy of the Japanese during World War II allowed them to humiliate many of the West's greatest countries or empires. The stalemate in the Korean conflict during the 1950s brought about by Chinese interventions humbled Western allies before an implacable Asian foe. More disastrously, the bloody nose given to first the French and then to the American military-industrial complex by the Vietcong and North Vietnamese armed forces engendered respect for the ability of Asians to hold their own ground and more. More ominously, modernization of the Chinese People's Liberation Army in the 1990s allowed an expansion of its naval presence that strengthens its claims to most of the South China Sea. These claims include most of the resource rich seabed around the Spratly and the Paracel Islands, and, of course, Taiwan.

Certain social factors have also contributed to recognition by the West of advances by Asians. The democratization of travel has allowed Westerners to become more aware of the richness of other cultures, thereby dispelling an

21

uninformed sense of superiority over other cultures. Similarly, massive Asian immigration to other parts of the globe has provided firsthand exposure to their admirable sense of discipline and work ethic. Successful integration of Asians into Western educational institutions has contributed to a deep insecurity about the ability of Westerners to compete with the perceived Asian commitment to hard work.

One side effect of the growing economic stature of Japan and other countries in East Asia has been their capacity to influence events even in America. There is considerable evidence that Japan's industrial and political leaders have spent considerable sums on either acquiring American ideas or attempting to influence them. The activities of Japanese lobbyists are well documented and have become a source of great concern to the American polity. American colleges and universities, as well as think tanks, have been recipients of large sponsorships from Japanese companies whose ulterior motive is to spread views favored by Tokyo. In later discussion, it will be shown that other countries attempt to influence public opinion in much the same manner. Certainly as the economic clout of countries in the region expands, they will begin exercising greater influence over the policies of other nations and international organizations.

However, it would seem that the most compelling indicators supporting the likelihood of Asian dominance are found in the context of the globalization of markets. Specifically, an impression of Asian commercial prowess is fostered by the increased quantity and quality of imports from the region. Besides the ubiquity of *karaoke* lounges and a wide range of Asian restaurants, Asian products have proliferated and competed favorably with or displaced domestic products. More significantly, many of the Asian economies were able to generate impressive rates of growth while much of the industrialized world was dealing with the woes of a recession and the pains of restructuring. These impressions were reinforced by the general decline in the value of Western currencies, especially the dramatic slide of the American dollar against the Japanese yen prior to 1996.

Many observers have come to accept these partially supported impressions of Asian superiority through the sheer weight of repetition. The proclivity among Western commentators for self-critical analysis has led to unnecessarily negative reports of waning economic fortunes in their own countries. As though to compensate for having expressed an earlier sense of superiority, Westerners seem to have imposed upon themselves a mass inferiority complex. Part of the problem with this cultural self-effacement is that it may reinforce a siege mentality of 'them against us' that could spark a new Cold War based upon economic rather than political conflicts. Transient problems associated with restructuring in response to the demands of the new global marketplace have been exaggerated into a signal of the end of an era of economic ascendancy for Europe and North America.

Asian navel-gazing turns outward: Asian views on 'Asia'

Asians also began to develop changing attitudes about their place in the world due to their 'discovery' of the New World in the late 19th Century. It then became widely accepted that Europe and North America could serve as the (temporary) source of advanced technologies to facilitate modernization. Upon studying in the West, Asians developed sufficient self confidence to allow a change in their attitudes whereby they no longer equated modernization with Westernization. By the middle of this century, Asian perspectives on their self-propelled emergence found a voice in nationalist movements and communism that were often blended together. While interest in communism has now waned, there is an apparent tendency for some Asian leaders to flirt with nationalism. However, such nationalist movements are paired schizophrenically with Pacific internationalism driven by economic pragmatism. Globalization has great momentum, but there is a residual historical reluctance on the part of Asians to unite the region along economic, military, or ideological lines. Perhaps one of the greatest challenges is to reconcile attempts at greater regional integration with the demands of globalized trade and strategic relations.

Images of the impending global ascendancy of Pacific Asia have been most aggressively touted by non-Asian observers in Europe and North America. After many years of hearing these announcements from Western commentators, certain East Asian regimes have begun to exploit the promise of Asia's future dominance as the legitimating basis for their authoritarian rule. Leaders of Japan and of some of the so-called miracle economies have begun to promote their approach to economic development as a model that has universal application just as Western powers did in previous decades.[11] In the face of such excitement, challenges to the projection of an 'Asian Century' have gone mostly unnoticed or have been dismissed altogether. It may be only a slight overstatement to suggest that the wide acceptance of the rising fortunes of Asians and the decline of the West is a generous mixture of ignorance and opportunism. For the most part, support for the 'Asian Century' is based upon superficial and anecdotal evidence. These evidentiary shortcomings will be explored more fully in Chapter Nine.

It is widely known that the foreign policy of 'Japan, Inc.' has been driven by commercial considerations. Given this deep concern for facilitating Japan's continued economic progress, opening a dialogue toward the formation of some sort of Pacific Community would serve several of its national purposes.

It was clear that Japan's export-oriented industrialization strategy depended upon open access to markets in the mature economies. However, in order to capture more immediate benefits than would be garnered by a more universal approach, a regional program toward greater trade liberalization was initially adopted. While this was probably a theoretically valid strategy, the initial emphasis upon regionally based trade relations complicated subsequent attempts to develop more global arrangements. In order to avoid this tactical error in future, the Asian Development Bank (ADB) and the Economic and Social Commission for Asia and the Pacific (ESCAP) were institutionalized by wider bodies. Although there is presently substantial support for APEC and widening interest among prospective suitors to join, so too is attention being paid to suggestions for an East Asian economic sphere (EAEC). This is championed principally by Malaysia's long serving prime minister, Dr Mahathir Mohamad, with an aim to provide a regional force to balance the influence of America over the content and pace of trade policy negotiations.

During the late 1980s, technocrats in the Japanese Ministry of International Trade and Industry (MITI) and politicians became increasingly confident about the wide applicability of Japan's modernization policies. This caused a rift between the views of the World Bank and Japanese authorities concerning the relevance of government intervention. The World Bank had traditionally followed neoclassical economic theory in judging the policy mix of recipient countries. Buoyed by their own success, Japanese officials became increasingly convinced that their reliance upon industrial policy was a worthy contribution to the knowledge about the process of industrialization. Other countries in the region followed Japan's lead of systematic and selective market intervention over extended periods to similar effect. In order to establish their approach as a model, and to showcase its impact on other economies in the region, the Japanese government commissioned the World Bank to produce a report on the East Asian 'miracle' economies.[12]

One of the most important conclusions of this report was that macroeconomic stability was essential for the high performance of the region's economies. Because these countries pursued prudent monetary and fiscal policies with the aim of controlling inflation, there was greater confidence in their banking sectors, which in turn encouraged the importation of technology by domestic, private firms. More in keeping with the expectations of their Japanese patrons, the World Bank researchers also pointed to the emphasis on manufacturing exports as a leading sector of growth. Finally, while acknowledging that the governments of the 'miracle' economies engaged in substantial market intervention, the conclusion was that it was more unusual that such actions produced beneficial results. However, the prerequisites for the positive effects of intervention were so rigorous that other developing countries would be unlikely to experience the same results.

In adopting the rhetoric of the 'Asian Century,' several East Asian regimes have aggressively promoted their own development models as being distinctively Asian, unquestionably successful, and easily transplantable. One element of this formula is the renaissance of a set of 'Asian values,' with some of the leading spokespersons found in what is commonly referred to as the 'Singapore School.' To a great extent, these values reflect elements of neo-Confucianism discussed in the previous section. In turn, the presumed existence of pan-Asian values provides the basis for a regionally-specific form of 'democracy' with Asian characteristics, accompanied by a uniquely Asian perspective on human rights. Given the wide diversity of cultures, traditions, religions, and languages throughout this vast region, it is not surprising that the debate over the content or existence of shared values remains unsettled. Nonetheless, a recent survey of prominent East Asians did reveal several interesting points of agreement.[13] First, many respondents expressed an impatience with the high-handed behavior of the US and the tendency for Western values to be imposed upon other regions. Second, just as many Asians resented the fact that leaders of Singapore's regime and its apologists would presume to speak for them.

Asian Century or Global Millennium?

No one doubts that the developing countries of Southeast and East Asia have achieved rapid export-led economic growth. However, the interesting questions concern what determined the pace of growth and whether their record is unique. Of equal concern is whether or not these record rates of economic growth are sustainable. As will be discussed, future prospects for sustained growth are a function of the operation of the institutional arrangements that have been relied upon up to now. Finally, an accounting of the toll of high rates of economic growth upon social arrangements and the consequences for the environment ought to be undertaken.

There is also little doubt that China's belated liberalization and modernization have been especially important elements supporting the expectation of an 'Asian Century.' Apart from the reorientation of China's markets toward world trade, there is enormous enthusiasm among foreigners over participation in some of that country's major development projects and public infrastructure schemes. With new frontiers opening in Burma-Myanmar, Laos, Vietnam, and perhaps Cambodia, Western businesses have a great incentive to focus upon opportunities in East Asia. Already the value of pan-Pacific trade flows have surged ahead of the value of trans-Atlantic trade.

Predictions concerning Asia's economic future have Japan surpassing the US as the world's largest economy by the year 2000, with China overtaking both by the year 2020. Others expect that the combined output of the four Tiger economies (Hong Kong, Singapore, South Korea, and Taiwan) will match the GDP of the US by the beginning of the millennium. If the other emerging economies of the region are included, East Asian production is projected to overtake North America by 2011 and Europe by 2015. In light of these forecasts, it might seem that the only growth industry likely to remain in the West is the publication of books on the rise of Asian economies.

An argument that will be offered here is that not only is the decline of the West exaggerated, but so are the prospects for Asia to be the dominant region over the next century.[14] Many industrial and political changes have been implemented in the West to correct some of the pressing problems there. Referred to as 'downsizing,' 'restructuring,' and 'decentralization,' these varied responses of Western businesses and governments are beginning to bear fruit. For example, the US economy has scored at or near the top in a world competitiveness ranking since the mid-1980s, and again ranked number one and number two in two international surveys in 1996.[15] Although the welfare state, the mammoth size of General Motors and IBM, and the public sector deficits of the French and Italian governments seemed to be permanent and immutable features of the Western landscape, they are undergoing fundamental changes.

As explained earlier, allusions to the 'Asian Century' rely upon an acceptance of the notion that the ascendancy of one region must be accompanied by the decline of another. Perhaps a better understanding is that over the next 100 years we will witness the beginning of a 'Global Millennium' where wealth is more broadly dispersed and evenly distributed. We can expect a post-millennium synthesis of cultural institutions from the East and the West that will evolve out of the ever widening access to communication facilities and information. This competitive outcome will be motivated and facilitated by the globalization of economic activities and the relentless search by mankind for efficient institutions that best allow collective and individual outcomes to be achieved. The past four decades of economic boom will rightly encourage Asian leaders to become increasingly independent and confident. However, those leaders who would seek to bar the evolution of Asian institutions will impede the emergence of the sort of moral, political, and military leadership that would be required for the promise of an 'Asian Century' to be fulfilled.

Notes

1   These policies reflect affirmative action programs for the indigenous, mostly Malay-speaking peoples. Although members of this linguistic group constitute the majority of the population, they were under-

26

represented as holders of economic power at the end of their respective colonial periods.

2 APEC participants include Australia, Brunei, Canada, Chile, China, Hong Kong, Indonesia, Japan, Malaysia, Mexico, New Zealand, Papua New Guinea, the Philippines, Singapore, South Korea, Taiwan, Thailand, and the United States. Together they generate 56 percent of the world's output worth about $13 trillion. Their combined populations account for 40 percent of the world total and occupy about 30 percent of the world land surface.

3 Formed in 1994 as a security deliberation body, ARF members include ASEAN countries (Brunei, Indonesia, Malaysia, the Philippines, Singapore, Thailand, and Vietnam) and observer countries from the region (Burma-Myanmar, Cambodia, Laos, and Papua New Guinea). Dialogue partners with interests in the region (Australia, Canada, China, the European Union, India, Japan, New Zealand, Russia, South Korea, and the United States) often attend the meeting.

4 J. Breslan, *From Dominoes to Dynamos: The Transformation of Southeast Asia,* New York: Council on Foreign Relations Press, 1994.

5 N. Macrae, 'Pacific Century: 1975-2075?', *The Economist,* 4 January 1975, pp. 15-35.

6 E. Vogel, *Japan As Number One: Lessons for America,* Cambridge, Mass.: Harvard University Press, 1979.

7 See C. Prestowitz, *Trading Places: How We Allowed Japan to Take the Lead,* New York: Basic Books, 1988.

8 Household savings as a percentage of income in Japan began rising in the 1950s, reaching 15 percent by 1960. It peaked at 24 percent in 1974 and remains between 15 and 20 percent of GDP. The saving rate in the US has fallen steadily until it bottomed out at 5 percent in the mid-1980s.

9 P. M. Kennedy, *The Rise and Fall of the Great Powers: The Economic Change and Military Conflict from 1500-2000,* New York: Random House, 1988. M. Olson, *The Rise and Decline of Nations,* New Haven: Yale University Press, 1982.

10 Some of the cultural attributes that have been associated with the high-growth East Asian economies are the importance assigned to education, a high regard for bureaucrats, deferred consumption and frugality, social reciprocity, respect for authority, and a high preference for social and political stability.

11 S. Chan and C. Clark, 'The Rise of the East Asian NICs: Confucian Capitalism, Status Mobility, and Developmental Legacy', in *The Evolving Pacific Basin in the Global Political Economy: Domestic and International Linkages,* Boulder: Lynne Rienner, 1992.

12   World Bank, *The East Asian Miracle,* op. cit.

13   D. I. Hitchcock, *Asian Values and the United States: How Much Con-
     flict?,* Washington, DC: Center for Strategic and International Studies,
     1994.

14   B. Cumings, 'What is a Pacific Century – and How Will We Know
     When it Begins?', *Current History,* December 1994, Vol. 93, No. 587,
     pp. 401-6.

15   *World Competitiveness Yearbook, 1996,* Lausanne: International Insti-
     tute for Management Development, 1996 and *Global Competitiveness
     Report, 1996,* Davos: World Economic Forum, 1996.

3 Imaging the 'Asian Century'

It is unsurprising that the confluence of so many favorable circumstances has led to an expectation of the Asianization of world affairs. The ongoing renaissance of Asian cultural institutions and the impression of political stability in the region, combined with recently unleashed economic dynamism, have generated unprecedented attention to the region. Rapid increases of per capita income registered first in Japan during the 1960s and then spread to Hong Kong, the Republic of Korea, Singapore and Taiwan in the 1970s and 1980s. Meanwhile, these economic success stories have been repeated in Indonesia, Malaysia, Thailand, and more recently, China. Most of these countries have also recorded notable social gains (e.g., improvements in education, health, and housing) along with economic progress. These results stand in stark contrast to developing countries in Africa and the Middle East and in many parts of the former Soviet Empire.

Out of these convergent factors has come a greater sense of self-confidence among Asians within the context of global economies and international politics. Westerners slowly and sometimes begrudgingly have come to realize the rising importance of the Asian Pacific economies despite the erratic signals of conflict and cooperation. One pressing issue concerns the question of the universality of human values versus an alleged cultural distinctiveness of these beliefs. As will be established in considerable detail in Chapter Six, the ongoing debate over 'Asian values' touches on a wide variety of issues relevant to interpreting Asia's past and predicting the region's future.

More immediately, this chapter will identify and explore those facts, events, and circumstances that have contributed to the recognition of the potential dominance of Pacific Asia over world affairs.

Modernization in Asia: From Westernization to Easternization

In the eyes of most observers, becoming 'Westernized' or more crudely, 'Americanized,' has been viewed as the touchstone of modernization. Given the spotty political and economic record of much of the rest of the world, there is considerably more behind this assertion than mere vulgar cultural imperialism. Western democratic ideals, even more than capitalism, served as the mobilizing premise behind the rhetoric and myths underlying the movements for independence from imperialism or feudalistic monarchies in Asia and around the world. Similarly, the wealth achieved by Western industrialized economies served as a benchmark of development, even if some leaders were to condemn the subsequent injustices associated with it.

Asians have become increasingly resentful of what they perceive as a lack of respect for their distinctive cultural traditions. At the same time, these complaints have resonated with multi-culturalist Western thinkers who reject any idea of the universality of cultural values and human rights. Some in both camps are interested in simply dismissing the validity of Western values, per se. By the 1990s, a significant shift occurred wherein the cultural hegemony asserted by America and the West over much of Asia seems to have been displaced. Instead, there is an anticipation of 'Easternization' or 'Asianization' as the way of the future that might have application outside the region. Many scholars in Asia and in the West allude to the apparent collapse of Western economic and social arrangements while extolling the vitality of these institutions' counterparts in Asia. Consequently, a new range of Asian models has been offered that refer to the impact of regionally specific values upon political, economic, and social institutions. Models of 'Asian values,' 'Asian democracy,' an Asian sense of human rights, and an Asian approach to economic development have appeared as the catch phrases of this view of the world.

Asian cultural distinctiveness: Neo-Confucianism and other 'Asian values'

Invocations for the rest of the world to imitate a superior set of values that are presumed to be peculiarly 'Asian' have come from diverse quarters. Proponents of these 'Asian values' combine in an unlikely alliance among British MPs and American members of Congress to the civil servants and leaders of selected Asian countries. Each of these champions of 'Asian values' is motivated by a personal agenda, whether it be a sense of conservatism, nostalgia, pragmatism, or pure political opportunism. These values are said to include commitment to hard work, a sense of thriftiness, emphasis on education, and well-defined family structures. Surely, most of these are human values that are no stranger to Western experience. What may be more distinctive is the addition of concepts like filial piety and an abiding respect for political authority, 'society above self,' and consensus building. This latter group of cultural institutions offers validations of the hierarchical social and political structures that are widely observed in East Asia. Although most of these values are still intact, they are undergoing transition due to modernizing influences. The forces of urbanization, changing demographics with an increased proportion of young in the population, increased wealth, income, and leisure, all combine to unravel attempts by opportunistic Asian leaders to inculcate these values.

Praise for these values from Western observers is most often directed toward finding a way to stop the decay of social institutions that is seen as the basis for the malaise that grips their mature economies. The offering of praise for 'Asian values' by certain Asian leaders, such as Lee Kuan Yew of Singapore and Mahathir Mohamad of Malaysia reflects their intent to use the issue to consolidate their influence over a one-party state. This is not to say that their pronouncements are purely cynical. However, most of these presumed values lend support to their authoritarian style of rule. For example, the so-called Singapore School and its progeny aggressively argue that Asia's distinctive cultural factors, especially filial piety and the subservience of individual to communal rights, have been the key to their continued economic growth and regional stability. Their point of view has struck a resonant chord among other authoritarian leaders in the region who have good reason to fear outside criticism. Armed with this argument, foreign commentary can be readily dismissed as cultural imperialism, an attempt to re-impose Western political dominance, or merely as an affront to national sovereignty.

After the victory of postwar liberation movements in casting off their colonial yokes, Asian nationalism had been mostly dormant except in communist regimes where nationalist rhetoric was used to thwart the encroachment of capitalism. More recently, brittle rejection of criticisms by outsiders has been manipulated by some authoritarian regimes in an attempt to inflame nationalist passions in order to disguise the goals of the ruling party as the goals of the country. Besides Malaysia and Singapore, the most vigorous rejections of Western criticisms have come from regimes in Burma-Myanmar, China, and Indonesia.

This new wave of nationalism has also been promoted by a new confidence among Asians, owing to the growing prosperity of the region. In addition, some of the early contributors to the notion of 'Asian values' were Westerners seeking to explain the recent accomplishments of the high-growth East Asian economies. Initially, attention was paid to the culturally-determined institutional and structural elements behind East Asia's rapid economic growth.[1] The common adherence of these high-growth economies to Confucian ethics was credited for the discipline and commitments of both workers and rulers that

31

served as the glue allowing rapid economic growth. The selective application of these neo-Confucian ethics supports the notion of 'Asian democracy' wherein virtuous rulers and loyal public servants claim to serve in the best interests of the people.

'Asian democracy' and political stability: Virtuous politics and economic prosperity

One of the presumed strengths of the political arrangements in most of the region is the stability and predictability of the political players. While East Asian economies have significantly different degrees of dependency upon foreign capital, an important motivation behind maintaining political stability is to provide reassurance to potential outside investors. Of equal importance is the ability of rulers to remain in power during the necessary shift away from the economically ruinous import substitution policies and other forms of protectionism. Thus, economic progress also depends upon the political strength of these leaders to impose policies that might not initially have wide support. A case in point was the capacity of some East Asian leaders to embrace policies that attracted investments and technology transfers from multinational corporations. These choices proved to be especially prescient and reflected an openness that had been rejected by most developing countries in the rest of the world.

Part of the perception of political stability is driven by the region's traditional respect for hierarchy and order. Thus, a defining element of Asia's political structure is the region's long experience with rule by strongmen, e.g., Kim Il Sung and son Kim Jong Il in North Korea; Chun and Park in South Korea; Lee Kuan Yew in Singapore, Mahathir in Malaysia, Marcos in the Philippines, and Sukarno followed by Suharto in Indonesia. These strongmen-rulers were often leaders who encouraged the dominance of single-party states in the region, e.g., the Liberal Democratic Party (LDP) in Japan; the Kuomintang (KMT) in Taiwan; the National Front (NF) in Malaysia; and the People's Action Party (PAP) in Singapore.

The really insidious threat to personal liberties is that so-called democracies based on the 'Asian Model' are masking the reality of creeping authoritarianism. By masquerading under the guise of self-styled Asian democracy, neo-authoritarian regimes are able to have their cake and eat it too. On the one hand, they gain a cloak of respectability to supporters of democracy in the region. On the other hand, their claims to a regionally-specific democratic arrangement allow criticisms by non-Asians to be dismissed as impositions of cultural imperialism.

Nepotism and dynastic succession: Asian family values?

Among the 'Asian values' credited for the recent economic success in East Asia are a dedication to hard work, respect for education, consensus seeking combined with a respect for authority, and strong family ties. However, in its modern political incarnation, the venerated Confucian tradition of strong family bonds leads to what amounts to dynastic succession and an entrenched policy of nepotism. By preventing the rise of a political meritocracy, nepotism may very well hinder a continuation of the recent enviable record of growth enjoyed by many of the countries in the region.

There is a long history of Asian political leaders providing family members with special privileges or installing them as their successors. Even today, many Asian governments operate under a dominant single party that in turn may be presided over by a single domineering figure or family. Although one-party states are known in the West, the 'one-family state' seems to be a peculiarly Asian phenomenon in today's world.

Nepotism is consistent with the culturally imbedded commitment to family that is said to define social relations in much of Asia. In its modern form, nepotism represents a form of corruption that naturally thrives in a situation where the authority and decisions of leaders are seldom challenged. This might involve passing the political mantle from parent to child, or the use of political connections by family members to promote their own commercial interests. Whatever their familial maneuverings, most regimes rely upon their bureaucracies to oversee the economic transitions. It is no simple task to smooth the shift from economies based on agriculturally-based family enterprises governed under a feudalistic system, to one dominated by manufacturing juggernauts under some form of representative democracy. Aspects of bureaucratic corruption can be rather more subtle. Nevertheless, they can be expected to place an institutionalized drag on future growth. Governmental institutions, including such 'agencies of restraint' as courts, independent electoral tribunals, anti-corruption bodies, central banks, auditing agencies, and ombudsmen are needed to check abuses by other public agencies and branches of government.

It is possible that nepotism and intra-familial succession contribute to political stability. However, where nepotism is prevalent, there are also a variety of costs to the community that should be considered. Political costs can be measured in terms of the loss of political rights. In politicizing market activity, nepotism invites economic inefficiency from the diversion of resources toward a single family or their cronies in a dominant political party. By interfering with the transparency of market transactions, nepotism will impose costs upon the greater community by reducing returns on gross investment.

Before receiving the mantle of political power, the progeny of rulers use their privileged status to develop their own power base. For example, this may involve grants of national monopolies over certain economic sectors. According to a 1995 rating survey by Transparency International, Indonesia was considered to have the world's most corrupt regime. It is probably no coincidence that family members of President Suharto are often at the heart of economic corruption. Similarly, the offspring of China's rulers use family influence to provide privileged access to markets for their supporters without regard to merit or to the rules of market efficiency. Children of the Chinese *nomenklatura* have gained so much economic clout that they are widely referred to as 'princelings.'

Besides bestowing economic advantage upon family members, there are also pervasive attempts to impose secular dynasties in many Asian countries. The unilateral transfer of political control to family members is often found where there were anti-colonial movements led by charismatic autocrats. This form of non-monarchical dynastic succession often reflects an attempt to maintain family fortunes and property. In other cases it may be deemed necessary to insure that the autocrat's family can survive the consequences of often brutal political competition. Few challenges can be made by a citizenry that is usually ill-educated and subject to severe reprisals if they voice dissent. As a result, Asian autocrats can decide in the best interest of their families, regardless of the impact on the country. In the end, it is not surprising that family politics spill over into national politics in much of Asia.

While similar arrangements have been gradually eroded in the West by experience and exposure to democracy, Asian political dynasties generally refuse to go quietly. In post-independence India, not only was there a near monopoly for the Congress Party, but Nehru or his descendants among the Gandhi family held a firm grip on leadership. Despite the entrenched corruption associated with Congress Party rule, Indira Gandhi extended her family's dominance by setting the stage for son Rajiv to be able to succeed her upon her assassination. After Rajiv's assassination, there were repeated attempts to encourage Rajiv's wife, Sonia, to stand for election despite her Italian heritage.

Politics in Sri Lanka followed along a similar path. The two strongest political parties are controlled by a single family and reflect sibling rivalry. The daughter of a former prime minister, Chandrika Kumaratunga, was elected president in November 1994. She appointed her mother, Sirimavo Bandaranaike, for a third term as prime minister.[2] Perhaps piqued by the voters' preference for his sister, Anura Bandaranaike awaits his turn at the dynastic political throne as a member of the opposition.

In death, Generalissimo Chiang Kai-shek and Kim Il Song of North Korea were able to bequeath leadership to their sons. In Singapore, there has been considerable controversy over whether the eldest son of Lee Kuan Yew is actually the heir apparent. In Cambodia, King Sihanouk's ambitions for his family are not limited to monarchical succession. Both his son, Prince Norodom Ranariddh, and the king's brother, Prince Norodom Sirivudh, have been groomed to succeed the King in his role as secular ruler.

It is obvious that Siti Hardijanti Rukmana, the eldest daughter of Indonesia's President Suharto, has her own presidential ambitions. Ms Rukmana is currently vice-chairwoman of Golkar, a government-sponsored political party that is dominated by the military. With such solid links to the military and her business connections, she is considered a likely candidate for vice president of Indonesia, and is in line to succeed her father. Ironically, Megawati Sukarnoputri, the daughter of Suharto's predecessor and arch rival who was deposed in a bloody struggle, has become an active candidate for presidency.

Politics in the Philippines is also rife with nepotism and is run by clans. President Marcos' wife became a cabinet minister and governor of Metro Manila, and his mother had an appointment to the nuclear power commission despite her lack of knowledge or experience in the field. Even Corazon Aquino's presidency was an incorporation of two of the biggest and most powerful clans in the Philippines, the Cojuangcos and Aquinos.

In addition, it is not altogether clear that Asia's strongman rulers will blithely step aside when their term in office expires. There is an expectation that some, like Prime Minister Mahathir of Malaysia and President Suharto of Indonesia, may hold on to their power by creating and assuming the office of 'senior minister,' as in the case of Lee Kuan Yew of Singapore. Under this scheme, titular power is relinquished, but substantive influence is not.

The institutionalization of the 'Asian values' of nepotism and dynastic succession is in conflict with the modernizing forces of marketization and democratization. This being the case, many Asian rulers invite accusations of hypocrisy for their actions. In earlier incarnations as pro-independence democrats, they demanded a form of government that was based upon self-determination and that reflected an expression of the will of the people. Nepotism and dynastic succession are practices that are more compatible with imperial colonialism than with modern democracy.

Eventually, it is likely that popular access to expanded media coverage will limit the ability of Asian autocrats to unilaterally decide what is best for their citizens. Feudalistic inter- and intra-familial transfers of political power and economic privilege will be challenged by modernized institutions in a global economy. As the losses due to corruption and inefficiency mount, investors and voters will ultimately decide if the economic costs of ancestral power grabs outweigh the presumed benefits.

Prosperity first, rights later

An authoritarian adaptation of the new Asian development model prescribes trading civil rights and freedoms for immediate economic growth; in other words, 'prosperity first, rights later.' This approach is evident in the one-party regimes of Indonesia, Malaysia, and Singapore. By placing a priority upon economic progress instead of political development, the explicit presumption is that individual rights are meaningless in the absence of basic material well-being.

The development record of the authoritarian East Asian regimes is often interpreted to suggest that rapid economic growth and political freedom are incompatible. It is thought that authoritarian, even totalitarian, regimes have an advantage over democracies in mobilizing production during the early stages of economic development because they are able to disregard the demands of competing interest groups. Leaders are therefore free to make the tough choices that might contradict popular calls for the redistribution of income or wealth to serve short-term preferences. In avoiding these pressures, authoritarian regimes seem better able to expedite the course of economic progress by extracting a relatively large amount of savings to be used for social investments. In contrast, democratic regimes must obtain public concurrence in order to attain a specific level of savings or to generate additional tax revenues. Instead of an informed consensus, authoritarian regimes can rely upon imposed acquiescence without the messiness of community dialogue.

However, authoritarianism does little to guarantee successful economic development. The regimes in Burma-Myanmar, Laos, (pre-Deng) China, and Vietnam are cases where autocracy has borne little fruit in terms of shared economic development. In the end, those countries that follow the policy of 'development now, rights later' will see short-run gains neutralized by unanticipated long-run costs. Just as it is impossible to 'fool all of the people, all of the time,' it is unlikely that a given regime will be capable of accommodating the dynamic pressures of changing preferences of a rapidly modernizing society. An autocratic regime long accustomed to having its way is almost certain to lose touch with the masses. The specific nature of the resulting impairment to the dynamic spirit of a modernizing community will be addressed in Chapter Seven.

Fast-paced economic development

An enormous amount of data is available which points to a remarkable process of growth and development among the menagerie of East Asian 'Tiger' and 'Dragon' economies. A first wave of books offered great technical detail in examining the underlying sources of this growth.[3] Building from these impressive statistics, yet avoiding the technical rigor, a second wave of books went into print in anticipation of the high degree of curiosity that would be aroused by the earlier literature.[4] Most books in this second wave offer an initial blizzard of numbers that is followed by breathless prose and praise for the unstoppable momentum of the East Asian economies. For example, in *Megatrends Asia*, John Naisbitt opines that '...Asia will become the dominant region in the world: economically, politically and culturally.' Ironically, the numbers that are the basis of this thesis are quickly set aside and the force behind the pro-Asia arguments depends upon personal anecdotes and casual generalizations. In the rush to judgment, shaggy dog stories are granted as much validity as is hard evidence, perhaps more so since the anecdotal rendering makes the arguments easier to digest for wider audiences.

Obviously there is little question that the developing countries of Southeast and East Asia have achieved rapid economic growth.[5] However, there is considerable controversy over how it was achieved and whether or not such a record is unique. One interpretation offered in a World Bank report on East Asian 'miracle' economies focuses heavily upon the success of market-oriented reform.[6] In a much quoted summary, the annual average growth rates of 5.5 percent during 1965 to 1990 experienced by the high-growth East Asian economies were accomplished by 'getting the basics right.' Most important of these basics was to establish macroeconomic stability by implementing prudent fiscal and monetary policies combined with competitively-determined exchange rates. This arrangement encourages thrift and rewards investment by establishing confidence in the financial system. Because a steady balance in the overall economic climate was maintained, savings were protected from the ravages of inflation, and there was some security in the ultimate values of investments. Another of these 'basics' included heavy public expenditures on social infrastructure, especially education. By encouraging the development of human capital, these countries were better able to enjoy 'shared growth' and to develop a stock of relatively high-quality civil servants.

One striking anomaly in the World Bank report is the implication, despite ample evidence to the contrary, that these countries relied upon a relatively honest and incorruptible civil service. Although the civil servants of Hong Kong and Singapore are generally considered immune to corruption, business dealings in most other countries often require numerous bribes and payoffs.

According to this same report, another key feature was the emphasis upon export-oriented manufacturing as the leading sector for domestic economic growth. Finally, selective government intervention as part of industrial policy was seen to promote job creation by raising the countries' economic growth potential. Furthermore, in the case of Japan, Korea, and Taiwan, development was facilitated by cooperative arrangements and information-sharing among firms and between the private sectors, including the coordination of investment plans within an otherwise competitive environment.[7]

Instead of identifying the approach of the East Asian Tigers as a model for other developing economies, emphasis was placed upon 'market friendly' development policies. For example, success with export-oriented development strategies depends upon the presence of certain external conditions. First, foreign markets must be large enough to absorb the exported products of the developing country. East Asian countries accounted for only 3.1 percent of the imports of manufactures by the European Community, Japan, and the US in 1988. Second, a successful export program depends upon a capacity to meet industrialized country standards in a global economy that must remain relatively open.

In describing the record of the high-growth East Asian economies, the World Bank suggested that their 'miracle' growth was based upon export-oriented growth strategies and prudent investment policies. The report's conclusions offered mixed signals as to the impact of government intervention as an element in the development process. Interventionist policies within these countries involved the promotion of specific industries, mild financial control combined with directed credit, and export-push policies. On the one hand, technocratic involvement in heavy industries with high-growth potential was credited with job creation in the early development stages of Japan, South Korea, and Taiwan. Similarly, the early and continued encouragement of export goods manufacturing was identified as a basis of the rise in domestic output.[8] On the other hand, these beneficial effects were deemed to be unique to the countries studied, and there was no claim that similar interventions should constitute the development strategy for other countries.

The uniqueness of the experience of these East Asian economies was also attributed to a variety of internal conditions that preceded their economic takeoff. One of the most important of these conditions was the presence of universal primary schooling leading to a relatively high level of education and literacy among the general population in the 1960s. By implication, skill levels and thus productivity of the labor force were generally higher than in other developing countries. These higher education levels also facilitated the transfer and adoption of foreign-sourced technology, and made it easier to find competent staff for the civil service. Relatively high education levels may have contributed to the fact that fertility and mortality rates were lower in East Asia than in other developing countries with similar levels of income. Perhaps not unrelated to the wide access to educational opportunity, measures of economic inequality in East Asia were relatively low, as measured by income and land ownership. Economic equality either contributes to growth by lessening political tensions, or it may reflect the presence of a middle class large enough to support an expanding market for domestic manufactures.

38

Of equal importance to the record of the high-growth East Asian economies was the general absence of market interferences by their governments. Unencumbered market forces therefore played an important role in their remarkable economic growth. Perhaps most significant was the decision to control inflation through a sensible approach to fiscal and monetary policies, including competitively-determined foreign exchange rates. Another important element of government policy was the decision not to provide welfare as transfer payments or income subsidies. This policy was partly a function of practicality that was supported by cultural norms. The inability of governments to generate sufficient levels of state revenues for social welfare payments was offset by the citizenry's strong commitment to family. As national incomes and government revenues rose in the high-growth East Asian economies, their leaders directed more of their expenditures toward social investment and infrastructure.

By contrast, the Western welfare state dedicated increasing sums for consumption. In this sense, there was no grace in the Asian 'miracle.' However, as will become apparent in Chapter Four, governments can afford to mandate individual self sufficiency only during periods of high growth. It will be seen that the level of public involvement increases when reversals of economic fortune occur. Nonetheless, the mixed results generated by East Asian government policies with regard to economic growth leaves the question unanswered. However, by examining the nature of these interventions in the past we can discern some implications for the future. This analysis will be undertaken in greater detail in Chapter Four.

Another perspective on the ability of countries in East Asia to have generated such high growth rates is offered by Mancur Olson. As mentioned in Chapter Two, he suggests that the economic power of countries tends to decline in response to the redistributive pressures and interferences demanded by special interest groups. Alternatively, the absence of these 'interest coalitions' should allow for higher rates of economic growth. Most of the high-growth East Asian countries underwent radical changes in their power structures that upended traditional hierarchical relationships. Those countries that escaped colonial rule saw their historical power centers evaporate and be replaced by nationalist rulers. As such, they benefited from the autocrat's ability to expedite development by weakening interest groups who would have promoted their own narrow concerns at the expense of national growth. Nonetheless, except for Singapore, it is unlikely that the pressures of regional interests can be resisted. Obviously, rice farmers in Korea and Japan have been able to exploit consumers by flexing their political muscle. The Japanese have provided huge subsidies to the islands of Hokkaido and Okinawa as appeasement with a stunning lack of success. As economic growth slows down, these pressures will become politically irresistible.

Japan as forerunner and engine of growth for East Asia

As the first East Asian economy to experience high-paced economic growth, Japan has provided the archetypal model to be followed by other industrializing countries in the region. In more recent years, the process of recycling Japan's large trade surpluses has also served as an economic locomotive for the rest of East Asia. The investment of industrial capital in neighboring countries continues to be spurred by the yen's perennial strength. Growing trade surpluses in the 1980s led to the initial phase of global investing by Japanese firms that was concentrated in North America and Europe. More recently, their attention has turned to East and Southeast Asia in search of lower labor and raw material costs, as well as expanding consumer markets. Direct investment in neighboring Asian countries has targeted assets with bargain prices. While investments in East Asia only constitute about six percent of total Japanese foreign direct investment, it is concentrated in manufacturing and involves a greater use of local partners as well as more reliance upon local financing. Two-thirds of Japanese investments in Asia are in manufacturing, while the comparative figure for the US is only about 20 percent, and the figure for Japan's worldwide investments is only 25 percent.[9]

Just as Japan was able to provide the lead for a period of rapid growth in the region, the deflationary cycle and excess production capacity in the Japanese economy are likely to herald a retreat in the fortunes of the other high-growth East Asian economies. This is unavoidable with over 5,000 Japanese firms operating in the region and employing more than 1 million people. In reaction to five straight years of falling corporate profits, private capital investment in Japan continues to decline and consumer spending is weak. Since these combined expenditures account for about 80 percent of the Japanese economy, there are probably more serious problems ahead.

Newly industrialized countries in East Asia: Dragons, Tigers, and 'miracles'

With Japan's successful industrialization, it became apparent that economic modernization was not limited to Western economies. Following Japan's business leadership, a 'virtuous cycle of growth' in the region began to take shape. As technology became outmoded due to domestic cost structures, it could be transferred to another country where it might be more suitable. East Asia benefited from Japanese direct investment was driven by both push and pull factors. The high value of the yen and rising domestic costs in Japan pushed capital spending to non-Japanese markets, while ground floor opportunities in nascent markets served as a pull factor.

At the same time, many of the leaders in the region began to discard the irrational import substitution policies that raised barriers against entry of foreign made goods with the aim of inducing domestic growth. A similar change in attitude led to the implementation of capital friendly policies designed to encourage investments by multinational corporations that were once derided as the scourge of the Third World.

Hong Kong was already well positioned for entry into the global marketplace. However, in its capacity as an important entry port for China, Hong Kong suffered from the fits and starts associated with Chinese internal affairs. Its neighboring colonial cousin, Singapore, was endowed with some of the same benefits of engagement with the international market through the British Commonwealth. Both were well placed by virtue of their experience with the world trading language as well an understanding of the rule of law and contracts. Meanwhile, Taiwan and South Korea made their own way into uncharted territory, aided in part by military engagement with America. Each of these early East Asian success stories had one leg in the Orient and the other in the West. Their strategic ties guaranteed more favorable terms for access to markets in the US and, to a lesser extent, in Europe.

Passing the baton to China

No account of Asia's progress or any allusions to a 'Pacific Century' could pretend to be complete without incorporating China. As the brinkmanship associated with the Cold War subsided, the priority of being a military superpower has been subordinated to the goal of becoming an economic superpower. China is well suited to accommodate this shift in strategic concerns. The lifting of the Maoist-inspired economic straight jacket, coupled with the normalization of relations with South Korea and increasing interaction across the Taiwan Straits, has led to one of the greatest economic booms, and perhaps the largest economic bubble, in history.

China's prospective role in global affairs is based heavily upon the support of Overseas Chinese in 'Offshore China.'[10] This diaspora of about 55 million Chinese throughout East Asia controls up to $3 trillion in liquid assets and is responsible for production of goods and services worth about $450 billion each year. Their annual output exceeds by nearly 25 percent that of the entire Chinese mainland of 1.2 billion people. Most of the inhabitants of Hong Kong are recent émigrés of neighboring Guangdong province. The flows of capital and goods between Hong Kong and Guangdong are mirrored by similar connections between Taiwan and Fujian province, though the dealings are obviously a bit more circuitous through shell companies.

41

Although the Overseas Chinese constitute a minority in most countries apart from Singapore and of course Taiwan, they or their descendants dominate private enterprise activities in Indonesia, Malaysia, and Thailand. They also have considerable influence in the Philippines. However, this group is not cohesive. Although there are interwoven patterns of contacts across these national boundaries, these are based upon ethnic or language groupings. Being Chinese is less important than are family and clan ties, or the networks established on the basis of one's origin in a specific village or province in the homeland. The businesses of Overseas Chinese have been mostly limited to patriarchal, closed corporations based upon family relations. However, this organizational structure has limited their abilities to expand or to mobilize capital. This is beginning to change in response to new opportunities on the mainland and the threats posed by the takeover of Hong Kong in 1997. In the same manner that economic reform on the mainland has boosted cross border investments of the Overseas Chinese, the uncertainty about the future of Hong Kong has prompted this group to shift their attention toward North America's western coast, to Australia, and beyond.

The Overseas Chinese are not the only ones who depend upon informal networks to guide their capital spending. Japanese companies have found a warmer reception in parts of their former colony of Manchuria, especially the area around Dalian in Lianoning province. Pragmatic considerations have allowed these Japanese investors to find partners who are willing to overlook past transgressions. Likewise, the presence of several million ethnic Koreans in the northeast provinces of China boosted trade and investments from South Korea after the normalization of relations. By 1992, Korea had become China's fourth largest trading partner. Further economic ties will be developed despite China's ambivalence over the issue of the divided Korean peninsula.

Whatever the remarkable advance in China's production and trade figures or the promise of its enlarged consumer class, the fact is that China's economy remains at only about one-tenth the size of Japan's. Even Korea and Taiwan, with significantly smaller populations, record higher GDP figures. Also, most of the impressive development been concentrated in the special economic zones (SEZs) and mostly along the coastal provinces with a few pockets of high growth in the interior. However, regional underdevelopment is but one of the challenges facing the leadership. Neglect of the infrastructure required for the development of internal markets will contribute to continued gaps in the development of the hinterland. The continued reluctance to rationalize and downsize the state-owned enterprises will be a haunting legacy of the forsaken economic policies of communism. Another grim specter is environmental degradation, which in China constitutes some of the worst in the world.

The upshot of all this is that China's continued cohesion depends upon two conditions. First, the interior and coastal provinces must remain loyal to the power center in Beijing and work to overcome the tensions generated by their wildly divergent development status. Second, the actions of the Overseas Chinese, whether intentionally or not, must provide some kind of glue to hold it all together. It remains to be seen if the carrot of prosperity will be successful, or whether the regime will resort to the stick of repression to keep China whole.

Who's next and at what pace?

A true frontier spirit is sweeping East Asia. The degree of confidence is so great that there is no question about whether there will be another round of high economic growth; the only question is which Asian country will be the next Tiger. The answer will be based upon a presumption that other countries in the region will follow the same trajectory path made possible by introducing market reforms mixed with judicious industrial policies. As in the case of the original Tigers, the export sector is expected to lead the rush to development.

Indonesia, Malaysia, and Thailand have already served notice of their intention to stake their claims to industrialized status. The other obvious candidates in the next round are the former socialist economies that are transitioning to market-driven economies, including Burma-Myanmar, Cambodia, Laos, and Vietnam. Even the economy of the Philippines is beginning to shake its image as the 'sick man of Asia.'

However, all the excitement about the economies in the region is belied by a closer inspection of the numbers. Dramatic changes will not come quickly for most countries in the region. For example, Malaysia's own government economists do not expect the country to be fully industrialized until 2020. Liberalization of Indonesia's economy is only now being put into place to allow for an industrial takeoff. Until recently, most of its growth was based upon a rich resource base and a large, pliant workforce. With growth of six percent a year, it will require 16 years for Indonesia's economy to match Malaysia's per capita income in 1993. Under the same conditions, it would take China over 20 years to reach that level, while Vietnam would catch up only after 40 years.

Globalization and the rise of regional economies

The projections mentioned above are based upon a conventional notion of the nation-state while ignoring the importance of economic activities that transcend geographic or political borders.[11] In large part, the observed achievements of East Asia have relied upon and fostered the growing importance of regional economic zones that cross frontiers. One of the imperatives of the global economy is that contiguous territories exploit their comparative advantages regardless of political and bureaucratic intent or protest. The fluidity of the international capital markets means that borders and government policies are increasingly porous. In turn, the stage is set for opportunities to develop region-based prosperity.

Examples of the regionalized economic areas can be found in the spread of Hong Kong's influence over the Pearl River Delta, growth triangles connecting Singapore and parts of Malaysia and Indonesia, and the Tumen Delta project that overlaps the borders of North Korea, Russia, and China. In this setting, nationalism, and protected domestic markets, become obsolete tools used upon only by politicians in a feeble attempt to preserve their political position.

In this context, income level thresholds become more important than geographic or political borders. For example, when GDP reaches $5,000 per capita, individual incomes provide enough margin for citizens to become aware of their consumption opportunities and to compare their positions with others. Government appeals for sacrifice in the name of patriotism will therefore become an increasingly tough sell. Political leaders can expect a lukewarm reception to outmoded nationalist rhetoric in the face of diffuse public perceptions. Appeals to national interest can be expected to founder on the shoals of economic rationality. In all events, countries like China and Indonesia will become increasingly ungovernable in their present political configuration due to the dispersed nature of geographic units and massive populations.

Tracking the Asian development model

Several features define this new Asian development model. Specifically, some of the common elements include: keeping a steady hand on macroeconomic indicators, a high rate of saving and investment, a reliance upon competent technocrats to implement industrial policy, and directing resources toward extensive development in infrastructure and people. Roads, ports, and bridges cannot contribute to growth unless workers acquire the requisite skills and education to contribute to economic production. Another key feature of Asia's growth strategy involved focusing upon exporting manufactured goods and importing technology. In addition, most countries in East Asia experience significant amounts of government involvement or regulation of their economies, sometimes involving force fed growth by directing capital toward favored sectors. In all its variations, however, the Asian development model acknowledged the value of the market.

In terms of inhibiting long-term growth, one of the most damaging forms of government intervention is the attempt to control or manipulate information flows. Pre-modern rulers in Japan limited their citizens' access to foreigners and their ideas due to a deep sense of xenophobia. Although that fear gave way to pragmatism and modernizing influences in Japan, some of the more authoritarian regimes in East Asia continue to view foreign influences as a corruptive force. Thus, there are media restrictions in Burma-Myanmar, China, Indonesia, Singapore, and Vietnam. These countries share an authoritarian style of governing that has evolved into one-party states. While many other countries in the region may have a dominant political party, they have matured enough to be able to forsake their autocratic ways.

One major oversight on the part of promoters of the 'Asian Century' is that the enviable economic progress observed in East Asia is not matched by social or political developments. On the one hand, it is perhaps unfair to expect these countries to be able to progress so rapidly on all fronts. Surely Western countries required several centuries to achieve the moral, scientific, and political advances that served as the basis for world leadership. On the other hand, it would be ill mannered to depict the valiant struggles by East Asians to improve their standard of living as a fixation upon materialism. However, if this impression does stick, it is probably due to the fact that some Asian leaders worship regularly at the altar of GDP to ensure their grip on political power. With one economic following hard upon another, there seems to have been little time for collective reflection on the implications of their newfound wealth. Nevertheless, while the emergence of economic power in East Asia is undeniable, it may be unreasonable and unfair to expect that these countries can adjust their other institutional arrangements in a commensurably short period of time.

Certainly the high rates of economic growth experienced in the region will be volatile due to lags in the modernization of other institutions. It remains open to question whether promoting growth while neglecting political and social reform can be consistent with maintaining the sort of supercharged economic growth realized in recent years. There is ample evidence that a fragile foundation is behind Asia's progress. It is to this issue that we turn in the next chapter.

Notes

1   R. Hofheinz and K. E. Calder, *The Eastasia Edge*, New York: Basic Books, 1982.
2   Sirimavo Bandaranaike become the world's first female head of state after her husband was assassinated. Her first term spanned from 1960 to 1965 and the second from 1970 to 1977.
3   A selection of this first wave of books is as follows: B. Balassa, *The Newly Industrializing Countries in the World Economy*, New York: Pergamon Press, 1981; E. Chen, *Hyper-Growth in Asian Economies: A*

Comparative Study of Hong Kong, Japan, Korea, Singapore and Taiwan, New York: Holmes & Meier Publishers, 1979. E. Lee (ed.), *Export-Led Industrialization and Development*, Geneva: International Labour Office, 1981; L. Turner and N. McMullen (eds.), *The Newly Industrialising Countries: Trade and Adjustment*, London: Allen and Unwin, 1982; and G. White (ed.), *Developmental States in East Asia*, New York: St. Martins Press, 1988.

4   Books in the second wave are: A. Chowdhury and I. Islam, *The Newly Industrialising Economies of East Asia*, London: Routledge, 1993; G. L. Clark and W. B. Kim (eds.), *Asian NIEs and the Global Economy: Industrial Restructuring and Corporate Strategies in the 1990s*, Baltimore: Johns Hopkins University Press, 1995; G. Gereffi and D. Wyman (eds.), *Manufacturing Miracles: Paths of Industrialization in Latin America and East Asia*, Princeton: Princeton University Press, 1992; Y. C. Kim (ed.), *The Southeast Asian Economic Miracle*, New Brunswick, NJ: Transaction Publishers, 1995; and W. Overholt, *China: The Next Economic Superpower*, London: Weidenfeld & Nicolson, 1993.

5   Estimates for East Asia's share of world output project an increase from 17.4 percent in 1980 to 23.7 percent in 1990 and 28.2 percent in the year 2000. Similar gains are expected for East Asia's share of total world trade from 13.7 percent in 1980 to 19.3 percent in 1990 and 33.1 percent in the year 2000.

6   World Bank, *The East Asian Miracle*, op. cit.

7   C. Johnson, *MITI and the Japanese Miracle: The Growth of Industrial Policy, 1925-1975*, Tokyo: Charles E. Tuttle, 1986.

8   Gereffi and Wyman, op. cit.

9   Abegglen, *Sea Change*, op. cit.

10   S. Seagrave, *Lords of the Rim: The Invisible Empire of the Overseas Chinese*, New York: Putnam's Sons, 1995.

11   K. Ohmae, *The End of the Nation State: The Rise of Regional Economies*, New York: The Free Press, 1995.

4 Economic realities and Asian illusions

The prediction of an approaching 'Asian Century' is based upon a number of questionable premises. Foremost among these is the presumption that past economic growth is a reliable indicator of future economic performance. Contrary to popular opinion, it will be argued here that East Asia is seriously vulnerable to failures in the economic arena. In part, this conclusion concurs with Weber's conclusion about the retarding impact of the institutional arrangements in Asia, but perhaps for different reasons.

Alternative interpretations of the past naturally give way to different understandings of the future. This chapter explores some views that challenge the conventional wisdom of the previous growth record and prospects of the high-performing East Asian economies.

Technocratic involvements in industries with high-growth potential have been credited for job creation in the early developmental stages of heavy industries in Japan, South Korea, and Taiwan. Similarly, the early and continued encouragement of export goods manufacturing has been identified as a basis for the rise in domestic output. However, the relatively unique preconditions existing prior to economic takeoff for these countries imply that the results cannot be easily replicated. The 'Asian Model' therefore does not constitute a relevant development strategy for other countries.

Although there is no expectation of a dramatic reversal of fortunes for East Asia in the near future, there are reasons to question the predictions of an uninterrupted economic growth path. While the formidable gains in output of the high-growth East Asian economies are without a doubt noteworthy, there is evidence to suggest that these results are not truly miraculous, nor is the level of growth without precedent. Indeed, there are other cases where a solid consensus on bullish economic forecasts has proved to be wrong. These cautionary remarks should not be seen as promoting an apocalyptic vision for East

Asia. Instead, it is hoped that the introduction of some contrarian views to the unbridled optimism for the region will point to mistakes that can be avoided.[1]

Bouquets and brickbats for the 'Asian Century'

Interestingly, the prediction of an approaching 'Asian Century' has produced a mixture of excitement and foreboding. On the one hand, there is an assortment of optimists, some of whom see recent developments in Asia as more of an opportunity than a threat to the existing world economic order. For example, as more Asians reach middle class status as consumers, world trade can be expected to expand dramatically. In the face of growing demand from such large demographic groups, the agricultural surpluses generated by the US and Europe will find expanding markets for their exports. Those countries that are able to export other basic commodities will also benefit not only from the larger number of customers, but also from the likelihood that the price of these commodities will increase in real terms.

Unfortunately, many of the optimists who believe in the 'Asian Century' are apologists for the authoritarian regimes in Asia. Many promote certain 'Asian values' that are identified as culturally superior, while Western values of individualism and liberalism are condemned. These critics' complaints are inadvertently abetted by the often self-effacing introspection of Western thinkers and the self-critical obsession of the media in the West. It is important to note that the manipulation of this idealized view of the future in order to serve narrow political purposes will inevitably spark interregional tensions.

On the other hand, protectionist-minded 'pessimists' in the West justify their nationalist agenda by invoking the dreaded image of a calcified industrialized world that is unable to compete with the surplus labor conditions and market-friendly policies of developing countries in East Asia. This viewpoint incites an adversarial atmosphere and, by so doing, encourages the costly imposition of restrictions on international trade flows. Politicians are tempted to interfere with international trade as a matter of political expediency. Such political posturing occurs despite the wide understanding that protectionism imposes costs on the greater population of consumers and taxpayers, while conferring benefits to specific groups of producers and workers.

Among the optimists and the pessimists are those who regard tomorrow as simply an extrapolation of today; where current growth rates in parts of Asia are taken to be a reliable indicator of the region's future. However, simplistic thinking along these lines ignores the impact of dynamic change. To be prepared for the competitive challenges of the next century, myopic thinking that is based upon static conditions must be rejected. The globalization of commerce along with the high degree of fluidity in capital markets requires that decision makers must become increasingly flexible in order to accommodate an unknowable future. Only those models that incorporate the dynamic element of long-run adjustments offer useful insights. As is starkly illustrated by the recession-bound Japanese economy in the 1990s, there can be no living on one's laurels in the new global marketplace. As elsewhere and always, life at the top will remain precarious.

Fortunately, many Asian regimes are making significant strides toward greater political decentralization in tandem with their economic liberalization. The most obvious cases of increased democratization are the Philippines, South Korea, Taiwan, and Thailand. Not surprisingly, leaders of some of the one-party states in the Pacific Basin claim that their countries' recent economic progress is the consequence of an immutable set of circumstances, especially the political status quo. In adopting this logic, former socialist regimes hope to maintain their one-party rule as the vanguard for rapid economic growth. However, rigidified political institutions, like the one-party or one-family regimes that control political arrangements in some East Asian countries, will ultimately prove to be a long-run detriment.

Political repression too often masquerades as political stability contributing to economic growth. Long-run economic prosperity is better served by the moderating influences of non-governmental organizations that evolve spontaneously under democracy. These non-governmental associations serve to counterbalance the governing elite, thereby insuring a more comprehensive expression of the community's economic preferences and potential. In contrast to more open societies in the West, authoritarian regimes in East Asia try to control the political opposition by placing strict controls over communication and information flows. These controls discourage investors by obstructing the independent corroboration of data. They also hinder technological advance by stifling the birth and circulation of new ideas on the premise that free thinking among the citizenry might undermine the security of the regime.

As the Soviet experiment showed, it is impossible to separate the economic from the political. Eventually an attempt to partition politics from other aspects of life will lead to the emergence of conflicts and disruptions in the social order that will have economic consequences. The imposition of restrictions on freedom of thought will constrain the potential for economic growth. East Asian authoritarian regimes may be successful in marginalizing their domestic political opponents through the application of strict social controls. Eventually, however, it will also be necessary to interfere with domestic commerce so that economic power cannot be used as a lever against the ruling party. Such politically motivated interventions will inevitably weaken private property rights, and will interfere with contractual arrangements. Consequently, with the passage and enforcement of law in the hands of autocrats, 'lawless order' will be substituted for law and order. Thus, while there may be a *system* of law (as in China), there is no *rule* of law to serve as a foundation for business confidence. In the end, an economic system built upon the exchange of favors for party loyalty will produce a distorted incentive structure. A derivative problem is the likelihood of political corruption stemming from the necessarily cozy relationships between favor-givers and favor-seekers.

Any political equilibrium observed under such conditions would have to be short lived. Without loyal supporters earned in open democratic contests, authoritarian regimes will find it increasingly costly to buy peace with an increasingly prosperous and autonomous middle class. Generous compensation must also be paid to civil servants to insure their loyalty. However, the lure of a high-paying government job may deter the limited pool of well-educated citizens pursuing more productive careers in the private economy.

Governments following this strategy will inhibit the emergence of indigenous entrepreneurs, who are a key ingredient for sustained economic progress. It is their creative and independent actions that generate growth. By definition, their search for profit opportunities requires that they constantly take risks and undertake challenges to the economic order, and if need be, to the political status quo. In contrast, people who choose to be political cronies are unlikely to be risk takers. Attempts by authoritarian regimes to institutionalize the free-enterprise process by appointing party faithfuls cannot succeed, because the attributes of entrepreneurship involve more than programmed trading. Being truly free thinkers, entrepreneurs will always constitute a potential threat to the political status quo.

However, attempts to suppress or co-opt them may lead to a ruinous brain-drain. In attempting to control entrepreneurs, authoritarian regimes are damned if they do, and damned if they do not. Perhaps the most damaging result of government policies that restrain free thinking is the glaring absence of innovative design and technological research in much of Asia. While it is true that some of the Tigers have begun to export some technology to neighboring countries and have registered an increased number of patents, much of this activity reflects the efforts of multinational corporations (MNCs) that operate in the region. In East Asia, foreigners have been patenting inventions at a faster pace than have Asian residents. For example, in 1990 foreign inventors in Singapore and Hong Kong were awarded 99 and 98 percent, respectively, of all patents issued.[2] Accounting for 95 percent of Asia's US patents, Japan is the only East Asian country that has kept pace with Western industrialized countries.

The tendency of most East Asian governments to avoid conflict and to work toward 'consensus building' has the unintended consequence of strengthening staid hierarchical structures by limiting open debate. In the absence of any counterweight to the strict adherence to hierarchical decisions of politicians or managers, short run gains from building consensus may be offset by related long-run costs arising from corruption, social injustice, or economic inefficiency. The swift pace of technological change and innovation in management practices undertaken by competitors will overwhelm whatever advantages may have been derived from imposed consensus under authoritarian or hierarchical rule. The multi-layered decision making process typical under a hierarchical system is too rigid and time consuming to allow nimble responses. The rapid pace of change inherent in the emerging global economic order is therefore drastically reducing the effectiveness of authoritarian rule, especially as citizens develop greater economic autonomy. Perhaps more effective is the discipline of global capital markets, which punishes political leaders for implementing economically irrational policies.[3]

Those countries with a tradition of hierarchical structures are likely to find their competitive advantages slipping away in the modern global economy. This is because the requirements for economic prosperity in the future will require the adoption of some culturally-alien arrangements. Perhaps the most pressing of these is a reliable system for the strict enforcement of contracts and a commitment to private property rights. Commercial law must be transparent, and a system of courts must provide fair and equal protection to all parties involved in contracts. What may be problematic for the hierarchical regimes of East Asia is that contract law is by its nature a method of protecting the interests of individuals. These protections exist regardless of whether the issue involves a commercial transaction or a political dispute. Most Asian regimes operate under rules that de-emphasize the importance of individuals. The continuation of enforced hierarchical business and political structures in East Asia can therefore be expected to stunt economic growth potential.

While it is generally thought that business can be conducted in a few Asian countries like Singapore without resorting to bribes, many of the other neighboring economies are riddled with corruption. According to a poll of international businessmen and financial journalists collected by Transparency International in 1995, 6 of the 10 most corrupt countries in the world were in Asia. In order, there were, Indonesia, China, Pakistan, the Philippines, India, and Thailand.[4] A similar Corruption Perception Index for 1996 revealed that Pakistan and Nigeria replaced Indonesia and China as the countries most affected by corruption, while 5 of the 10 countries with the worst rating were in Asia. In order, these were Pakistan, Bangladesh, China, India, and Indonesia. Being successful in most parts of Asia requires a skill for developing patronage and a nose for strategic bribery. With kickbacks so common, corruption in Asia is cosmic in its proportions. For example, it has been estimated that corruption adds about 30 percent to the cost of doing business in Indonesia.[5]

Another manifestation of corruption can be found in the actions of one-party states that establish judicial systems that follow the dictates of the executive branch of government. This form of corruption weakens business confidence in that it undermines the substantive application of commercial law by skewing dispute resolution in favor of political cronies. In addition, this arrangement is socially destructive in that corrupt leaders can remain in power while silencing those who demand more open government. Thus, personal rights can be curbed and human rights ignored.

Economic logic and sustainable growth in East Asia

Considerable statistical data have been compiled to suggest that an 'Asian Century' is inevitable. Seductively cloaked with an aura of scientific accuracy, this 'objective' evidence constitutes the cornerstone for arguments favoring Asian Pacific leadership in world affairs in the next century. Not surprisingly, many investment advisors, journalists, politicians, business leaders, and the general public have credulously accepted this pronouncement. However, there are alternative interpretations of the past that naturally produce different understandings of the future. For example, the region's high economic growth rates can also be explained by the transfer of technology from advanced economies, combined with the massive infusion of inputs into their production processes. This chapter will elaborate the contrarian view of the previous growth record and future prospects for Asia's 'miracle' economies.

The first question at issue is the identification of the underlying basis for the remarkably swift transition and modernization of these economies.[6] The concise explanation offered by the World Bank report on East Asian 'miracle' economies was that these governments designed and implemented proper macroeconomic policies. As a practical matter, this explanation can be distilled into an endorsement of policies that promoted export-led growth.[7] This view was taken by many Japanese government officials as validation of their highly bureaucratized approach to economic development. Even in Japan's own view, then, there is no 'miracle,' per se. Their economic results are attributable to the steady and visible hand of government directing the growing fortunes of its citizens.

By the late 1970s, several seminal studies appeared which brought the high economic growth of East Asia to the attention of the world.[8] Their analysis of the causal factors underlying the experiences of five of the fastest growing economies in the period 1955 to 1974 raises serious questions about the conclusions of the World Bank report. These studies examined the growth in the use of factor inputs (i.e., land, labor, and capital) and other technical considerations in order to determine their contribution to economic growth in the region. In examining the productive contributions of inputs with reference to a wide measure of technological change (total factor productivity or TFP), it was reported that increases in inputs accounted for about one-half of the recorded growth in income over the period studied for the five countries in the survey.[9] Since Japan, Korea, and Taiwan had relatively large farming sectors at the beginning of the period, they experienced a substantial growth impact owing to the shift of resources from the agricultural to the industrial sector. Interestingly, except for Japan, improvements in the distribution of income accompanied rapid economic growth in the other four countries.

Another survey examining the growth experience of Hong Kong, Singapore, South Korea, and Taiwan, found quite mixed results across countries and over time.[10] Although improvements in TFP appear to be an important source of growth, there is also some indication that distortions in the capital or labor markets led to a decline in efficiency.

This latter point was later confirmed by several economists who analyzed a more current data base.[11] Paul Krugman popularized the Alwyn Young study that concluded that East Asia's economic growth was neither miraculous nor surprising. Furthermore, given the evanescent nature of the conditions under which these growth rates were generated, they are not likely to be sustained in the long run. In their view, East Asia's exceptionally high economic growth rates were the inevitable consequence of a dramatic rise in the quantity of inputs into the economic system. On the one hand, there are physical limits to the resource base that can provide inputs into the economy. On the other hand, gains from such input-driven growth eventually run up against the 'law of diminishing returns,' and cannot continue unless there are accompanying increases in efficiency.[12] Increases in per-capita income can be sustained only if the quantity of output rises relative to each additional unit of input. Economic growth in these East Asian countries can be largely attributed to the expeditious mobilization of resources, a boost that can only happen once, coupled with the abstemious nature of consumers in the region. For example, even if its financial system problems are disregarded, the Japanese economy can no longer rely upon growth driven by increases in labor inputs because birth rates are declining, and the entry of women into the labor force has peaked.

A clear illustration of the law of diminishing returns is provided by comparing relative trends in Asian output growth on a per capita and per worker basis. As most rosy economic reports on the region like to emphasize, the general pace of economic growth in Hong Kong, Singapore, South Korea, and Taiwan has more than offset increases in population growth. Similarly, measures of annual growth in output per capita rank these countries in the top 5 of a total sample of 118 countries. These countries also compare favorably with the rest of the sample in terms of gains in output per worker, which are derived from rapid increases in labor and capital inputs. However, the gains in output per worker are considerably less than the gains in output per capital. Thus, the incremental *return* associated with increases arising from increases in labor force participation is now *diminishing*.

Such crudely-derived gains in output have been the driving force behind the extraordinary growth of East Asian high-growth economies over the past three decades. Another report estimates the 'miracle' component of this economic growth to be less than one percentage point of the recorded growth rates.[13]

As indicated above, dynamic, and thus sustainable, economic growth relies upon gains in total productivity. Increased labor participation rates, employment expansion, as well as increased investments in education, health, and physical capital are blunt, one-shot methods for generating economic growth. The perpetuation of high growth rates demands that qualitative improvements must coincide with quantitative increases in inputs. Interestingly, Botswana, the Congo, Egypt, Malta, and Pakistan recently outpaced the gains in productivity registered by the high-performing East Asian economies. Hong Kong, with the least amount of government intervention in microeconomic affairs, recorded the greatest gains in TFP. Apparently, the intrusive industrial policies of the governments in Singapore, South Korea, and Taiwan have resulted in rigidities preventing rapid and appropriate responses to market signals. Such government directed incentives for production tend to interfere with efficient resource allocation due to greater lags in the decision process.

Significantly, unlike Singapore, South Korea, and Taiwan, a much greater proportion of Hong Kong's rapid growth is attributable to gains in TFP. In the case of these other countries, the explanation for growth lies in government directed investments derived from taxes and forced savings.[14] Governments may be able to stimulate growth by offering subsidies and tax incentives to multinationals, but this can only be a short-run strategy. Just as in the early stages of development in the USSR, many of the high-growth East Asian economies have made large expenditures on physical and human capital.[15] Although there may be notable differences in their development paths, there are signs that returns on investments in East and Southeast Asia are diminishing in a manner reminiscent of the Soviet experience. In addition, this phenomenon does not appear to be lost on the financial markets: measured in local currency terms, declines in the stock markets of Singapore and Thailand in 1995 exceeded losses in the all-share index of Mexico during the same year.

Some confirmation of the Krugman and Young studies is found in the response of businesses to the rapidly rising operating costs in the region.[16] For example, China's regime announced an intention to rescind tax breaks that had been offered as a lure for new foreign investments. Moreover, foreign businesses have had to contend with soaring costs for expatriate housing in controlled property markets, continued interference and financial impositions from corrupt officials, a scarcity of skilled labor and management talent, and rising delivery costs due to regulations in the transport industry. When operating costs exceed productivity gains, production facilities will migrate to areas where greater profit opportunities are available. Businesses are beginning to reposition themselves to escape cost inflation in Japan and even China, by moving to Malaysia and Indonesia.

In polls of expatriate managers, most of the East Asian economies ranked very low in terms of desirable labor attributes.[17] It seems that there are a variety of problems that belie the impression of cheap, surplus labor in Asia. Not only is skilled labor in East Asia expensive due to its relative scarcity, but the tendency of these workers to be 'job hoppers' contributes to costly instability in the work place. Interestingly, the labor forces of most Western countries tended to rank higher than their East Asian counterparts when considering cost, quality, availability, and turnover.

Those who insist that the objective evidence points to continued growth in East Asia should remember that Soviet economic growth during the 1950s led many to be excessively optimistic about that country's economic prospects. For example, Paul Samuelson, a Nobel laureate economist, predicted that Soviet living standards would catch up and then surpass those of America by the early 1990s. He was not alone in this observation. Even the CIA offered similar predictions. If such highly esteemed economists and government intelligence services can err about this sort of projection, it seems wise for lesser mortals to question the capacity of the high-growth East Asian economies to sustain their enviable record. In all events, while various East Asian economies have certainly exhibited high rates of economic growth, the supporting data are often supplied on a tightly controlled and selective basis by the governments themselves. Since this data is not amenable to extensive outside corroboration or detailed analysis by independent sources, such reports should be interpreted with a healthy skepticism.

References to the failed communist experience are often provided as evidence that static, central planning will eventually be overcome by the dynamics of economic reality. However, it might also be said that communism failed to achieve the increases in productive efficiency necessary for long-term economic viability because of the absence of a free-thinking entrepreneurial class imbued with a sense of inventiveness. The stifling of individualism and creativity by authoritarian regimes in East Asia is likely to impose a fatal limit upon the capacity of these economies to grow faster forever. Since they have had and will have difficulty spawning indigenous sources of growth, they will continue to rely upon borrowed technology. This parasitic dependence upon foreign markets is not consistent with continued high rates of growth in the globalized marketplace.

More recently, the record of many of the Southeast Asian economies has depended in large measure upon the Northeast Asian economies, notably Japan and South Korea. All of the Asian economies will soon have to confront the inevitable shake-out associated with duplicative economic growth strategies and productive capacities. By mid-1996, a region-wide slump in the electronics industry signaled the beginning of this problem. Also, it can be expected that price competition from emerging economies in other parts of the world will undercut the growth potential of East Asia's 'miracle' economies and hasten the necessary economic restructuring.

Another question about the capacity of East Asian economies to sustain their high growth rates involves the nature of the growth cycle. In comparing the high-growth experience of East Asian economies with that of the West, the difference in their respective starting points must be considered. As Western industrialized economies entered the mature phase of their development, they experienced a flattening growth path at the time when the high-growth East Asian economies were entering the initial trajectory of their takeoff phase. The dramatically high rates of East Asian growth are hardly surprising given that these countries could draw upon established Western technologies to modernize their industries.

In general, modernization allows those countries with relatively low productivity to achieve more striking advances in income by expediting the 'catch-up' phase of economic development. This arises from the replacement of traditional techniques by advanced technology with a learning phase considerably shorter than that experienced by the country that originally developed the innovation. For example, Great Britain needed 60 years before doubling output per person during its initial industrialization, but the US economy accomplished the same feat in about 45 years. More recently, Korea was able to double its per capita output in only 10 years (1966-77), while China's Guangdong province took a mere 5 years to do so.

Other economies are poised to enter this race. With each passing day, competitive firms are entering the global economy from countries that have implemented privatization and marketization policies. By imitating the success stories of East Asia against whom they will compete, it will obviously not be different for many of these emerging countries to 'get their basics right.' Many countries in Latin America and Eastern Europe are at a growth phase similar to that of the East Asian emerging economies during the 1960s. It is therefore likely that restructuring pressures on East Asia's high-growth economies will come first from the Latin American and East European rather than the second round of 'miracle' economies in the region. Unless the East Asian economies can effectively cope with the pressures to downsize or to increase productivity, their economies will not be able to lead others in the region into next century.

In sum, recent East Asian economic growth is probably no more sustainable than the high-growth phases experienced by other countries during their early development stages. Similar to Germany and America prior to World War I, the high-growth East Asian economies have probably benefited as much from exogenous forces, such as widening product and resource markets, as they have from their own choice of development strategy. However, the dependence of East Asian economies upon technology and markets in the West must be replaced by greater self-reliance.

The more inclusive and transparent nature of political relationships necessitated by a modern economy poses a challenge of equal magnitude to the ability of East Asian economies to remain on a high-growth path. Since these progressive political relationships are incompatible with authoritarian leadership, one-party regimes will find the adjustments most difficult to make. As will be discussed in Chapter Six, the limits to growth and global leadership imposed by authoritarianism and economic logic may be exacerbated by traditional institutions common to many of the East Asian high-growth economies.

Politics and limits to high growth in East Asia

As mentioned in Chapter Three, authoritarian leaders in East Asian regimes insist on a development path of 'prosperity first, rights later.' Left to their own devices, people might choose material progress over political freedom. However, authoritarian rule deliberately erects serious barriers which prevent citizens from communicating their preferences for greater individual autonomy. In one-party states with deep traditions of hierarchical rulers, political conversation is unidirectional, from the elected to the electors.[18]

Contrary to the 'cruel choice' approach to development prescribed by Asian authoritarian leaders, one author has offered the compelling argument that democracy does not inhibit development.[19] Suggestions that the absence of democracy was the determining factor behind super-charged growth in East Asia overlook the impact of other initial conditions. His analysis draws four general conclusions concerning the relationship between political and economic institutions. First, the absence of both democracy and free markets (e.g., as was the case in ex-communist regimes) weakens incentives for production and innovation and leads to a deficiency in productivity and growth. Second, the lack of free markets may nullify democracy's advantages over authoritarianism, as in India prior to its ongoing reforms. Third, democracy on its own may or may not drive significant economic growth. Fourth, free markets can deliver growth with or without democracy, as in some of the East Asian economies. The explanation offered here is that high growth in those East Asian economies ruled by autocrats was more the result of the diffusion of Western technology and access to international markets, rather than authoritarian political arrangements. Recent experience in East Asia indicates that authoritarian regimes can oversee consistent growth and development while allowing for a reasonably equitable distribution of income. However, as argued above, democracy coupled with markets can best promote long-term development by encouraging the sort of individualism that promotes sustained entrepreneurship and innovation.

Thus, the 'miracle' economies in East and Southeast Asia may be no different and no more sustainable than was the exceptional growth of the Soviet economy or the post-war economy of Germany. Clearly, despotic regimes can initially have considerable success in directing the development of immature economies by resolutely implementing policies that do not violate economic rationality. However, the East Asian high-growth economies have been following, rather than leading, the rest of the developed world, by relying upon ready access to Western technology and open markets. As the 'age of mass industrialization' passes, the competitive advantages of many East Asian economies will be challenged. Without producing their own domestic entrepreneurial talent and self-generated technological advance, these countries will continue to lag the developed economies in what could prove to be a perpetually dependent relationship. Despite high scores in international competitions for Asian primary and secondary science and math students, there is a dependency upon institutions of higher education in the West. Whatever the shifts in economic prowess, the West continues to have the greatest centers of higher learning, thanks to its tradition of intellectual freedom. As such, these centers attract and produce the bulk of the world's great scholars and innovators.

Generally speaking, it is relatively easy to implement a set of competent policy initiatives in the early stages of development. Given the tremendous opportunities afforded by a global economy, it would require a substantial number of truly inept policies and remarkably unstable or inefficient institutions to hold back economic development. For the most part, this was the situation in China between Liberation in 1949 and 1978. Furthermore, the complicated political relationships that evolve in conjunction with a modern economy are certain to impose limits upon the gains generated from authoritarian leadership. This issue will be addressed in more detail in Chapter Eight.

Some Asian leaders point to material advancement as an indisputable justification for the physical or intellectual imprisonment of their citizenry, as well as for the controls and restraints upon their media. However, there is no reason to expect that Asian autocrats will have any greater long-term success than observed elsewhere. A slowdown in the rate of economic growth will cause an unraveling of the social contract under which political rights had been traded off for prosperity. This will weaken the official legitimacy of the authoritarian regimes and political stability will be shaken.

Economic limits to political stability in East Asia

Generally, East Asian economies are characterized by a number of structural weaknesses. However, this need not be taken as a prognostication of dramatic reversal in the fortunes of the region. Nonetheless, these deficiencies can be expected to impose constraints on the ability of these countries to continue their heretofore high rates of economic growth. Since the governments in the region must deliver continued economic prosperity as the price for their political survival, these issues are of considerable importance to the region's stability.

Continuation of economic growth will be hampered unless the infrastructural weaknesses that exist in many of the high-growth Asian economies are remedied. The great commercial potential of China and Vietnam remain largely dormant because they have poor internal communication and transportation facilities. These facilities are crucial for the development of their own domestic markets and to enable foreigners to access consumers.

For the most part, East Asian exports are in narrow product lines that are not included among the necessities of life (e.g., food and energy). Therefore, there will be enormous pressure to operate with great flexibility in response to an uncertain demand. For example, Japanese exports are heavily concentrated in consumer electronics and automobiles. They export much less in other categories, such as high technology items. At the same time, similar or even less sophisticated exports are produced by other economies in the region. As markets become saturated with durable consumer items, future export production will rely principally upon the replacement market. Export earnings are jeopardized further by a secular decline in electronics industry pricing that appeared in the latter half of 1996.

It has become increasingly evident that East Asian economies must develop a capacity to export services and other value-added products in order to widen their economic base. Increased participation in the information revolution is also becoming a practical necessity. However, political arrangements in many East Asian countries deliberately hinder the free flow of information. The pressing question is whether control and censorship of information deemed politically dangerous can be consistent with a thriving information-based economy.

East Asian exports depend heavily upon sales to advanced industrialized economies, especially North America. While Japan has provided the impetus for manufacturing growth in the region, the demand for its output is largely a function of economic activity in Europe and North America. Although global trade has probably been permanently liberalized, there are risks that trade relations may be mismanaged in the name of nationalism. Unfortunately, this problem is not limited to Asia. China's obsession with dominating Tibet precipitated a confrontation with the Disney Corporation over a film about the Dalai Lama's life. Alternatively, there are intermittent protests by US citizens against NAFTA or WTO membership that are motivated by a fear of losing national sovereignty.

Most East Asian economies depend heavily upon imported raw materials, including energy, and will remain so for the medium term. The region contains considerable natural resources, especially oil in the South China Sea and in Siberian Russia. However, development of these reserves will continue to be hampered by internal political instability and international disputes. Even if these disputes were resolved tomorrow, development would most likely still be stymied by the shortage of skilled labor in the region. As these shortages drive up wages in the more advanced economies of the region, they will lose their comparative advantage of relatively cheap labor.

As mentioned previously, traditional institutional arrangements in Asia serve to inhibit original research. Even though Asians hold education in high regard, most schooling is based upon rote learning. Hierarchical structures inhibit free thinking and the challenging of conventional wisdom that generates new ideas or approaches. As a result, those contributions that have emerged from East Asia are in narrowly focused areas with limited applications.

East Asian bubble economies?

Speculative bubbles involve the mass delusion that asset prices will rise relentlessly.[20] These bubbles are typically the result of some distorted incentive structure that causes market participants to make 'irrational' decisions. Often it is the excessive expansion of the supply of money and credit. Because governments or their central banks control money and credit policies, public policies are the most probable source of speculative manias that can affect an entire economy. Past financial frenzies have been famous for wild gyrations in market valuations for tulips or swampland. In their more modern incarnations, this fever often directs funds into financial instruments and away from cash-starved, real assets.

In the case of Japan, bureaucratic control over the economy set the stage for a classic speculative bubble.[21] Apparently, Japan's prior economic ascendancy supported the illusion that technocrats, bureaucrats and politicians could replace the decentralized decisions of entrepreneurs and other economic agents. Because many countries in the region have adopted the Japanese development model, it is instructive to examine the Japanese experience as a trailblazer for events in the rest of East Asia.

While the details are different in each case, the blueprint being followed by most of the East Asian economies is basically the same.[22] In general, unusually high rates of growth induce natural economic consequences that eventually slow the economy's pace. This moderation of excessively high-paced growth tends to occur through the export-dampening effects of general inflation, coupled with an appreciation of the real exchange rate. Exports will lose their competitive advantage and experience a downturn as they become more expensive due to rising domestic production costs and the appreciation of the domestic currency.

However, in the case of most East Asian economies, the rise in the domestic price of goods will be limited because central bank actions can be expected to thwart inflation. An obsession with preserving competitive exchange rates may induce some governments to interfere with the other adjustment mechanism, i.e., the increase in the international cost of their currencies. Because exchange rate management is an integral element of the strategy to facilitate exports, it is unlikely to be abandoned, especially in the early stages of export-led development.

When the prices of goods and exchange rates do not rise sufficiently, then the adjustment burden is shifted elsewhere. The most likely outcome is a rise in the price of property and other tangible assets. This mechanism has been conspicuously at work in the rental of office space and the cost of housing in Hong Kong, Singapore, and Tokyo, for example. These increased costs have a significant impact on the profitability of corporations, and upon the economy as a whole. As inflated asset prices work their way into the operating costs of business, profit margins of these companies begin to shrink. Eventually, the competitive advantage of the overall economy will be eroded as foreign firms find it too expensive to maintain a presence in the country. The effect is comparable to a tax increase on the use of building space. In time, as foreign firms relocate or downsize their operations, growth-related pressures are relieved in the same way as with the other mechanisms.

By interfering with normal market processes, policy-induced distortions will exacerbate the severity of the inevitable adjustment. Indeed, Japan's difficulties during the early 1990s can be attributed in large part to an inability to deregulate the economy.

Japan's economy has been gripped by a recession since the early 1990s, and its retail sector has been in a slump for over three years. It is more disquieting that its financial sector has all the signs of a full-blown banking crisis. Although a large scale restructuring was necessary to avert a financial disaster in Japan, neither the Ministry of Finance nor Japanese politicians has taken sufficient steps to restore global confidence. The Ministry of Finance has not been forthcoming with accurate details of the severity of the problems, and bankers have been instructed to avoid revealing information about the magnitude of bad loans. Until resolute actions are taken to provide greater certainty of a permanent fix, financial operations in Japan are certain to be harmed in the long run.

A complete understanding of the severity of Japan's problems is obscured by large and continuing trade surpluses with its Western trading partners, coupled with the aggressive expansion of Japanese investment in overseas production facilities. Meanwhile, the chronic strength of the yen also serves as a deceptive indicator of financial stability and economic vitality.[23] However, the Japanese government and businesses are becoming aware that the high value of the yen may cause disturbing increases in unemployment as a result of the 'hollowing out' of their economy. An economy experiences this 'hollowing out' process when firms maintain their headquarters at home, but shift manufacturing jobs to overseas locations. For example, many Japanese manufacturing firms have moved offshore in response to rising domestic costs and the strong yen, both of which limited profitability for goods produced in Japan. At the same time, domestic industrial production has been slow or declining while business inventories have been rising. Hollowing out is likely to worsen due to the overemployment of domestic labor ('labor hoarding') by Japanese firms, and the existence of excess production capacity. Indeed, one of the proud features of the Japanese economy, permanent or 'lifetime' employment, is unlikely to survive the economy-wide restructuring imposed by the strictures of the global marketplace.[24]

Japan's current economic malaise is the result of a chain of events beginning with the expansionary monetary policies put into force after the September 1985 Plaza Accord. In order to spark growth in Japan, discount rates were lowered from 5.0 percent to 2.5 percent by February 1987. At the same time, the Japanese financial sector was liberalized. Financial commitments became increasingly 'securitized' as funds began to circulate outside the conventional banking sector.[25] The catalyst for Japan's bubble was cheap and readily available credit that led to a boom in the property and stock market. During the 1980s, the price of real estate rose by a factor of five. The price of golf course memberships that were bought and sold like other tradable commodities, rose to a level equaling the cost of building an entire golf course in most other countries. At their respective peaks, it was claimed that the total estimated market value of Japanese land constituted 60 percent of world property values and that Japanese stocks accounted for nearly 40 percent of world stock market values. These claims were met with wide-eyed greediness rather than incredulity. In turn, Japan's real estate industry overestimated the pace of economic growth and began construction on many new commercial buildings.

The boom in collateralized lending against the inflated paper value of real estate and stocks meant that an increasing proportion of borrowing against land and stocks was heavily leveraged against unsustainable valuations. Eventually, commercial property in some of the larger cities declined 30 to 70 percent from their peak values, while the Nikkei Index fell by at least 60 percent.[26] To date, the Nikkei has recovered only about one-half of that loss. Real estate prices, however, have continued their decline. In the six month period up to September 1995, foreclosed properties sold at auction for about 20 percent of the collateral value of their loans. However, even at those low prices, only about one-third of the properties were sold. The remaining two-thirds did not sell; the minimum bidding price of 18.7 percent of the original loan was obviously considered to be too high.

In November of 1995, the Ministry of Finance announced that problem loans in Japan amounted to $371 billion (37.4 trillion yen). Many others believe the actual amount to be between $444 and $460 billion.[27] Both estimates put the figure for unrecoverable loans at about $100 billion. These unserviceable private debts account for nearly 10 percent of Japan's GDP. This percentage is three times greater than the proportion of American GDP involved in its Savings and Loan fiasco. As was the case in the US, Japanese housing loan companies (*jusen*), with $60 billion to $70 billion in problem loans on their books, will be bailed out with taxpayers' money. Similarly, the collapse of Japanese National Railways (JNR) may involve losses of $200 million. Should land prices continue to drop or not recover, those financial institutions holding real estate as collateral will be saddled with increasing bad debts and eventual write-offs.

By the end of 1995, various financial institutions were on the brink of collapse, including Cosmo Credit Corporation in Tokyo, Hyogo Bank in Kobe, and Kizu Credit Cooperative in Osaka. Collapse of these three financial houses would absorb the entire amount of Japan's deposit insurance funds.

Subsequently, a reactionary wave of consolidations swept through Japan's banking industry. For example, Mitsubishi Bank merged with the Bank of Tokyo after acquiring Nippon Trust Bank. Similarly, Sumitomo Bank and Daiwa Bank engaged in merger talks. In November 1996, the Ministry of Finance ordered the closing of Hanwa Bank and continued investigation into Asahi Bank for irregularities at its New York branch. This was the first government-ordered closure of a bank in post-war Japan. Others are faced with the possibility of a downgrade in their credit ratings. Having grown accustomed to insulation from competition due to bureaucratic regulation, Japan's banks are now immobilized by its previously protective web.

Official Japanese involvement in the scandalous loss of $1.1 billion at Daiwa Bank in New York reflects a systemic problem. In September 1995, it was discovered that Japan's Finance Ministry had been informed about Daiwa's financial irregularities as early as April 1994. By not notifying American bank regulators, Daiwa's management breached federal and state banking regulations, and the Japanese government ignored an important intergovernmental protocol. Their joint actions have led to a major loss of credibility of Japan's private and public sector. This lack of transparency is a common obstacle in economies that have deep traditions of bureaucratized regulations within a hierarchical political system. In this context, the system of accountability is designed to protect existing institutional arrangements, governments, or political figures rather than customers, shareholders, or citizens. As a result, there is a contrived consensus that tends to sidestep the tough issues of restructuring or deregulation. Ironically, the bureaucratization of economic relations thought to be so useful to Japan's initial development has led to rigidities hindering the prompt policy responses required to accommodate rapidly changing market conditions.

Losses in the stock and property markets destroy real wealth even though there is a total or partial rebound. Economists speak of 'wealth effects,' where these transitory losses lead to a heightened sense of caution when it comes to consumption. The slump in retail sales can be explained by such negative 'wealth effects.' Similarly, positive 'wealth effects' inspired by the Japanese bubble-induced high levels of consumer debt due to heavy borrowing. Continued uncertainty over the eventual market value of property, along with increasing doubt about job security, have combined to stifle consumer confidence. The sagging retail sector, the strong yen, and overinvestment based upon debt-based capital spending in response to cheap credit, all contribute to the growing amount of excess productive capacity in Japan.

Because Japan's deflationary cycle is driven by the high international value of the yen, aggressive macroeconomic stimulus packages designed to aid its recovery have been largely ineffective. In order to encourage investment spending and boost bank profits, the Bank of Japan reduced its official discount rate (ODR) to banks from 6 percent in 1991 to 0.5 percent at the end of 1995. The crux of economic weakness, however, is debt deflation that places strict limits upon the formation of new credits. In a declining price environment, the real interest rate is high even if the nominal interest rate is low. Fiscal stimulus begun in 1992 led to increases in central government spending that totaled nearly 14 percent of Japan's current GDP. Growth, however, continues to lag. It is structural reforms, not the conventional route of cyclical stimulus, that are necessary for Japan's economic recovery.[28]

A variety of factors account for Japan's sluggish growth in the 1990s. One of the most critical problems confronting the Japanese economy is the low level of productivity. The growth in output per worker has decelerated from an average of 6 to 8 percent over the previous century, to 4 to 6 percent in the mid-1980s, and to about 3.5 percent by the mid-1990s. Despite a sustained investment effort that exceeded the pace of American capital accumulation over the past half decade, Japan's productivity gains lagged behind those in America. Apparently, the average returns on new investment in Japan were considerably less than those associated with similar ventures in America.

Concurrent with the increase in debt in the private sector, Japan's public sector debt is now among the highest of all industrialized countries, amounting to the equivalent of a year's GDP (about $5 trillion). Although the government's budget deficit in the 1990s was in a manageable range of less than 4 percent of GDP, it may rise to as high as 20 percent by 2030 if problems with pension spending are not brought under control.[29]

These issues are all the more important since Japan serves both as the engine of growth and as the model for development in the region. Uncertainty about Japan's recovery from its various economic ills therefore does not bode well for the rest of the region. This is no surprise since these economies have followed Japan in a 'flying geese' pattern of development. In the first instance, the failure of Japanese industrial interests to serve as a source of intra-regional support for capital investment may short-circuit the growth path of East Asia's emerging economies. In the second instance, those countries that follow the Japanese model for development are likely to encounter the same economic problems now evident in Japan. In emulating Japan's export strategy to attain high economic growth, it can be expected that East Asia's high-growth economies will eventually experience the same sort of slowdown that Japan experienced in the first half of the 1990s. Regardless of the problems in the financial system caused by debt deflation and falling growth rates, the Japanese economy can no longer rely upon input-driven growth.

There are signs that the problems observed in Japan are already beginning to appear in neighboring economies. Dramatic rises in property prices in Hong Kong and Taiwan have been followed by precipitous declines. Similarly, after rising sharply from 1992 to 1993, the stock markets of the region declined just as dramatically during 1994. This volatility suggests that cautious, long-term investment has given way to short-term speculation.[30] The absence of stable, long-term capital belies all the ample lip service paid to the 'Asian Century.'

Land prices have soared in Singapore for various reasons. Clearly, domestic needs for the island's small amount of land area is in heated competition with the demands of multinational corporations operating there. In the early 1990s, many firms operating in Hong Kong dreaded the uncertainty surrounding the 1997 takeover by communist China. To maintain a regional presence, they either shifted their operations to Singapore or opened representative offices there. Although locals are somewhat shielded from the ensuing increases in property costs due to the provision of public housing by the government, the economy as a whole cannot be considered immune.

As in the case of Japan's bubble economy, many investments and purchases in Hong Kong and Singapore are leveraged against collateral of inflated real estate and stock holdings. In such a tight market, even small increases in interest rates could trigger dramatic adjustments requiring repayments that would reverberate to other sectors of the economy. For example, some who have purchased stocks on margin accounts may be forced to dump their shares on the market. Similarly, those with debts to repay from borrowing to purchase big ticket items may simply default. A resultant sharp plunge in the stock market would have a negative impact on real estate prices. In Singapore, this prospective situation is worsened by the fact that one of the largest players in the real estate market is Temasek Holding, a quasi-governmental organization. To avert a collapse of Temasek, the government would be forced to honor its obligations by drawing on the funds held in the publicly-mandated pension accounts, the Central Provident Fund (CPF). In one stroke, the savings and gains of the past three decades could disappear. It is especially disconcerting that there is little disclosure about the financial status of Temasek, or of any other quasi-governmental organizations.

Among the most important contributors to East Asian economic growth are the family firms operated by the Overseas Chinese. In diversifying their wealth outside their home countries, members of this group have become the largest source of cross-border investments in Hong Kong, Indonesia, Malaysia, the Philippines, Thailand, and Vietnam. Since 1978, they have also provided $50 billion of capital to China. This sum represents 80 percent of all foreign investment that is placed in China through over 100,000 joint ventures.[31]

The dominant type of enterprise operated by Overseas Chinese involves a concentration of ownership among family members with management control residing with the family head. Initially, this coincidence of management and ownership can be advantageous for growth, but numerous problems will emerge over time.[32] For example, selection of company leadership is often guided by bloodlines rather than proven management talents. Tight ownership limits expansion because outside investors typically demand a level of transparency that is anathema to such closed corporations. This lack of openness inhibits long-term strategic planning, and the development of independent structures for corporate governance that are necessary to attract investors from outside the wider Chinese community.

It is especially problematic that many of the larger commercial empires held by Overseas Chinese families are concentrated in property investments and financial services.[33] Because prices in the region have surpassed those in the developed economies by a wide margin, the asset value boom is likely to peak soon, if it has not yet already reached its zenith. An extended period of slower overall economic growth may therefore be in store for the region. A more pessimistic scenario would be a hard landing as the result of the bursting of a region-wide property bubble. Worse yet, with the end of the building boom and subsequent collapse in real estate prices, there would inevitably be knock-on effects upon the service firms that provided support.

The welfare state in Asia?

It has become commonplace to hear proclamations of the decline of Western civilization as the result of its devolution into a welfare state. However, this postmortem may be slightly premature. Likewise, it may be equally erroneous to suggest that East Asia has escaped from the costs and moral hazards of implementing Western systems of social welfare. In truth, these systems merely take a different form in much of Asia. For example, large industrial concerns in both Japan and China hoard labor, principally as a tool to ensure social peace. However, the high costs of labor hoarding tend to contribute to declining productivity and falling profits. Like a government program, the corporate sector will encounter limits in its ability to continue this welfare scheme forever. Similarly, the Japanese system of 'lifetime employment' operates as a private approach to public welfare. In both instances, acceptance of higher national unemployment rates will be necessary if Japanese or Chinese companies are to effectively compete in the global economy. Thus, although 'lifetime employment' has been declared an important element of Japan's post-war strength, economic realities will force the abandonment of this tradition-bound institution.

China's unofficial welfare system takes the form of subsidized credit loans to inefficient, loss-making state-owned enterprises (SOEs). The decision to keep nearly 100,000 SOEs on a lifeline of easy credit reflects concern for the employment of nearly 100 million workers, but this short-term fix has resulted in an extended period of labor market disequilibrium and inflationary pressures. Other examples of the Asian variant on the welfare state include the provision of publicly-managed pension funds and housing in Hong Kong and Singapore.

In an economic upswing, the costs associated with these forms of welfare are both less visible and less intrusive than they would be in an economic downturn. Nonetheless, popular pressure to expand welfare will increase as various Asian bubbles begin to burst or deflate. At that point it will be evident that culturally-driven private mechanisms will be insufficient to deliver the type of social stability and economic prosperity that has recently characterized much of East Asia.

An agnostic look at East Asia's 'miracle' economies

Considerable excitement has been generated by the impressive economic performance of Hong Kong, Singapore, South Korea, and Taiwan. Indeed, their vigorous growth prompted them to be known poetically as 'Dragon' or 'Tiger' economies. Recent references identifying them as 'miracle' economies suggest, however, that hyperbole has overtaken poetry.

It is encouraging that East Asia's collective progress represents a shift in their economic record from worst toward first. The rest of the world can breathe a collective sigh of joy and relief as millions, perhaps billions, of people are raised from centuries of grinding poverty. However, about 80 percent of East Asia's population continues to live in economies where annual per capita income is less than about $600.

One major explanation for the region's brisk economic advance can be found in the massive infusion of capital and labor inputs into the system, a growth process that has both logical and physical limits. High rates of investment in physical capital, education, and health, combined with increased labor force participation rates and employment expansion, are effective but unsustainable means for generating economic growth. Assertions that these exceptionally high rates of real economic growth will continue indefinitely have considerable appeal as simplistic extrapolations of the recent past into the near future. However, long-term continuation of high growth rates requires that qualitative improvements in inputs match the quantitative increases. Without a boost in productivity, diminishing returns will unavoidably lead to a slowdown in economic growth. Sustained long-run growth depends upon increases in the total productivity of the factors of production.

A comparison based on gains in 'total factor productivity' places the 'miracle' economies of Asia substantially behind other economies that have less impressive nominal growth rates. In this light, there is no more reason to believe that the 'Asian Model' of government-directed development is any more 'miraculous' than was the now-discredited Soviet development model. As in the case of the Soviet experiment, there is little indication that the East Asian economies can maintain above average growth rates.

Beginning in the early 1990s, Hong Kong's economy has experienced lagging productivity growth combined with persistent double-digit inflation. In turn, these factors have led to an international cost-competitiveness problem that is the essence of the territory's current economic difficulties. As in Japan's 'bubble economy,' the remedial adjustments needed to cure Hong Kong's malaise would include a strong dose of industrial restructuring, asset deflation, and a slowdown in the rate of overall economic growth. It is not enough to suggest that Hong Kong is insulated from a sharp downturn or has no need for such remedies because of its position as China's window to the outside world. It is true that Hong Kong has in the past exercised a near-monopoly on the handling of China's trade through port facilities at Kwai Chung, but the bulk of its China-related traffic is of the 'trans-shipment' variety where containers are transferred from one ship to another. As such, Hong Kong's value-added role in these transactions is that of a service provider.

Thus, Hong Kong no longer plays the independent role of exporter of domestically-produced goods.

Rising operating costs due to shortages of skilled labor and land plague most of the 'miracle' economies. Real estate booms in Hong Kong and Singapore have most of the characteristics of a speculative bubble that could burst at any time. Deflation of this bubble will have dire consequences for long-term economic growth.

As prior experience shows, the creation of financial bubbles requires that market participants temporarily suspend their belief in economic reality. It is not surprising, therefore, that even intelligent and aware investors are willing to equate real value with inordinately high real estate and land prices in Singapore. Political leaders and technocrats in Singapore apparently believe that past successes in guiding their economy will enable them to contain the bubble. Such belief ignores centuries of evidence to the contrary.

By the end of 1996, Malaysia had fewer problems with long-term competitiveness than did Singapore. Some short-term problems, however, threaten the international value of the ringgit that could lead to dramatic shifts in domestic interest rates. In addition to lagging productivity and increasing labor costs, the Malaysian manufacturing sector is beginning to slow after an extended run of high growth. Factory output growth in the third quarter of 1995, although a respectable 14.1 percent annual rate, was the slowest since 1991 and is likely to herald the beginning of an unavoidable retreat from unsustainable rates of growth. When wage increases exceed gains in output, shrinking profit margins undermine short-term competitiveness.

To remedy an overheated economy, the normal course is for economic growth to slow in response to an appreciation of real exchange rates and a general rise in prices. However, it is unlikely that the international values of the currencies in the region will be allowed to rise. Most of the economies rely upon export-led growth, and these governments are aware that growth would be slowed if exchange rates rose. Similarly, inflation in most of these economies is likely to be held in check by the heavy hand of their central banks, so as to avoid the political fallout from the impact of rising prices upon low income earners. Increased attempts to impose price controls on basic commodities would signal such concerns.

Economic logic therefore requires that adjustments must take place elsewhere. If neither commodity prices nor exchange rates are allowed to rise, then the prices of other non-controlled assets must do so, especially in the real estate sector. These increases will raise business operating costs and lower corporate profit margins, thereby leading to a loss in competitive position.

APEC: Dream or unfulfilled fantasy?

One ray of hope for the future of the Asian Pacific region is the rapid pace at which the 18 Pacific Rim countries that comprise APEC are achieving consensus, even if it is not matched by supporting action. Any understanding among a group of countries that accounts for half of the world's economic output and 46 percent of global trade is welcome. Indeed, it is no exaggeration to say that APEC certainly ranks in potential importance with GATT, the IMF, and the World Bank. Initially, there was an impression of considerable advances arising out of APEC summits due to a broad agreement on the principles of free trade. APEC agreements were also in harmony with developments on the wider world stage in connection with formation of the World Trade Organization (WTO).

Unfortunately, the grand promises made at the end of widely publicized international meetings have become forgotten press releases. At the Osaka meeting, an 'agreement to reach an agreement' was announced whereby each government would propose individual plans for action to further liberalize trade and investment, as well as economic cooperation on infrastructure development. More advanced countries like the US and Japan were given a deadline of 2010 for implementing a more liberal trade regime; other APEC participants were expected to reach the same goals by 2020.

Similarly, follow-up sessions to the Asia-Europe summit held during March 1996 were stalled due to Southeast Asian insistence that any scheme to promote direct investment between the two regions be based on a non-binding agreement. The seeming futility of such summit negotiations was underlined by one of the Southeast Asian co-chairmen of the meeting when he said: 'In Asia we agree to things only if they are subject to change without any advance notice. If we want the governments to endorse the plan, then it is important to make it clear from the beginning that they will not have to follow it.' Such a view clearly violates the underlying understanding of contractual obligations that underpin Western market economies.

Concerning trade, promises are easy to make, hard to keep. Domestic constituencies in all countries make it difficult for trade bureaucrats to come up with answers for sensitive issues like trade in rice and textiles. Similarly, grand trade strategy has lost some of its attraction in the US after a bruising fight over approval of the North American Free Trade Agreement (NAFTA). In the end, fulfillment of these agreements requires more than photo-ops and soundbites of the expressions of goodwill among heads of state.

The next century will witness a continuation in the rising fortunes and growing political importance of East Asia, but a simplistic extrapolation of recent economic activity in the region is not an accurate harbinger of the next century. This may be best illustrated by examining developments in China as presented in the next chapter.

Notes

1   There have been a number of authors who have questioned the dawning of the 'Asian Century.' For example, see M. Abromowitz, 'Pacific Century: Myth or Reality?', *Contemporary Southeast Asia*, Vol. 15, No. 3, December 1993; C. Coker, 'The Myth or Reality of the Pacific Century', *Washington Quarterly* (1988, Vol. 11) pp. 5-16; B. Cumings, 'What is a Pacific Century', op. cit.; A. Dirlik (ed.), *What is in a Rim? Critical Perspectives on the Pacific Region Idea,* Boulder, Colo.: Westview Press, 1993; and G. Hicks, 'The Myth of the Asian Century', *Asian Wall Street Journal,* 26 October 1995.

2   See NSF (1995), *Asia's New High-Tech Competitors* (NSF 95-309) Arlington, Virginia: National Science Foundation.

3   L. Bryan and D. Farrell, *Market Unbound: Unleashing Global Capitalism,* New York: John Wiley and Sons, 1996.

4   *1995 TI Corruption Index,* Berlin: Transparency International, 1995.

5   'A Great Slide Backward in Southeast Asia,' *Business Week,* 5 August 1996, p.51.

6   A. Fishlow, C. Gwin, S. Haggard, D. Rodrik, and R. Wade, *Miracle or Design: Lessons from the East Asian Experience,* Washington, DC: Overseas Development Council, 1994.

7   This echoes the results of a much earlier study, E. Lee (ed.), *Export-Led Industrialization and Development,* Geneva: International Labour Office, 1981. See especially the conclusions by I. M. D. Little, 'The Experience and Causes of Rapid Labour-Intensive Development in Korea, Taiwan Province, Hong Kong and Singapore; and the Possibilities of Emulation.'

8   E. Chen, *Hyper-Growth in Asian Economies,* op. cit. and B. Balassa, *The Newly Industrializing Countries in the World Economy,* op. cit.

9   This method of assessing market performance is known as growth accounting. An estimate of economic growth is calculated as the result of a combination of increases in the quantity of factor inputs (capital and labor) and a measure of efficiency of how those inputs are used. The latter is known as total factor productivity (TFP).

10 Chowdhury and Islam, *The Newly Industrialising Economies of East Asia,* op. cit.

11 A. Young, 'Lessons from the East Asian NIE's: A Contrarian View', *European Economic Review* (1994, Vol. 38) pp. 964-73. For supporting

argumentation, see P. Krugman, 'The Myth of Asia's Miracle', *Foreign Affairs* (1994, Vol. 73, No. 6) pp. 62-78; and, L. Lau and J-I Kim, The Sources of Growth of the East Asian Newly Industrialized Countries, *Journal of the Japanese and International Economies* (1994).

12   D. Rae and A. Orr, 'Grow You Good Thing, Grow', *International Review* (September 1996), National Bank of New Zealand.

13   A. Wood, 'No Future in the Past', *The Weekend Australian* (14-15 October 1995), p. 27.

14   For example, the average annual real growth of GDP for Singapore in the period 1960-91 was 8.5 percent. Of this, only 1.75 percent of that total are the consequence of increases in the productivity of factors of production. R. van Elkan. 'Accounting for Growth in Singapore', in K. Bercuson (ed.), *Singapore: A Case Study in Rapid Development*, Washington, DC: International Monetary Fund, 1995.

15   Unlike the East Asian economies that pursued export-oriented industrial strategies, resources in the Soviet Union were mobilized under a system of autarky. Another critical difference was the near total absence of private property rights under authoritarian-socialist regimes.

16   M. Simon, 'Asia, You Cost Too Much', *Asian Wall Street Journal* (28 October 1995).

17   *Asian Intelligence* (Number 469) Hong Kong: Political and Economic Risk Consultancy, Ltd., September 1996.

18   The above discussion points to the long-run interdependency of economic and political freedoms. This interdependency is most evident in the pressing challenge faced by political leaders in seeking to implement policies that support a well-ordered society while promoting individual freedoms. Despite the collapse of authoritarian socialism (communism), authoritarian regimes of East Asia pose a new challenge to Western democracy. In place of communist rhetoric, a new authoritarian credo insists that rapid and orderly growth requires strict limits upon individual freedoms and rights.

19   J. Bhagwati, *India in Transition*, Oxford: Clarendon Press, 1993.

20   C. P. Kindleberger, *Manias, Panics, and Crashes: A History of Financial Crises*, New York: Basic Books, 1989.

21   A good description of the conditions behind Japan's financial problems is in C. Wood, *The Bubble Economy: The Japanese Economic Collapse*, London: Sidgwick & Johnson, 1992.

22   P. Krugman, 'Dutch Tulips and Emerging Markets', *Foreign Affairs* (1995, Vol. 74, No. 4), pp. 28-44.

23   In trading at around 100 yen to the dollar, the Japanese currency is as 'overvalued' as was the dollar in 1984. Then the problems in the world

currency markets resulted in the adjustments agreed to the following year in the Plaza Accord.

24   So-called lifetime employment in Japan is generally limited to male workers and to companies with 300 or more employees. It is a norm to which many companies aspire, but it has no legal basis. Counting public sector employment, only about 9,500,000 out of 65,000,000 workers in Japan have this arrangement.

25   Securitization of debt involves transforming loans into tradable securities. This method was used by the US government to deal with the S&L fiasco.

26   On 29 December 1989, the Nikkei stock average hit a peak of 38,916. In November 1996, it remained as low as 21,000.

27   Because of their private ownership and lack of independent, outside audits, less is known about Japanese life insurance companies. However, it is becoming apparent that many of them are facing serious cash flow problems.

28   Following upon his work on Japan's bubble economy, see also C. Wood, *The End of Japan Inc.: And How the New Japan Will Look*, New York: Simon and Schuster, 1994.

29   'Japan's Debt-Ridden Future', *The Economist,* August 3, 1996, p. 31.

30   A. Downs, 'The Coming Crash in Asian Real Estate', *Asian Wall Street Journal*, 28 October 1995, p. 11.

31   M. Weidenbaum and S. Hughes, *The Bamboo Network: How Expatriate Chinese Entrepreneurs are Creating a New Economic Superpower in Asia,* New York: Free Press, 1996.

32   Many of the most successful Overseas Chinese entrepreneurs have outgrown the networks that they might have relied upon initially. The *huiguan* or Overseas Chinese associations that appear in many of the villages, towns, and cities across Southeast Asia are becoming moribund. The services they provided (scholarships, cultural events, food for the poor or providing small business loans) have been taken over by other institutions. Meanwhile younger generations resist the ordering of their lives through such community associations.

33   This proclivity for rapid turnover for high profit may be partly a function of their social insecurity arising from being a minority group that often holds a disproportionately large share of income and wealth.

5 The China challenge: Control, corruption, crowding, costs, Cold War II, and crime

Despite numerous contradictions and deficiencies apparent in China's economy, many observers are unreservedly bullish on its prospects. In many instances, this *Sinophoria* reflects wishful thinking about the country's theoretical economic potential, supported by little more than an extrapolation of China's recent growth momentum that is assumed will continue unabated. However, there are reasons to believe that China's growth process may soon begin to unravel. In particular, conservative factions among the Chinese leadership are pressing for the continuation of existing institutional arrangements. Ironically, the same arrangements that have been viewed as a source of strength for the Chinese economy in its early phase are likely to become the source of future weakness.

As indicated in Chapters Two and Three, optimism about China's economic future is based upon observations of high growth in the recent past. At the same time, the success of its export-oriented strategy has led to steadily increasing international reserves that are expected to reach between $90 and $100 billion by the end of 1996. China's foreign debt, at about 15 percent of GDP and 70 percent of export earnings, is considered to be at manageable levels.[1]

Despite all this good news, all is not well in the Middle Kingdom. The subtitle of this chapter constitutes a non-exhaustive list of probable sources of economic infirmity. Some of these flaws are a function of the Chinese leadership's demonstrated obsession with controlling economic and political development. As the legacy of China's imperialist, nationalist, and communist past, extensive bureaucratic interferences with the economy have resulted in widespread corruption. This problem is both cause and effect of the inability of the central or provincial governments to combat petty or organized crime. More ominous for its neighbors and others with economic or strategic interests in the region, Chinese government policies motivated by nationalist sentiments seem bent upon a course that threatens to sow the seeds of Cold War II. Other negative factors include certain spillover effects related to high-paced economic growth. Crowding as urban congestion has combined with rapidly rising labor and land costs to begin stripping away one of the main sources of China's economic competitiveness.

Doing business in China and doing business with China

Commercial progress is made more complicated by the nuisance impact of pervasive corruption, crime, and crowding. Congestion in the coastal cities and special economic zones (SEZs) has resulted from the inadequate development of transportation and communication infrastructure. Increasing operating costs and the announcement in 1996 of the government's intention to eliminate tax incentives for investments in the SEZs, have squeezed both profit opportunities for foreign investors.[2] In sum, these factors combine to lessen the competitive edge of China's economy on the world stage.

One beneficial side effect of an expanding private sector is that the percentage of total national income paid to China's central government has shrunk. However, as revenues shrink for Beijing, its 'small' government status will mean that most of the urgently required infrastructure projects will have to be financed by government debt issues. Given the expected magnitude of these needs, the Chinese public sector will probably continue to dominate domestic capital markets. China's growing status as a debtor nation represents a dramatic change from the 'miracle' development that was initially boosted by equity financing in the country's stock markets.

Ironically, China has a dependent sector that rivals the 'welfare state' in Europe in terms of its exaggerated costs and the drag it places on the economy. The government continues to finance state-owned enterprises, most of which are not economically viable. The great majority of China's SOEs produce a glut of low quality goods amid numerous higher quality alternative products. Most are not earning a profit and so have required subsidized loans from government banks. In turn, most of these loans are never paid back so that these banks also operate at a loss. In the first quarter of 1996, losses among state industrial firms rose by 41 percent from the previous year.[3]

Unprofitable SOEs could either be privatized, consolidated with other healthier SOEs, or simply allowed to declare bankruptcy. Yet privatization cannot go forward unless these economic dinosaurs are downsized or reorganized. Bankruptcy is even less acceptable to the leadership since there would be losses of perhaps millions of jobs that would certainly lead to substantial social unrest.

Unfortunately, there are also signs that official corruption in China is rapidly reaching epidemic proportions.[4] By interfering with market-driven asset allocation, this corruption perpetuates the inefficiency of centrally-directed infrastructure projects. China's industrial enterprises include white elephants akin to the defunct projects of mammoth scale associated with the Soviet Union. Decisions about financing and spending tend to be based upon political connections or the private ends of corrupt officials, rather than commercial viability or economic rationality. Unhappily, with the leadership's offspring parlaying their family connections into lucrative business deals, it is likely that attempts to purge corrupt influences from China will become increasingly difficult.

Besides encouraging inefficient economic policies, corruption also exerts a corrosive influence on China's political and social institutions. For example, commercial law is administered in a disturbingly arbitrary manner. Meanwhile, enforcement of court orders is spotty, and tends to favor the interest of domestic litigants, especially those with ties to the People's Liberation Army (PLA) or the ruling party.

China's present generation of rulers seems unable to recognize that unnecessarily extensive regulations and inappropriate rules add to the problem by providing irresistible incentives for corruption. Rather than taking preventative measures like refraining from extensive economic interventions or reducing bureaucratic control over markets, the leadership periodically arrests or executes corrupt officials. The elimination of specific individuals is a poor substitute for instituting an incentive scheme that rewards ethical and economically efficient behavior.

Understanding China's market socialism

There is evidence that the Chinese authorities have an imperfect comprehension of, and scant trust in, the outcomes of market processes. It may be true that individual Chinese entrepreneurs understand the market, but that is another matter. However, the senior leadership views a vibrant economy as merely an incidental means to a greater political and social end. Social control and economic power are seen as indispensable tools for maintaining political stability in a fractious country peopled by groups with competing and often contentious interests.

In light of the foregoing, it is not surprising that China's program of modernization is seen to move forward in fits and starts. Indeed, the oxymoron chosen to refer to their system, 'socialist market economy,' indicates that the leadership does not appreciate the contradictions that they confront in implementing the transition program. Their attempt to implement economic reforms without surrendering political hegemony insures that neither the market nor the system of governance will operate inefficiently. In the end, one will succumb to the demands of the other.

The nature of the transition process in China, as elsewhere, must be understood within a historical context. Decades of central planning under communism have habituated the current leadership to extensive state intervention in economic affairs. When combined with the regime's obsessive intent to maintain political power in the hands of the Communist Party, it is no wonder that the heavy hand of government remains widely evident. Thus, the gradualist transition policies adopted by China's leadership are not the product of some theoretically sound, strategic economic plan. Instead, this half-hearted approach to marketization reflects the insecurity of the regime as it tries to retain political power through macroeconomic control. These quasi-interventionist policies have had mixed success in dealing with inflation and unemployment, and have resulted in some economic and social dislocations. Thus, the hidden, non-monetary costs of socialism (e.g., shortages and queues) have now been replaced by the obvious, tangible costs of rising prices and unemployment.

Attempts to perpetuate centralized rule despite the collapse of its legitimating ideology involve an obvious incongruity. Symptomatic of this inconsistency is the continuing issuance of five-year plans that purportedly provide guidance for what is meant to be a burgeoning market economy. Admittedly, substantive differences have become apparent in the extent and nature of China's economic planning after reform was initiated in 1978. For example, the most recent plan lists preferred areas for foreign direct investment, thereby suggesting an extraterritorial dimension to government planning. As part of this more outward-looking approach, Beijing has identified certain foreign ventures that are consistent with the 'plan,' with special emphasis on high technology areas. It is as though Beijing presumes to guide the behavior of foreign firms simply by unilaterally incorporating them into its official scheme.

In any event, foreign businesses are discouraged from contributing to the plan due to government policies regarding exchange controls, coupled with China's underdeveloped and highly politicized financial system. Beginning in July 1996, the renminbi began moving toward partial convertibility, with full convertibility targeted for the year 2000. By the end of 1996, it will be fully convertible for 'current account' transactions, such as the net balance on goods and services. Full convertibility will also apply to remittances, so that foreign ventures can repatriate their profits without special permission. However, transactions on the 'capital account' side of the balance of payments ledger will remain under bureaucratic control.[5] This being the case, repatriation of profits from direct and portfolio investments continue to require approval by various civil servants or politicians in Beijing or in provincial capitals. With these continuing exchange controls, China's leaders impede the international component of the economy's capital flows.

At the same time, the lack of restraint shown by China's lending authorities has also contributed to a major weakening of the entire banking sector. Indeed, a potential banking crisis looms in China due to accumulated bad debts that total the equivalent of hundreds of billions of dollars. Most of these are held by state banks and account for about 70 percent of the country's lending operations. The problem loans stem from the government-controlled nature of the industrial framework. The prevalence of bank lending arose out of Deng-era reforms wherein bank loans replaced subsidies. State banks are prohibited from foreclosing on state-owned enterprises, so they are unable to liquidate SOE assets to cover delinquent payments. Furthermore, unless and until there are credible controls over credit to the SOEs, there will be relentless inflationary pressures. Resisting reform of the banking sector therefore will preclude the establishment of long-term macroeconomic stability.

Government policies are creating a mini-bubble in financial speculation that is likely to do long-term harm to the economy. Banks in China are paying deposit rates well in excess of the inflation rate. This is possible because the banks hold government bonds that provide a healthy spread over the rates paid to depositors. Non-bank financial institutions attract depositors by paying interest rates that are higher than those offered by the banks, and fund these liabilities by investing the deposits in the soaring stock market. Unfortunately, this sort of financial pyramid drains funds from those sectors of the economy that produce goods and services. This speculative fever will therefore inhibit domestic consumer demand and choke off investment in real production.

As if this were not bad enough, bad loans for the 'Big Four' banks in China amount to between 30 and 40 percent of their assets.[6] Of the Chinese bank affiliates operating in Hong Kong, eleven of them were given low credit ratings by Moody's Investor Service due to poor financial disclosure on the part of the Bank of China. Perhaps the reason why a full-scale banking crisis has not yet erupted is that the saving rate in China is about 40 percent. At some point, however, rising inflation or political instability could provoke mass withdrawals, thereby leading to a system-wide financial collapse.

One of the justifications for adopting gradualist transition policies is that socialist conditioning has left the affected populations ill-prepared to cope with the sudden rigors of competitive capitalism. On balance, the strategy behind gradual transition is to tinker with reform and to delay indefinitely the badly needed fundamental reforms of their institutions. Popular support for reform may actually be diminished under this piecemeal approach. Gradualism may lengthen the period of painful economic adjustment, and cause citizens to confuse the symptoms of the socialist hangover with the prescription for the cure.

The reactions of Chinese peasants to the initial reforms of the agricultural sector provide a convincing counterargument to gradualism. Despite their lack of experience with free markets, they were able to respond with great enthusiasm and success to the 'household responsibility' system of land allocation begun by Deng Xiaoping in 1979. Under this system, farmers are able to sell a portion of their grain production for profit in local markets. However, the failure of the government to extend agricultural reform to include the creation of clear and legally defensible land ownership rights, has discouraged farmers from making the sort of investments necessary to enhance long-term production.

Even so, China's gradual approach to modernization is often cited as a successful experiment in transition policy. In turn, the presumed superiority of the Chinese model for slow and gradual reform will likely lead to a similar approach in other transitional socialist economies like Cambodia, Laos, and Vietnam.

However, there is ample evidence to suggest that an accelerated approach to economic reform is more effective than gradualism. For example, one of China's neighbors in the Pacific region, New Zealand, is one of the most notable success stories associated with accelerated economic transition policies. It has enjoyed a remarkable recovery from the suffocating effect of decades of interventionist market policies imposed by socialism. Similarly, various East and Central European economies are quickly showing benefits from massive sell-offs of SOEs.

In the case of China, such remedial action would reduce the burden of subsidizing loss-making SOEs with ready access to credit. By the end of 1995, the debt-to-asset ratio for China's SOEs had risen to 80 percent from 18.7 percent in 1980. In addition, only about 28 percent of all SOEs were showing a profit. Delays in privatization allow inefficient state-owned enterprises to absorb scarce tax receipts, thereby jeopardizing the marketization process for the entire economy. Specifically, nearly 10 percent of the government's revenues is spent on subsidies for SOEs. In all events, rapid transformation forces hidden unemployment into the open, while Chinese-style gradualism provides an unsustainable illusion of full employment in inefficient SOEs.[7] During marketization, high and rising rates of joblessness may be observed, along with falling production and declines in productivity. However, these phenomena should be understood as residual elements of the failures of socialism. The full and sustainable benefits of marketization will ultimately be achieved when there is a more complete removal of lingering, state-sanctioned impediments to free market processes.

The issue of universal applicability with regard to China's gradualist approach raises various questions. European transition began with democratization. In contrast, reformers in China, as in Vietnam and Laos, continue to operate within authoritarian regimes. Attempts to control an economy involve different constraints within a democracy than under dictatorship or autocracy. Democracies tend to allow citizens to seek out the individual means for fulfilling their life purposes, allowing entrepreneurs to fulfill their role as a motor for economic progress. If citizens wish to undertake new enterprises, democratic governments usually try not to get in the way. Additionally, democratic governments encourage entrepreneurial activity by enforcing a system of private property rights. However, in order to realize the full benefits of marketization, socialist economies must follow suit. Provision and protection of property rights will eventually give rise to a code of personal rights and freedoms. Interim steps require that government intervention be scaled back, along with the socialist tendency to hoard labor. Furthermore, a reasonably brisk withdrawal of the communist state sector is the best hope for China and East Europe. Tentative reductions in state intervention will only inhibit future growth prospects. In addition, restraints upon political freedom tend to retard the development of individualist institutions, including private property rights, which are necessary for entrepreneur-driven growth.

Thus, the 'success' of China's reforms should be viewed as a short-run outcome based on an opportunistic political agenda that will limit long-term economic growth. Thus, the present growth rate of China's economy cannot be considered sustainable. Like other East Asian authoritarian regimes, the Chinese leadership can ignore democratic trends, at least in the short run. They may be able to stimulate export-led growth by relying upon prison labor to create a momentary competitive advantage. Similarly, trade unions may be suppressed or co-opted to prevent wage hikes. However, these abusive practices combined with gradualist reform spell disaster for the long run, especially if they prop up morally and politically corrupt regimes. Ultimately, it is doubtful that such regimes can insure political stability.

In reality, China's piecemeal reform agenda has had less impressive results than expected. First, many objective successes depended heavily upon the entrepreneurial skills and capital provided by Overseas Chinese who served as trading partners, financiers and intermediaries. Second, China's reform approach has actually interfered with economic development more than the reported growth statistics suggest. For example, these favorable data overlook the existence of an incredible mass of migrant labor consisting of from 100 to 200 million peasants searching for employment.

A major flaw in China's approach to macroeconomic policy is the continued lack of independence of its central bank. As a result, China's crude monetary system is guided by short-term political expediency rather than economic rationality or commercial viability. As mentioned previously, continued subsidies to loss-ridden SOEs through the provision of easy credit means that efficient firms become capital starved. The preeminence of such politically-motivated decisions has resulted in a policy of negative real interest rates. In 1994, the nominal annual interest rate was 11 percent while the inflation rate was well over 20 percent. Since the real cost of borrowing is negative, it will encourage a high demand for, and inefficient use of, investment funds for capital expenditures. Attempts to decide upon and to implement a stabilization policy reflect the confused nature of the reform program. Austerity measures imposed during the Summer of 1993 were later abandoned by the Third Plenum of the 14th Central Committee of the Chinese Communist Party in order to promote 'maximum growth.' At the 8th National People's Congress, however, new policies were again announced as a means to restrain economic growth. Instead of a commitment to restrain credit formation and monetary growth rates, price controls were instead instituted in order to rein in inflation.

Despite the wavering, the Chinese authorities are seen to have made a credible effort to lower inflation. Early estimates were that by the first quarter of 1996, the annualized rate of price increases has slowed to less than 8 percent, down from nearly 20 percent one year earlier. However, these near-miraculous results strain credulity. Actually, the lack of ready access to Chinese data sources and the ever-changing nature of the government's formula for calculating the consumer price index, suggest that stated inflation numbers could be contrived. All China watchers are aware that Beijing's reported statistics have a history of being manipulated to suit political purposes.[8]

And so it is that China's unpredictable macroeconomic stabilization policies inspire little confidence for future economic or political stability. Selective price controls continue to be imposed on some of the most widely used commodities and services, such as food staples, energy sources, public transport, and fees for schools and hospitals. Price controls reflect an inability or unwillingness to tackle monetary growth as the cause of inflation. This strategy also exposes an ignorance of the long history of price controls' failure as a tool to correct underlying economic problems.

Appropriate macroeconomic remedies are simple, if not easy, to implement. Interest rates must be allowed to rise so that a more rational use of capital, and greater intensity in the use of labor, will be encouraged. If accomplished through tighter monetary policy to rein in money supply growth rates, this should also restrain inflation. Inefficient state enterprises should be liquidated or restructured through privatization so that capital will begin to be invested in new commercial activities that are responsive to market signals. As indicated earlier, the debt problems of the SOEs have reached crisis proportions. Due to excessive leveraging of debt and poor performance, somewhere between 20 and 30 percent of their debts are non-performing such that payments on interest and principal are overdue. Until these problems are resolved, the entire progress of economic reform will be jeopardized.

A sound and just commercial code must accompany complete elimination of exchange controls in order to increase the confidence of foreign investors. In the end, the Chinese regime must refrain from political expediency and make economic rationality a priority. Otherwise, it will become increasingly difficult to achieve economic growth rates that will absorb the addition of 50 million or so new entrants into the labor force each year.

Unfortunately, the bureaucracy and party structure of China are imbued with the dogma and mechanics of the communist state. Old habits will die hard. For over four decades, they have been concerned with consolidating power instead of seeking efficient solutions. Although many mainland Chinese exhibit a great affinity with making money, there is no real commercial culture with a commitment to mutual fulfillment of contractual obligations.

Another practical problem associated with operating in China is the speedy saturation of markets. Reports of huge and growing numbers of consumers have attracted a multitude of outside investors eager to exploit virgin territory. All too often, however, the market is rapidly saturated by foreign producers who soon find themselves with excess capacity in their production facilities. This over-capacity is largely due to poor strategic planning in the face of heady competition to exploit China's huge potential markets. For example, telecom companies from around the world rushed in and built state-of-the-art factories in China in hopes of capturing a share of the 30 million new telephone land lines being added each year.[9] A glut resulted from foreign firms adding to the output of existing domestic suppliers. Consequently, the price per line has fallen to about $70 or about one-third less than American prices.

Exporters to China can face other problems. Despite the ebb of central planning, there are still areas of the economy where the state intervenes either as purchaser or producer. Orders from foreign producers can be cut or canceled abruptly if domestic output rises unexpectedly. The figures on production used by the Chinese government are notoriously unreliable. Whereas *caveat emptor* (buyer, beware) guides commercial decisions anywhere, those selling in China should closely heed the slogan, *caveat venditor* (seller, beware).

China's territorial policy: Romance or rape of Hong Kong and Taiwan?

At midnight of the last day of June 1997, the fate of Hong Kong will forever more be decided by a regime, that despite recent successes, is characterized by an obsessive fixation on control and power. It was this obsession that led to the starvation of millions of its own citizens in the ill-conceived experiments of the Great Leap Forward and the Cultural Revolution. Recent attempts to disrupt democratic elections in Taiwan by threat of military action provide evidence of the determination of the Beijing leadership to impose its will at any cost.

Despite the rhetoric of 'one country, two systems,' there is good reason to doubt that China's communist regime will be able to maintain the cognitive dissonance necessary to respect the autonomy guaranteed to Hong Kong in the Joint Declaration that was co-signed with Great Britain in 1984. However, reneging on this important agreement will be less important than the likelihood that China's embrace will have a smothering effect on Hong Kong's economic future. Various observers offered skeptical assessments of Hong Kong's future as the deadline neared.[10] Equally significant, the fate of Hong Kong will not be lost on the Taiwanese. Nonetheless, whatever happens in what the Chinese call the Hong Kong Special Administrative Region (SAR) will shape the economic fortunes of China and its relationship with the rest of East Asia.

A disturbing sign of bad faith is found in the Chinese government's announced intention to dissolve the freely elected Legislative Council (Legco), the only democratically elected body in Hong Kong. This insistence comes despite the fact that a majority of the citizens of Hong Kong expressed their preference for democratic government in the last election. In asserting an unqualified and unilateral right to impose their will to determine the destiny of Hong Kong, it appears that the mainland leaders have little appreciation for the role played by individual autonomy in the island's success.

In an increasingly globalized environment, it may seem trivial to suggest that future developments in Hong Kong will have an impact beyond its tiny geographic space and its six million inhabitants. However, the economic fortunes and political circumstances of Hong Kong are a bellwether for the region. By virtue of their unique and, in the short run, irreplaceable nature, the institutional structures in Hong Kong will remain a critically necessary conduit for trade and capital, as well as a political and economic safe haven for all of East Asia. It is evident that Hong Kong's role is at risk when one considers the striking similarities between Hong Kong and Taiwan. Unfortunately the prognosis is not encouraging.

One of the biggest questions is how Hong Kong might avoid the effects of the corruption that is so ingrained in China. This contaminating influence will come from several sources. First, newcomers to the bureaucracy appointed by Beijing are likely to be chosen based upon their political loyalties instead of upon their skills. If so, and if they are not as qualified as their predecessors, their presence will demoralize the current civil servants while lowering the esteem in which Hong Kong's bureaucracy is held by the rest of the community. Second, the many enterprises that are expected to emigrate from the mainland to Hong Kong will bring with them bad habits developed in the mainland's polluted business environment. Most will be long accustomed to using political connections to impose their will over a given situation. This will set a bad example for those businesses domiciled in Hong Kong. Indeed, many local businessmen have eagerly signed on as advisers to Beijing, presumably to insure access to those who will pull the levers of power.

Corrupt practices will be especially problematic when it comes to the Securities and Futures Commission (SFC) of Hong Kong. Functionally similar to the US Securities and Exchange Commission, the SFC sets and enforces rules governing the futures and stock exchanges of Hong Kong. One persistent problem is the traditional proclivity of Chinese leaders to exercise strict control over the institutions under their command. A second set of problems can be seen in the erratic performance of the stock markets in Shanghai and Shenzhen, both in operation since 1992. The overseer of these markets, the China Securities Regulatory Commission, has a record of abruptly imposing regulatory changes. This is due in part to the disruptive effects of speculation and insider trading. The futures market has also been shaken by blatant manipulation.

It is unlikely that the police or the SFC will vigorously prosecute business enterprises that might have ties to the PLA or the communist party and its leadership. Even if there were such prosecutions, mainland interests have a demonstrated knack for beating back proceedings. Similarly, they also have a poor record for abiding by adverse rulings. In sum, Hong Kong's institutions are only a small dog that will be unable to wag a tail so large as China.

Friction will inevitably arise over sharing the economic spoils of Hong Kong. There will certainly be disputes over collection and disbursement of tax revenues. Much else can be expected to unravel. Milton Friedman and other commentators have predicted that the Hong Kong currency will be unable to maintain its traditional peg against the American dollar. When this happens, the Hong Kong dollar will depreciate in line with the renminbi, and the local Hang Seng stock index will also plummet in value. Eventually, the Hong Kong dollar will disappear because it will no longer serve any functional purpose.

Hong Kong and the future of East Asia...?

It would be easy to underestimate the importance of Hong Kong in the growth equation for the rest of East Asia. Without continued stability and economic growth in Hong Kong, China is almost certain to face a slowdown in its own dash toward material prosperity. Hong Kong cannot simply be replaced by another trading and financial center either in China or elsewhere. Despite suggestions that Shanghai is being positioned to resume it preeminent status as financial center for East Asia, it will be many years before the necessary physical and institutional infrastructure could be in place. With market capitalization of over $405 billion at the end of 1996, Hong Kong had the fourth largest stock exchange in the world. It also has the third largest international banking center and the fifth largest foreign exchange market.

Even if the physical infrastructure could be created elsewhere overnight, it would not be possible to replicate Hong Kong's reputation for enforcement of the rule of law. These internationally recognized standards of regulation, so important for China's own growing international economy, are the result of more than a century of exposure to English Common Law institutions. Only in Hong Kong are contracts that relate to China enforced. On the mainland, there is no credible rule of law; legal disputes are usually resolved by the government in an arbitrary fashion. In any case, the issue is not whether the rise of one trading and financial center will emerge only at the expense of another. Even with considerable diminution in recent growth trends, there will be room for several other such ports and financial centers in the region.

Until recently, no great cultural gap existed between the people of Hong Kong and the mainlanders. This is not surprising given that in most of the population of Hong Kong are actually émigrés from China's coastal provinces. However, it must be remembered that they came to Hong Kong to flee oppression while pursuing their fortunes. In the interim, a new identity was forged for the citizens of Hong Kong that is distinct from the rest of China. According to a 1996 poll, most of Hong Kong's citizens think of themselves first as part of a modern, internationalized culture. Being Chinese was considered secondary. For the most part, their interest in the politics of the mainland was related to a concern over the impact that reversion would have on Hong Kong's affairs.

In the 1984 negotiations for the handover of Hong Kong and the New Territories, the future of the citizens of the Crown Colony was transferred to a country whose leadership has one of the worst human rights records in the world, and who have had little experience with or respect for the rule of law. The people of Hong Kong are often perceived as being basically apolitical, with little motivation for taking risks to protect Hong Kong's modernized institutions. Actually, the reality is something quite different. With the approach of that fateful date in 1997, it appears that the residents' distinct identification with Hong Kong has been strengthened. This was evident in the 1992 elections when Martin Lee and other like-minded democrats won a majority of the contested seats in Legco. While this result was a pleasant surprise to many observers, it was viewed with confused alarm by the Chinese authorities and their sycophants. Prior to the poll in September 1995, it was viewed as politically expedient to obtain the endorsement of the ruling elite in Beijing. Instead, such obsequious behavior only earned the contempt of voters. Hong Kong's citizens clearly wanted to protect their civil liberties after June 1997, and registered decisive approval for candidates who identified with democratic values.

Having lost Maoist communism as a legitimating ideology, the regime in Beijing has now chosen the risky route of playing the nationalist card. The reversion of Hong Kong fits into their single-minded goal of territorial unification. However, their bullying tactics are unlikely to attract those Chinese in Taiwan whose own system provides more upward mobility and freedom from oppression. The communist regime must understand that economic dynamism on the mainland is necessary for legitimation of its rule. Of equal importance, the current leadership must realize that the preservation of Hong Kong's legal and sociopolitical institutions is the key to stability, and therefore survival.

Inevitably, the uniquely democratic identity of Hong Kong's citizens will cause them to come into conflict with their new rulers. This has already been evidenced by the mainland's clear disregard for the voice of the majority by branding pro-democracy legislator and rights activist Martin Lee as a 'counter-revolutionary.' With the prospective forced dissolution of Legco, the only body in Hong Kong with genuine political legitimacy will be destroyed.

In order to provide a democratic veneer to the post-reversion government of what the Chinese refer to as the Hong Kong Special Administration Region (SAR), a Chief Executive was 'elected' by a group of 400 eminent citizens. This electoral college, known as the Selection Committee, was itself selected by Beijing. The affair had most of the trappings of democracy with candidates engaging in campaigns followed by open voting. It was announced by Vice-Premier Qian Qichen that the regime had no favorite candidate. However, only a handful of Selection Committee members was associated with pro-democratic parties. After two rounds of voting, Tung Chee-hwa was chosen as Hong Kong's first post-colonial leader. In another act of 'Asian democracy,' the committee selected legislators from among themselves to replace the popularly elected Legco.

Unfortunately, Mr Tung Chee-hwa comes with a great deal of baggage, including serious questions about conflict of interests. It is widely known that Beijing bailed out his family-owned shipping company when it experienced some financial difficulties during the 1980s. Unless he earns the trust of Hong Kong's people, he will have no credibility. Unfortunately, Mr Tung will have to embody a combination of conflicting attributes. If he behaves in an overtly pro-Beijing manner, he will not be trusted by the citizens of Hong Kong. Without this trust, there are likely to be challenges to his authority. If these actions precipitate the imposition of martial law, it would certainly be a public relations disaster for China with substantial economic consequences. It therefore might have been better if a senior civil servant from Hong Kong's highly respected bureaucracy had been selected.

The economic and political issues relating to the administration of Hong Kong are complex. On the one hand, the economic implications are of paramount concern. It has become likely that the appointment will fall to a prominent business person with close ties to the regime in Beijing. But the choice of someone with loyalty to one particular ethnic group or business clique will introduce another source of instability into Hong Kong's future. Even if government contracts and licensing were to be handled with perfect probity, everyone will believe that there were informal agreements of that provided privilege or bureaucratic shortcuts to favored players. This perceived loss of integrity in commercial dealings will undermine the attraction of international capital to Hong Kong.

From a political standpoint, once steps are taken to dissolve Legco, Mr Tung will be forced to choose sides. By coming down on the side of Beijing, his credibility Hong Kong's champion will be diminished. As a result, the Chief Executive's usefulness to the Chinese authorities will decrease. Alternatively, siding with the interests of Hong Kong and pro-democratic forces would mean an intolerable loss of face to Beijing. Even if the Chinese authorities do not dissolve Legco, there will be innumerable opportunities for them unilaterally to impose their will that is destined to spark outrage in the global community.

By virtue of its role as an international news hub, events in Hong Kong are widely publicized. Beijing authorities will inevitably be tempted to muzzle or control the press. Things may be different on the mainland where dissidents such as Wei Jingsheng or Wang Dan can be arrested or disappear without most of the world taking note. Denouncements from outsiders can readily be rebuffed as interference with China's internal affairs. However, the use of brute force in the Hong Kong Foreign Correspondents' Club would probably have much greater impact on world opinion.

Even if Beijing insists that their treatment of Hong Kong is an 'internal matter' that brooks no outside interference, it will be the end to China's pretense of being a modern, civilized state. This is important since even modest turmoil in Hong Kong will reverberate along the entire Pacific Rim.

There is more at stake than political ideologies. All sides, whether democrats or communists, are rather more pragmatic than passionate. Instead, it is a clash between the forces of modernity and feudalism. Unfortunately, because all players are effectively Chinese, there is no role for outsiders to act as mediators.

On the one hand, citizens of Hong Kong are familiar with the joys and sorrows of modernity. This comes from their immersion in a culture that has been guided and well served by following the rule of law in open dealings with the rest of the world. On the other hand, mainlanders tend to be inward looking from years of self-imposed autarky. In the mainland's feudalistic world of power and control, the rule of law is an alien concept, and will be viewed by the leadership as a nuisance. Due to ingrained autocratic ways, the leadership in Beijing will dismiss pluralism as out of the question. By insisting upon its

own sense of order, Beijing will suppress criticism and even spontaneous political humor.

In response to each misstep in administering Hong Kong, the Chinese can
be expected to pull the reins of power ever tighter. With each constrictive action, a little more of the creative life that drives Hong Kong's economy will
slowly be choked out of it. This behavior need not be motivated out of malice
aforethought or from a lack of appreciation for the market. Even though Western democracies had extensive exposure to markets, they stifled the creative
juices of entrepreneurs with the welfare state. The Chinese communist regime's obsession for orderliness will almost certainly have a much greater
negative impact on the productive spirit of Hong Kong.

If economic and entrepreneurial freedoms prove to be expendable to the
Chinese leadership in Beijing, democratic interests can expect even less consideration. To mitigate this dismal prospect, democratic forces in Hong Kong
ought to establish contacts with their counterparts in the rest of Asia. Those
who represent the liberalizing conscience of modern Asia must hang together
or they will surely hang alone in the face of authoritarian repression. Contacts
with officials in London, Paris, and Washington may remain an important
source of moral or financial support. However, more solid links need to be
forged with democrats and dissidents in Bangkok, Jakarta, Manila, Rangoon,
Singapore, and Seoul.

In sum, given the compulsive drive for power and domination exhibited by
China's leaders, it is unlikely that they will accommodate or tolerate Hong
Kong's democratic tradition. Therefore, Beijing's administration of Hong
Kong appears to be doomed to failure.

Hong Kong and Taiwan: Siamese twins?

Just as the fate of Hong Kong will determine China's economic future, so too
will the post-1997 relationship between Hong Kong and Taiwan. In terms of
actively facilitating the progress of China's economic reform, Hong Kong and
Taiwan have fulfilled important and complementary roles. It may be true that
Taiwan can survive separation from its Siamese twin. However, by virtue of
their symbiotic relationship, Taiwan's economy will not subsequently be as
healthy, and an identity crisis is almost certain to follow.

Once Hong Kong enters the embrace of the motherland, with Macao soon
to follow in 1999, Beijing's hegemonic attentions will focus on Taiwan.
Clearly, Taiwan's continued autonomy is one of the greatest threats to the legitimacy of the communist rulers of the mainland. As long as Taiwan remains
democratic and prosperous, it belies the myth that the Chinese people are incapable of making their own choices for leadership. With the stakes so high, it

is no wonder that there has been so much saber-rattling and missile launching across the Taiwan Strait.

Doubtless, the hard-line position of the Chinese authorities with respect to Taiwan was intended to serve in part as a warning to independent thinkers in the coastal provinces and Hong Kong. Such bellicose behavior reveals an obsession with power and control on the part of Beijing. Even if these leaders can appreciate the importance of the economies of Hong Kong and Taiwan to China's growth prospects, they seem prepared to sink them both into the sea rather than relinquish eventual control over them.

This rigid stance reflects a profound misunderstanding among China's current leaders about their shared economic destiny with, and dependency upon, the existing institutional arrangements in Hong Kong and Taiwan. For example, Taiwan is the third largest exporter to China. Also, Taiwanese investors are believed to be the source of about $20 billion of foreign direct investment in China. Most of these funds were and are likely to continue to be routed through Hong Kong, owing to the integrity of its financial and judicial systems. This flow will only continue as long as the institutional environment provides the same kind of assurances and security that was provided in the past. Economic relationships thrive and survive in markets characterized by stability, transparency, and a credible rule of law. All of these conditions will be in jeopardy once Hong Kong is handed over to Beijing.

China's media policies

The proliferation of privately owned media outlets has created an illusion of expanded media freedom in China. These include chatty magazines, scandal sheets, and even pornography. The broadcast media has also become increasingly creative and daring in their programming. Within this new media structure, political criticism is tolerated within tight limits. One area of zero tolerance and outright censorship is the advocacy of independence for Taiwan or Hong Kong. Despite what might be considered encouraging signs, the list of taboo subjects can arbitrarily be changed at the whim of the leadership.

Beijing has already signaled its intention to control information flows. In early 1996, the Chinese government adopted a broad plan for the regulation of news and other information. One notable feature of this plan is the imposition of access fees paid to the official New China News Agency by all foreign media services. Ultimately, this allows the agency to control the dissemination of information from outside sources to China's citizens. As a result of this strict scrutiny, foreign news providers can more readily be prosecuted under China's draconian rules covering libel or the preservation of national security interests. With the courts obliged to do the bidding of the ruling party, Chinese reporters have been successfully prosecuted for revealing economic information that is treated as routine in most of the rest of the world.

There is considerable ambiguity and uncertainty when it comes to media freedom in Hong Kong after 1 July 1997. The Director of the Chinese State Council's Hong Kong and Macao Affairs Office, Lu Ping, has sent mixed signals to journalists on what to expect. It is unsettling that the official line has been that freedom of the press will be *regulated* instead of *protected* by the law. Doubtless, the laws will be changing after Britain's handover.

Beijing has indicated that it expects Hong Kong's media to be 'patriotic' toward the motherland. With patriotism a mere euphemism for acting as a communist party supporter, press freedoms will be severely curtailed. Apparently, Beijing's view is that reporters must present the government's positions in an uncritical and unqualified manner. In a post-colonial Hong Kong, unauthorized advocacy of viewpoints or causes by journalists or publishers will not be tolerated. An ominous note of caution has been offered that members of the media might be held accountable if their statements led to 'action.' The implication is that published arguments which convince the public that the government's policies are wrong will subject journalists to prosecution by the state.

Clearly, China's leadership will not shrink from heavy-handed treatment. At least one journalist has been imprisoned under the pretense that he leaked state secrets. However, enforcement of Beijing's media policy for Hong Kong may follow the approach that Singapore has taken. Rather than incarcerate the offending journalists, the Singapore authorities prefer to bankrupt or financially impair media owners through lawsuits for libel, or by withholding advertising revenues from those who antagonize the ruling party.

Hong Kong's freewheeling media has a long and illustrious history of independence. Loss of this freedom will not merely be a matter of nostalgia. Surely the cozy confines and the encounters with quirky Asia hands at the Foreign Correspondents Club will be missed if it is shut down. The disappearance of press freedom in Hong Kong should not be viewed merely as the loss of another historical artifact. By blocking information access from the rest of the world, press censorship will jeopardize future economic growth for Hong Kong and China. Press freedom provides the basis for all information flows, including financial data demanded by long-term investors. Interference with information flows will introduce distortions in the market that will unavoidably inhibit Hong Kong's role as a regional financial center. After all, it is the markets, and not political pressures, that guarantees efficient adjustments to a rapidly changing global economy that will be connected electronically and driven by intensive competition.

China, MFN and the WTO

Pre-election promises to 'get tough' on China's human rights record created an issue that confounded the Clinton administration. Eventually, human rights were jettisoned as the litmus test for renewing most-favored nation (MFN) status. However, a shift from political to purely economic arguments actually strengthens the case for revocation of MFN and rejection of China's application to the World Trade Organization (WTO), which is the successor to the General Agreement on Tariffs and Trade (GATT). However, this is not to suggest that trade with China should be limited. On the contrary, trade with China should be actively encouraged, but with several caveats.

Regarding the WTO, there are various reasonable arguments that support delaying China's membership in the world trading community on an equal basis. For example, persistence of internal trade barriers among Chinese provinces and high external hurdles that block foreign imports create formidable obstacles to commerce. WTO membership entails delicate give-and-take bargaining, which requires skills that Beijing seems to lack, judging from its intractable negotiating style over Hong Kong. Also, rampant corruption and the dubious quality of China's judicial system do little to inspire confidence for protection of foreign or even domestic business interests.

China held membership in GATT until communist forces 'liberated' the country in 1949 and resigned from the world trading body. An appropriate question to ask is whether a political regime whose rigid ideological commitment led to the impoverishment of one-fifth of the world's population for over 45 years has changed enough to be a worthy partner in the WTO.

China's supporters posit a variety of gains from its entry into the WTO. First, the increased economic interdependency from broadened trade links should induce China to become a more responsive and responsible global citizen. Second, by promoting high-paced economic growth, increased trade will give rise to a Chinese middle class, that will act as a moderating force against the repressive political regime. Third, China is pictured as a vast market of virtually unlimited commercial opportunities for its prospective trading partners.

In the first instance, China's trade policies are a mosaic of external as well as internal obstructions. Although there have been substantial decreases in external barriers to trade, Chinese provinces have their own tariff regimes and threaten trade sanctions against one another. Therefore, before its application to the WTO can be taken seriously, China must introduce its own internal free trade area. A second issue relates to external trade barriers. In order to qualify eventually for WTO membership, China must implement substantial, unilateral reductions of these tariffs. Although tariff levels are being reduced, they have been as high as 100-200 percent on many goods. China continues to follow 'import substitution' policies designed to protect and promote domestic production, e.g., as in the case of automobiles. Even with the removal of all tariffs, many other non-tariff barriers to free trade would remain, such as requirements for foreign companies to enter into joint ventures with Chinese partners or local content requirements.[11]

Additional problems stem from the fact that most of China's state-run enterprises are grossly inefficient and heavily subsidized. Despite the onerous burden that the SOEs put on the central authorities and the rest of the economy, political expediency demands that their financial lifelines remain secure. Besides the distortions introduced by subsidies, some exporting enterprises are known to enjoy a contrived competitive advantage from their access to forced labor. This would not present a barrier to WTO entry, per se, if it were not for the contentious manner in which prisoners are tried and sentenced. The presence of prisoners of conscience in China's penal system gives pause to most concerned observers who might otherwise support China's WTO application.

The presumed political advantages of granting WTO membership to China's bureaucratic and centralized regime are also questionable. World Trade Organization members will be required to engage in negotiations over sensitive and difficult issues. Successful conflict resolution must involve mutual understanding and confidence that other parties will abide with the outcomes. Examples of Chinese intransigence in their 'negotiations' with the British government over Hong Kong's fate do not bode well on this score. Specifically, China's threats of economic retaliation against the Walt Disney Company concerning the making of a film on the life of the Dalai Lama violate the spirit, if not the letter, of WTO obligations. Similarly, the inability of the Chinese leadership to muster the political will to shut down factories that pirate CDs and software does not inspire faith in their capacity or willingness to uphold international agreements. In an especially troubling episode, the regime was embarrassed by the arrest of three senior officials of China North Industries Group (Norinco) who smuggled assault weapons into San Francisco in early 1996. Norinco is under the direct tutelage of China's State Council and is equivalent to a cabinet level department.

The broader argument is that China's admission into the WTO would gradually undermine the regime's repressive politics. This optimistic line of reasoning depends upon several assumptions. One is that economic growth estimates are reliable; another is that this new wealth will be evenly distributed among China's regions. Regarding the former, the statistics often cited as indication of China's successful modernization program are highly problematic and probably inaccurate.[12] A report in the Chinese government's mouthpiece, the *People's Daily*, admits that China's statistics are 'at best suspicious and spurious at worst.'

Although economic prosperity may be a necessary condition, it may not be sufficient to mobilize a politically-relevant bourgeois class to counteract the repressive brutality for which the Chinese regime has been noted. There are important prerequisites to the formation of an autonomous and politically viable middle class. Real and transferable private property rights are a primary need. As a general rule, efficient markets and a new set of economic interests tend to prosper when private property rights are well defined *and* clearly enforced. Neither of these preconditions is met in China. Peasant control over landed property is tightly circumscribed, and subject to stringent restrictions for access and transfer of title. Ownership of urban property involves similar stipulations on the right of acquisition and transfer. Furthermore, the lack of procedural integrity in the application of legal codes in China means that enforcement of property and business contracts is arbitrary and subject to political whims. WTO membership in itself is unlikely to hasten remedial changes in property arrangements in China.

The narrow concentration of increased wealth in China's coastal provinces, coupled with continuing restrictions on private property rights, implies that the emergence of a landed middle class is largely illusory. There is no indication that the architects of post-Mao reform intend to implement the necessary changes to allow full property rights to be held by private individuals. Vice-Premier Zhu Rongji projects that socialist state ownership will continue to distinguish Chinese property ownership from its private, Western counterpart. Thus, it is at best premature to contemplate the remedial impact of a property-owning middle class upon bureaucratic rulers bent upon maintaining power.

The basic conflict in China is between a ruling class of bureaucrats and party apparatchiks on the one hand, and a productive class of entrepreneurs and workers on the other hand. This modern ruling class uses the tools of the state (violence, control and coercion) to maintain power, enriching itself and its supporters at the expense of others. In contrast, the productive class relies upon market processes (cooperation, voluntarism and exchange) for its livelihood. For the moment, most of the trump cards in this 'class struggle' are with the administrative classes, i.e., the socialist bureaucracy. From this interpretation, the Tiananmen Square Massacre can be seen as merely the first round in a fierce battle against the rigid authority of the Chinese bureaucracy.

The present Chinese regime seems oblivious to the fact that its complex regulatory scheme creates an almost irresistible temptation for corruption. On its own, WTO membership can do little to stem the levels of public profiteering that have been described by China's General-Prosecutor as the worst ever since 1949. The epidemic proportions of this problem is symptomatic of an economy adrift with a compass that instinctively guides it away from market institutions.

Market relations cannot stabilize without commercial laws that are applied in a rational and evenhanded manner. Otherwise, corruption and arbitrariness prevail. In many known cases, the interpretation of contract law by the judicial system appears to be rigged in favor of the Chinese parties. Without the incentive

93

for mutual advantage that a credible system of contract rights fosters, economic growth based upon market transactions will be undermined.

Assessment of China's membership in the WTO requires full consideration of China's record on internal politics and economic policies combined with its international reputation. On these counts, there is little indication that the current Chinese regime can be expected to behave as a reliable partner in WTO. As mentioned previously, relations between Beijing and London over the handover of Hong Kong have provided little assurance of China's willingness to abide to either the letter or the spirit of international agreements. Perhaps worse, there are questions about the capacity of the leadership in Beijing to hold the country together in its current configuration.[13] It appears that there is too much uncertainty about China's future stability for its trading partners to enter into agreements that they would treat as binding, while the Chinese behave as they like.

Trading with China: Politics as business as usual...?

It is ironic that while the US and most Western countries have abandoned diplomatic or moral pressures as leverage in trade negotiations, China's leaders have refined the art of mixing non-economic issues with commercial transactions. China's leadership seamlessly blends the public with the private and the political with the commercial. Such diplomatic legerdemain has enable China to have increasing influence over the content and outcome of future discussions. Not surprisingly, politics have become a primary consideration on the Chinese trade agenda. Worse yet, the authorities in Beijing have placed their own internal priorities onto a collision course with the interests of other countries.

The ability of China's leaders to mix politics with trade is enhanced by continued government controls over capital flows and the extensive regulatory approval framework that overlays all business conduct. Several high level business deals have been held hostage or have fallen victim to China's politics as business. This is evident in the recent announcement of an order for 30 A-320 Airbuses from the European rivals of America's Boeing Company. Chinese authorities have also reached a preliminary agreement for a $2 billion project to produce a 100 seat regional aircraft in partnership with the trans-European conglomerate, *Aerospatiale*. Most observers accept that the timing of these announcements was intended as a display of disaffection with America's decision to send aircraft carriers to the Taiwan Strait in response to China's attempts to use military force to influence the outcome of Taiwan's first democratic election of a president. China's leadership can therefore be expected to apply various political litmus tests as conditions for trade with increasing frequency.

In stirring up a diplomatic firestorm due to Taiwan President Lee Teng-hui's visit to the US in September 1995, China's leaders served notice that they will attempt to influence the domestic agenda of its trading partners. The collective pout of China's leaders over the threat of free elections in the region reflects a wish to marginalize the homegrown forces of democracy in Hong Kong in the runup to July 1997.

An interesting case in point is found in the ambivalent reception extended to Martin Lee, leader of the Democratic Alliance in Legco, during his visit to the US and Canada in June of 1996. In previous trips to Washington, Mr Lee had been feted as a legitimate voice for the democratic aspirations of Hong Kong's citizens. However, the Clinton administration initially snubbed him in what seems to have been a 'pre-emptive cringe' to Beijing's anticipated negative reaction to democratically elected officials of Chinese descent. After the *Wall Street Journal* exposed this shameful treatment, Mr Lee was received by various Republicans including Messrs Dole and Gingrich. Only then did Clinton Administration officials seem to warm to the idea of meetings, if not photo-ops, with Mr Lee. In a more shameful episode during a subsequent visit to Australia in late 1996, Mr Lee was totally snubbed.

In deciding upon how to receive Hong Kong's democrats in the future, Washington should note that Legco's leadership grew out of the spontaneous urge for democracy among Hong Kong's citizens. Indeed, the democratic movement took shape despite British opposition that was only slightly more hospitable than the Chinese. However, shunning Hong Kong's proven leaders is not merely shameful, it may also be injurious to the economic health of the region. As suggested before, the fortunes of East Asia depend heavily upon the stable, transparent, and efficient institutions that are presently best provided in Hong Kong.

The concept of 'one country, two systems' seems increasingly improbable when the differences in the systems at hand are considered. Hong Kong has an economy with a proven record of sustained growth, a free press, an elected legislature, and a respected legal system dedicated to the rule of law. It is valid to ask whether all this can be immunized against the corrupt business and legal practices presently associated with China and the power-hungry rulers in Beijing. Unfortunately, casualties are already evident in the run-up to the increasingly unfriendly takeover. Apart from insisting that the democratically elected Legco will be disbanded, Beijing has also suggested that Hong Kong's independent and honest civil servants should affirmatively pledge their loyalty to leaders on the mainland.

A likely area for conflict is the role of the People's Liberation Army (PLA) in Hong Kong. The ranking officer who will command Chinese forces in

Hong Kong after the 1997 handover, Major-General Liu Zhenwu, will earn less in one month than many businessmen can earn in a minute. Such enormous mismatches of power and wealth will make for a volatile cocktail. It is hard to imagine that the soldiers and officers who earn so little will not envy or resent the prosperity of those whom they are to 'protect.'

Interaction with China will be especially difficult for the US as its economic destiny becomes more enmeshed with developments in East Asia. This will require that a delicate balance be struck between economic and ideological goals. However, the US government is not in the business of choosing between principles and profits. Washington must avoid the temptation to place the interests of specific firms or industries above democratic principles. In any case, short-run economic gains achieved through such expediency can be expected to lead to long-run political losses. Since the continuation of the rule of law in Hong Kong depends upon the survival of pro-democratic forces, Mr Martin Lee and members of his alliance must be encouraged and supported. If Asia is going to play an increasingly influential role in world affairs, it would be better if it did so as a pluralistic democracy.

A chilling wind from China and prospects for Cold War II?

While the rising fortunes in East Asia spark confidence about future stability in the region, almost each passing day reveals yet another bone of contention between China and a variety of outside interests. These frictions are most evident in China's interactions with the US and some non-governmental organizations. Unfortunately, with so much disagreement over such a wide range of issues, it appears that Cold War II may be just around the corner.

This dire prospect arises partly due to differences in the way East and West understand the role of economic institutions. In the West, aggregate concepts like the 'US economy' reflect a convenient shorthand. In reality, the 'US economy' does not compete with the 'European economy' or the 'Asian economy.' Instead, some American firms compete with some firms in other countries. However, authoritarian rule in much of East Asia is closely identified with one family, person, or party. For them, countries do compete. This misunderstanding unfortunately hinders trade negotiations and contributes to international friction.

Over the past several years, the US has been locked in seemingly interminable disputes with China over a number of issues, including intellectual property rights, human rights, Taiwan, Hong Kong, trade imbalances as well as nuclear proliferation and testing. This list is only likely to grow as China's ambitions begin to be played out on the world stage. Fortunately, these issues are not more numerous or fundamentally more intractable than those that normally exist in the course of international relations among other countries.

This being the case, a protracted Cold War II pitting China against an array of opponents can be avoided. However, the current socialist-patrimonial institutional arrangements characteristic of China's current government may simply make this conflict inevitable. If this is so, it is important to understand why these frictions exist and to articulate clearly what is at stake for all sides.

In the first instance, it should be clear that there is no Western conspiracy to contain China in such a way as to thwart the aspirations of its industrious and proud peoples. After all, few in the West are threatened by the rising economic power of India or a democratic Taiwan. Neither are there signs of a clash of cultures whereby Confucian or Asian values are incompatible with those of the rest of the world. Asians' paranoia in this regard is based upon a fundamental misunderstanding of the give-and-take of negotiations that is a normal part of reaching international accords. Chilling aloofness should not always result from differences of opinion. Certainly, a lack of harmony will be unavoidable even among the closest allies. What is important is how disputes are resolved when they do arise.

Such fundamental differences in principles combined with a rigid ideology or set of nationalist interests may provide the basis for a prolonged cold war. These conditions are most likely to result in intransigence when there is a one-party regime with an authoritarian government. Under such hierarchical rule, leaders are unaccustomed to being questioned about their decisions. In the absence of domestic opposition parties, there are few challenges to their interpretation of the 'will of the people.' These matters may be further complicated when such regimes are so insular and autarchic that they lose touch with the realities of the rest of the world. Being immune to criticisms from their own citizens, and with no opposition parties to contend with, such regimes will tend to be insensitive to outside entreaties.

These conditions aptly describe China's current circumstances. The situation is exacerbated by the fact that China's military modernization and record rates of economic growth have occurred at a historic national juncture with the reclamation of Hong Kong after a century of colonial occupation. It is not surprising that this confluence of events has given the Chinese government new-found confidence, and prompted its leaders to assert their preferences while insisting that others defer to their wishes. At the same time, the disappearance of a Soviet military threat means that American and Chinese security interests do not overlap to the same degree.

A greater problem is that some hard-line factions in China's regime portray world events to the citizenry in very strong, adversarial terms. Such propagandizing elements have been instrumental in choosing words that define the relationship of China with America. Manipulation of translations from English

97

into Chinese allows the regime to create an unduly antagonistic impression. For example, official documents speak of American attempts to 'throttle' or choke off Chinese modernization in place of more mild terms used in English like 'containment.'[14] Clearly, this sort of inflammatory language is likely to stir up anti-American sentiments without actual provocation. Following similar nationalistic impulses, there have been deliberately unbalanced portrayals of America as a nation in cultural and economic decline. Ultimately, this intentionally distorted portrait of America will lead to foreign policy miscalculations that could seriously impair China's economic ascendancy.

As suggested above, the Beijing leadership can be expected to take strong exception to outside criticism. Ostensibly, there are residual fears stemming from a nationalistic paranoia about attempts by foreigners to weaken China by dividing it. In truth, this is a mere contrivance designed as a convenient shift of the public's focus away from internally generated dynamics that are forcing decentralization of political power. Beijing's insecurity leads to a treatment of any outside criticism as a direct challenge to sovereignty, and treats fault finding by outsiders as a potential 'loss of face' for the Chinese leadership.

Although the prickly nature of China's leaders makes constructive dialogue difficult, the leadership of Western countries must nevertheless endeavor to understand what is at stake and seek to define and defend their own long-term, fundamental interests. Principles of human dignity along with a commitment to the rights and freedom of the individual must not be traded for transitory economic advantage that might only serve a special group of commercial interests. Protection of individual rights and the preservation of institutions that promote human dignity must surely be seen as more universal and more valuable than is the market share of GM or Boeing or Motorola in the booming markets in China or other parts of Asia.

As mentioned earlier, there is some cause for optimism that Cold War II may not become an enduring feature of international relations. For their part, Western politicians can lessen tensions by seeking a 'strategic dialogue' with China to emphasize the areas of common concern that are taken for granted among allies. As it is, by allowing the discussion to have too much focus upon contentious issues, there has been an unnecessary escalation of hostilities.

It is to be hoped that the passing of the older generation of China's leaders from power will give way to a younger and more pragmatic leadership less likely to conduct affairs in a manner designed to allow them to 'save face.' With their increased exposure to contract-based cultures, the next generation of China's leaders might better understand the nature of negotiations with countries that have multiparty democracies. At the same time, the mitigating influences of the market may encourage restraint on adversarial posturing by all sides.

While frustrations in the short run may be enormous, benefits can be expected to accrue to all when the Chinese leadership becomes more willing to grant concessions to trading partners or their own citizens. As the Chinese and other Asian peoples are eventually released from the grip of their autocratic rulers, it is likely that the world will be a safer and more prosperous place for future generations in all countries.

Rising costs and waning advantages?

The cost of living for China's struggling citizens is rising due to inflation. Even though they may be dismayed by increases in the price of a bowl of rice, they would be astounded by what it costs for foreigners to live in their major cities. A 1996 survey by Corporate Resources Group of Geneva found that Beijing, Shanghai, and Hong Kong were ranked third, fourth, and fifth among the most expensive cities in the world for expatriates. Guangzhou and Shenzhen ranked 11 and 12, respectively.[15] By comparison, New York City was ranked 38 on the list of 139 cities.

The survey examined the costs of western-style amenities including nearly 200 products and services consumed by international workers and company executives posted in overseas locations. Extremely high housing rentals contributed significantly to these rankings. Beijing had the most expensive western-style housing, followed by Tokyo and Hong Kong.

The costs that are enumerated in the above study reflect only economic factors and do not include the psychic costs of congested urban living or the frustrations of operating a business or placing investments there. Among the complaints from those investing in China are extensive bureaucratic interference and exaggerated distortions in asset pricing and allocation arising from the imperfections in the market system. These add to the other considerable costs associated with operating in China and in many other parts of East Asia.

China's 'miracle' growth is no guide for the future

In short, the brisk pace of China's economic expansion over the last few years is likely to soon run out of steam either due to economic logic or political instability. To date, much of China's momentum reflected the non-repeatable gains resulting from the removal of irrational political barriers that had previously blocked market activity. Although these gains were substantial and did not require the legal infrastructure associated with capitalist development, future growth will be stunted unless a transparent and equitable legal system is established. These developments will not come easy to a leadership that is so obsessed with maintaining control. It is therefore unlikely that China will make the leap toward the implementation of separation of powers and a strict sense of legalism. Hong Kong, Japan, South Korea, Singapore, and Taiwan established a reliable commercial code with the assistance of outside patronage that is not available to China.[16] In this case, the absence of a dominant colonial power or an occupying army was a mixed blessing for China. While it was able to go its own way since 1949, China now pays the price for its isolation in terms of anachronistic institutions and a glacial pace toward reform.

A revisionist view of China's economic activity raises serious questions about the progress made to date. After years of unconditional acceptance and publication of economic data submitted by Beijing, the World Bank now believes that these numbers are deeply flawed.[17] For example, although there is no doubt that China has made progress, new estimates suggest that about 30 percent of the population is living in poverty. This figure stands in sharp contrast to the earlier estimates of seven percent. These new calculations reduce the estimates of China's GDP by about 25 percent so that per capita GDP is apparently $1,800 instead of $2,500. Now it seems that China's economy will not be able to overtake the US economy for at least 30 years, instead of earlier estimates of about 11 years.

This more sober outlook on China's economic prowess does not change the fact that its modernization process will generate numerous challenges arising out of economic and social transformation. As signs of social instability such as high and rising rates of crime as well as endemic corruption erupt out of China's modernizing experience, the regime's rigidity will render in incapable of accommodating the strains of change. Increasingly, the Chinese Communist Party will find that its mandate to rule is bereft of legitimacy. In the words of one observer, there is 'a relatively thin line between order and chaos' in China.[18] On this unhappy note, it appears that expectations of China's impending prominence as a world class economic power are greatly exaggerated.

An implied before, there is an interesting paradox concerning the institutions and values that have contributed to rapid economic growth in China and other parts of East Asia. There is no dispute that they might have contributed to short-run economic gains. The next chapter will examine the cultural, political, and economic institutions and the values reflected by them in terms of their impact upon the capacity of East Asian economies to sustain high rates of long-term growth.

Notes

1   The range that is considered to be safe is 30 percent and 165 percent, respectively.
2   Simon. 'Asia, You Cost Too Much', op. cit.

3   Those firms that did operate at a profit saw their earning fall by 55 percent.

4   H. Root, 'Corruption in China: Has it Become Systemic?', *Asian Survey*, Vol. xxxvi, No. 8 (August 1996), pp. 741-57.

5   The current and capital accounts represent indicators of international economic activities. The current account is a record of receipts from imports and exports, net interest income, plus net transfers. The capital account is the record of a country's international borrowing and lending transactions.

6   H. Sender, 'Small Change: China's Banks Labour with the Baggage of their Past', *Far Eastern Economic Review*, 8 August 1996, p. 62.

7   There are estimates that over 100 million peasants are roaming the Chinese countryside in search of work. In other words, one out of every twelve Chinese citizens is a migrant laborer, many of whom are unemployed.

8   A striking case in point is the assertion that China's measured unemployment resides in the range of 2 - 3 percent. In light of the tens of millions of displaced peasants, this figure must be considered to be fantastically understated.

9   Alcatel-Alsthom, AT&T, NEC, Northern Telecom, and Siemans AG have factories in China.

10   M. Yahuda, *Hong Kong: China's Challenge*, London: Routledge, 1996 and B. de Mesquita, D. Newman, and A. Rabushka, *Red Flag Over Hong Kong*, Chatham, NJ: Chatham House, 1996.

11   Although the SOEs are heavily subsidized, the government does not guarantee their external debt. Foreign creditors cannot count on the Chinese authorities to bail them out, unless they fall under priority projects as specified under the five-year plan.

12   C. Lingle and K. Wickman, 'Don't Trust the Reports of Supercharged Growth', *International Herald Tribune*, 19 January 1994. See also 'How Poor is China?', *The Economist*, 12 October 1996.

13   G. Segal, *China Changes Shape: Regionalism and Foreign Policy*, London: Institute for International Strategic Studies, 1994 and Lincoln Kaye, et al., 'Disorder Under Heaven', *Far Eastern Economic Review*, 9 June 1994, pp. 22-50.

14   E. Friedman, 'Goodwill, Lost in Translation', *Far Eastern Economic Review*, 1 August 1996.

15   All five of the most expensive cities were in Asia with Tokyo and Osaka taking the top two spots. The only European cities in the top ten were Moscow at 6, Geneva at 8, and Zurich at 9.

16   Many of the other emerging economies in the region carried over these influences from their colonial experiences.

17 'Poverty in China: What Do the Numbers Say?', *Background Note, East Asia & Pacific Region,* Washington, DC: World Bank, 1996.

18 K. Lieberthal, *Governing China: From Revolution Through Reform,* New York: W. W. Norton, 1995, p. 228.

6 Burdens of the 'Asian Model': Economic costs and political consequences

Political leaders in developing countries around the world are beginning take notice of the impressive progress of economic development in East Asia. Those countries must decide whether certain aspects of the 'Asian Model' should be adopted in their own pursuit of material gains. However, their choices are being muddled by the rhetoric that promotes the contrived notion of 'Asian values.' Those who assert the existence of a superior set of values that are peculiar to Asia found considerable comfort in a World Bank study of the region's 'miracle' economies that credited the leaders for their forthright, capital-friendly policies. Significantly, the most ardent supporters of 'Asian values' include authoritarian rulers and their apologists as well as a new breed of Asian nationalists.[1]

Supporters of 'Asian values' assert that developing countries must choose between two distinctive development paths. One is the 'Asian Model,' characterized by high economic growth achieved at the expense of individual civil liberties. The other option is a Western-style system, where individualism ultimately leads to cultural decline and economic stagnation. Under this dichotomy, Western guarantees of personal rights and freedoms are portrayed as a form of moral pollution that leads to selfishness and the destruction of the collective good. All too often, 'Asian values' are promoted in adversarial terms as the antidote to 'Western values' that threaten to alienate citizens against cherished institutions such as self-sacrifice and cooperation.[2]

As in most simplistic choices, there is more here than meets the eye. Ironically, due to a tradition of open self-criticism and public introspection about its economic, social and political institutions, much is known about the failings of the West. There is no question that these shortcomings are well-chronicled and freely discussed by observers from all cultures. By contrast, a different set of traditions allows deficiencies associated with the 'Asian

Model' to be readily overlooked. It is well known that criticism among Asians tends to be muted and restrained.

Consequently, there is often a failure to confront pressing problems that require prompt remedial action. Nimble decision making may also be obstructed by the hierarchical political structures that stifle initiatives by junior officials. Thus, policy inertia tends to arise out of bureaucratic rigidities in much of East Asia. Perhaps the clearest example is the continued domination of the Japanese economy by bureaucrats, despite evidence that their policies contributed to an extended recession and, according to news reports, exacerbated the Kobe earthquake disaster. Thus, what is often observed is a misleading 'constructed reality' and a contrived sense of stability within East Asian institutions.

Equally significant, the notion of a harmonious and homogeneous set of 'Asian values' common to the region is belied by in the undulating tide of nationalism that rears its ugly head in various countries from time to time.

Questions about the notion of 'Asian values'

As a starting point, the assertions of a homogeneous 'Asian Model' beg investigation. Because of the adversarial rhetoric often used by its proponents, the 'Asian Model' inspires troubling political division. In earlier ideological disputes, the 'rich' North was divided against the 'poor' South, or followers of communism vied with capitalism for supremacy. The promoters of 'Asian values' have instigated a new war of words that sets in stark relief unquestioned Eastern virtues against the allegedly unavoidable decadence of the West. In a manner similar to that of former communists, authoritarianism is justified on the basis of a 'superior' economic system. More problematic is that the authoritarianism identified with the new 'Asian Model' is justified as a safeguard against the decadence arising from a 'white peril' that will undermine Asian values and, in turn, weaken the economic performance of the region. Ironically, the first salvos in this new Cold War against the West have emanated from erstwhile strategic allies and deeply dependent trading partners, such as Prime Minister Mahathir of Malaysia and Senior Minister Lee Kuan Yew of Singapore.

Several other issues merit further consideration. First, the impression that the 'Asian Model' evolved from communities engaged in active public discourse is false. For example, while Mr Lee Kuan Yew of Singapore aggressively promotes his vision of 'Asian values,' his regime has implemented policies to insure that there is no open forum for the airing of controversial views. Singapore's domestic media seldom challenge the judgments of the PAP regime, while the foreign media are often censored and always subject to numerous restrictions. Satellite dishes and transmitters are manufactured in Singapore and the Singapore Broadcasting Corporation and Asian Business News beam programs to the outside world.[3] However, these same devices cannot be used in Singapore, and these transmissions are kept from the uncensored view of their own citizens.

In Singapore, as in the other authoritarian regimes in the region, attempts to air critical opinions of Asian culture or reports on repression in Asia are likely to be suppressed. Citizens can be subjected to detention without trial for an indefinite period, while outside criticism tends to be dismissed as an inappropriate intrusion into domestic affairs. While there may be a higher probability of becoming a crime victim in some places in America, there is a near certainty that East Asian authoritarian regimes will silence those who challenge their supremacy. The liberal application of libel laws, reliance upon compliant tax authorities, and use of character assassination of opposition figures are effective means to silence political dissent. Because of their insidious nature, these tactics may not attract the attention or ire of human rights campaigners, who are instead more likely to notice when political dissidents are detained without trial.

Second, if 'Asian values' truly exist, the distinguishing elements and their sources must be identified.[4] Interestingly, most of the outspoken proponents of Asian values favor authoritarian forms of government or some form of Asian nationalism, often as a unifying political force. As promoted by such autocratic forces, 'Asian values' are based upon a spiritual poverty that is matched with an obsessive adherence to authority. These values promote prayer by politically mute masses at the altar of GDP with the blessing of the new Asian autocrats.

In any event, the idea of a single 'Asian Model' based upon a truly pan-Asian culture is an illusion. Proponents are of several minds on this issue: at times they seem to speak of values common to East or North Asia (e.g., Confucianism), or they widen the focus to all of Asia. Nonetheless, all these alternative versions of 'Asian values' have one element in common. Family values are typically depicted as the binding force that will unify the region and which will save Asian culture from the moral decay and social chaos that is offered as a caricature of American culture.

However, if family values are key 'Asian values,' then the citizens of Burma-Myanmar, Pakistan and India would not be so impoverished. If family values are 'Asian values,' then Singapore's Tribunal for the Maintenance of Parents would not have been inundated with lawsuits brought by neglected parents seeking support from their children. If success requires that these family values be combined with repressive authoritarianism, then the economies of Vietnam and Laos would not have performed so badly. If family values, repression and dominance of Chinese culture are the required mix, China

105

should not have waited so long to experience strong economic growth. Clearly, it is difficult to believe that family is so important in Asia when children are sold into prostitution, or when gender-based infanticide is practiced.

Arguably, there may be some values shared by all Asians; however, most of these are also shared by peoples in other regions of the world. Several studies have investigated Asian thinking on the similarities of values held by other Asians and the differences of those values from the rest of the world. These studies relied upon interviews or surveys of an elite segment of the population of Asia.[5] The results imply that Asian intellectuals, businessmen, and government officials tend to rank certain values differently from their Western counterparts. However, most respondents work in the most modernized segments of their respective countries and rely upon institutions that are interlinked with other countries and cultures. thus, as the elite proponents of 'Asian values' gain more exposure to the value systems of other modernized regions in the world, the perceived gulf between East and West should diminish. This convergence is inevitable, given that the values mentioned in the referenced survey are already shared by all; it was just the rankings that varied.

The costs of corruption: Business as usual in Asia?

Whatever the definition, adherence to a set of 'Asian values' does not seem to be have been enough to stem rampant corruption in most countries in the region. Interestingly, because many of the most vibrant economies apparently also have the most pervasive corruption, there might be a temptation to think that it does not harm prospects for economic growth. Although growth can be achieved in the short run despite corruption, long-term prospects will suffer irreparable harm. Corruption leads to higher costs through excessive bureaucratic procedures, and increased uncertainty due to shifting legal frameworks. In sum, corruption breeds an environment that is hostile to commercial and contractual norms.

A 1995 report by Transparency International (TI), an international organization that monitors business attitudes about official graft, indicated that the most corrupt places to do business are concentrated in Asia with China and Indonesia considered to be the worst. In TI's 1996 report, Nigeria and Pakistan were deemed to have the most corrupt practices, while China and Indonesia remained among the top ten. It seems that international competition for bribery is beginning to replace international competitive bidding.

While corruption is worst among the emerging economies of Asia, South Korea and Japan face enormous problems of their own. Even squeaky clean Singapore was embarrassed in late 1995 by a high-profile bribery scandal involving the deputy CEO of the Public Utilities Board, Choy Hun Tim. It was revealed that he accepted nearly $8.5 million (about 14 million Singapore dollars) in kickbacks from Western contractors.

Ultimately, the political costs of corruption can include the collapse of ruling coalitions, as experienced several times in Japan, which is generally regarded by international businesspersons as having a low level of corruption. Similarly, the very foundations of stability and democracy have been shaken by the corruption scandals that have led to the trial and imprisonment of two former heads of state in South Korea on bribery charges.[6]

Obviously, it is in the economic and political interests of these governments to control perceptions about the extent of corruption. The tradition of 'saving face' that mitigates public humiliation for personal failure, has been subverted into a device for deceiving voters as well as prospective investors. Furthermore, by promoting consensus and limiting dissent, it is easier for leaders and entire governments to hide their failures. Thus, despite numerous and widely reported scandals involving corruption, a World Bank report on the 'miracle' economies of East Asia noted the 'relative lack of corruptibility of the public administrations in Japan and Korea.'. By rewarding businesses for non-productive behavior, corruption precludes efficient capital allocation and formation. 'Clean businesses' are therefore eliminated through a process of adverse selection, and macroeconomic growth prospects are greatly diminished.

Corruption occurs on many levels. The gamut runs from 'tea money' paid to petty bureaucrats, to gifts of liquor or gold watches to minor officials, to deposits in Swiss bank accounts for cabinet ministers. The costs of corruption observed at both a microeconomic and macroeconomic level. From the microeconomic standpoint, these costs are imposed at various points of daily interaction. Corruption leads to consumers paying above-market prices for poor quality products offered by protected firms. When it comes to state-run services, consumers may also have to pay bribes to jump the queue for driving licenses or for access to quality medical care. As citizens, they may be called upon to pay taxes that subsidize favored private firms or that sustain state-owned enterprises. As competitors, the economic costs of corruption can be measured as market shares lost to a less efficient rival.

Corruption also reduces production efficiency by encouraging a misallocation of resources through distorted incentive structures. These inefficiencies emerge when official and bureaucratic corruption afford less qualified business contractors an upper hand in bidding. By distorting the risk/reward profile of a particular project, resources are wasted and public funds are misallocated. At the corporate level, corruption raises the costs of doing business and diverts funds from more productive activity like worker training or capital investment. Corruption also sends false signals to the capital markets, in that the financial disclosure of companies that engage in paying bribes will overstate their performance and mislead potential investors.

The banality of the evil associated with corruption is seen in the loss of hundreds of lives when city officials in Seoul accepted bribes to ignore fatally-flawed workmanship in the Samsoong Department Store. Indictments for bribery at the highest levels have rocked the governments of India, Japan, and South Korea, while the rampant corruption that characterized the Marcos' regime is yet to be exorcised from the Philippines. Similarly, questions surrounding sweetheart condominium deals for Senior Minister Lee Kuan Yew and son Hsien Loong have tarnished Singapore's reputation for incorruptibility.

Pervasive corruption in East Asia invites the cynical view that it is an inescapable and harmless component of the new global economy. However, corruption involves a complex skein of economic and social costs that might derail the aspirations of emerging Asian economies, and undo the advances of those economies that are already integrated into the global market.

Among the social costs is a general weakening of the community's moral fabric, combined with apathy toward political and legal reform. On the one hand, it demoralizes honest competitors by creating an impression that 'honesty does *not* pay.' On the other hand, public sector corruption violates the notion that consent of the governed is a determinant of public policy. Instead, the private interests of public officials exert undue influence on official decisions, to the detriment of public welfare. Corruption also helps perpetuate authoritarian regimes by providing politicians with financial support that is not dependent upon their performance on behalf of the citizenry. Worse yet, the prospects for remedial action are not good, since those who are directly involved in corruption are protected by the very public officials who are responsible for fighting this evil.

Corruption leads to increasing politicization of economic activity, which in turn contributes to the bureaucratization, centralization, and the general politicization of life that lead to entrepreneurial stagnation. Unsurprisingly, corruption thrives in a setting of extensive government regulations. Under these conditions, bureaucrats effectively 'privatize' services that should be available to the general public by demanding payoffs that become their own personal income. These arrangements often lead to a concentration of power and a consolidation of wealth or income in the hands of those with the best political connections.

Government actions in some form (e.g., regulation, public ownership) are present in most countries. In modern economies, government interventions are often intended to offset breakdowns in market efficiency. Unfortunately, extensive government involvement will simply increase the opportunities for corrupt behavior, thereby deepening market imperfections. In a corrupt environment, government officials have a strong incentive to maximize the number of situations where they can collect the fruits of influence peddling. These payments might take the form of political advantage through promised votes, campaign contributions to political parties, or as outright bribes.

Ultimately, corruption is at best a zero-sum redistributive game. At worst, it may lead to a negative-sum outcome whereby the losses to one group exceed the gains to the rest of the community. Those who praise the virtues of the institution of *guanxi* seem to overlook its zero-sum nature, whereby if I have it, you cannot. From a community standpoint, all would be better off if no one could exploit such power networks. From an economic standpoint, markets work best when the rules of the game are transparent and consistent.

In much of Asia, corruption is the natural outgrowth of the necessity of acquiring *guanxi* in order to make business deals. Those familiar with commercial arrangements among Chinese traders are aware of the importance attached to the informal social networks and contacts known as *guanxi*, translated literally to be 'good relations' or simply, 'connections.' *Guanxi* is widely practiced in East Asia, and it is a crucial element of business dealings with large numbers of Overseas Chinese.

Some elements of *guanxi* reflect attempts to sidestep the red tape interferences of bureaucrats and can lead to real gains for the community at large by facilitating economically efficient plans. Yet these gains may be illusory if the obstructions were artificially created by unnecessary government actions. Corruption and connections too often replace legal precedent and impartiality as the basis for resolution of economic disputes.

The social waste arising out of most *guanxi* arrangements is likely to reduce long-run growth potential for the economy as a whole by clouding transparency and increasing the costs associated with transactions. *Guanxi* imposes structural limits upon economic activity by interfering with the process of discovering individually advantageous arrangements. In other words, *guanxi* is subject to the law of diminishing returns. As the number of contacts grows larger, the costs of nurturing each carefully forged arrangement begin to outweigh the attendant benefits derived from the relationship. Ultimately, dependence on *guanxi* will restrict the expansion of businesses that depend heavily upon it.

Guanxi is also likely to have a 'crowding out' effect upon socially beneficial economic activities through the diversion of profits from entrepreneurs into the hands of bureaucrats. The socially productive activities normally associated with profit seeking (greater competition leads to increased consumer choice, gains in efficiency, innovations, and lower prices) are lost when corrupt officials require that they receive payments before projects can go ahead. Competing interests among entrepreneurs and consumers functions like an 'invisible hand' that harnesses self-interested behavior to serve the general community. Corruption and the purchase of *guanxi* create a 'hidden hand' that picks the pocket of both consumers and producers.

At first glance, the custom of corruption appears to be a tempting institutional arrangement to exploit. Newcomers to Asia are apprised of the importance of cultivating the right sort of contacts. However, the logic of such arrangements is seldom thoroughly considered. Ironically, corruption involves several internal contradictions. If access is too exclusive, then there is little incentive for outsiders to attempt to penetrate a market. However, an extension of the existing corrupt arrangements to accommodate newcomers will also deflate its value.

Perhaps worse, if government officials try to enlarge the sphere of activities that involve corrupt behavior, this will lead to an increasing loss of efficiency that makes investment less attractive to outsiders. Similarly, because these arrangements are informal or at least outside the law, they may encourage violence or other criminal acts as a means of dispute resolution.

The good news is that the increased presence of multinational corporations in developing economies will demand that business dealings become increasingly transparent and have the force of law behind them. Certainly, the severe financial penalties associated with the Foreign Corrupt Practices Act provides US corporations with a strong disincentive to acquiring *guanxi*. In the end, the custom and tradition of corruption in Asia look to become a victim of the forces of modernity.

Economic growth versus (Asian) democracy?

It is no secret that many of the transitional communist regimes in China or Vietnam would like to develop a market economy under the present leadership while maintaining a monopoly over political power. In order to achieve these dual objectives, a model of 'authoritarian capitalism' is being aggressively promoted in many Asian countries.[7] Such regimes seek legitimacy through successes with limited, neo-mercantilist economic reforms.

The characteristics of various economic systems can be seen in Figure 6.1. This diagram indicates the extent to which there is economic and political freedom in various countries. The governing system of those countries with severe limits on both economic and political freedoms is identified as 'authoritarian socialism.' The system that allows substantial economic and political freedoms is identified as 'liberal capitalism.' The system that limits economic freedoms but is based upon multiparty democracy is identified as 'liberal socialism.' Systems that impose restrictions on political freedom but allow expansive economic freedom are identified as 'authoritarian capitalism.'

Countries emerging from years of isolation or the suffocating impact of central planning are seeking to prompt economic growth by implementing the same sort of export-oriented policies used by Japan and the other 'miracle' economies. However, this success is possible only because these countries are free-riding on a liberal global trading regime. Complaints about protectionist policies, especially those issued by their Western trading partners, are generally greeted with discourteous self-righteousness, and dismissed as neo-colonialist intrusions.

Political Freedoms

	(No, No) Authoritarian Socialism (PRC, USSR)	(Yes, No) Liberal Socialism, Social Democracy (India, Sweden)
Economic Freedoms	(No, Yes) Authoritarian Capitalism (Indonesia, Malaysia, Singapore)	(Yes, Yes) Liberal Capitalism (Canada, EU, USA)

Figure 6.1 Taxonomy of political and economic institutions

Supporters of economic reform in Asia too often turn a blind eye to the socially and politically repressive tendencies that characterize 'authoritarian capitalism.' This uncritical view is partly based on the hope that sustained economic growth will give rise to a liberalizing middle class. Hints of liberalization observed in South Korea, Thailand and Taiwan are often cited as examples that support this theory. However, the true extent of middle class influence is actually less than it appears. The liberalizing effect of an emerging middle class can be diluted through the co-optation of the bourgeoisie, either through crony capitalism or enlistment into the state bureaucracy. For example, in spite of decades of sustained growth and its enviously prosperous middle class, Singapore remains decidedly authoritarian.[8]

A variety of Asian authoritarian regimes encourage the 'commercialization of politics' whereby political parties or government institutions undertake business transactions that exploit insider information or political influence.[9] These activities are observed in the tangled web of commercial arrangements involving the ruling parties in China, Indonesia, Malaysia, Singapore, South Korea, and Taiwan. Such arrangements help perpetuate single-party dominance of political power by providing an independent and covert source of financing. This is especially important for the military in China. In particular, the PLA has been able to manipulate a wide variety of commercial dealings in order to finance their own modernization schemes. By affording the PLA an independent revenue source, such insider deals eliminate the need for tax

111

funding, which might place an additional strain upon intra-governmental relations, as discussed below. At the same time, the co-optation of the middle class, either through bureaucratic appointments or access to lucrative private sector arrangements, contributes to the same end. In sum, the politicization of economic activity breeds corruption and money politics in most of East and Southeast Asia.

In their search for an expedient economic model to facilitate rapid economic growth, many of the erstwhile communist regimes in Asia have reached the politically opportunistic conclusion that authoritarian rule is a 'necessary evil.' The purveyors of this snake oil assert that an escapable 'cruel choice' involves the tradeoff between political freedom and economic prosperity. Such arguments amount to sophistry designed to justify the imposition of authoritarian capitalism.

The logic behind the alleged tradeoff between high-paced economic growth and political freedom suggests that democracies are at a disadvantage relative to authoritarian, even totalitarian regimes, during transition or the early stages of economic development. The argument is that while economic freedoms may serve as a foundation for the development of political freedom, the reverse is not necessarily true. In this view, not only is political freedom not necessary for economic development, it threatens to obstruct economic progress. Reasons cited include the formation of powerful interest groups that demand redistributive policies that are inefficient and that reduce long-term economic growth. Similarly, tax revolts, open political debate and change of rulers place substantial fetters upon economic decisions by governments. Unlike authoritarian regimes, democratic rulers face political constraints in extracting a target level of savings or generating revenues through raising or imposing taxes. The partial truth in these observations provides dangerously seductive support for authoritarian rule.

In addition, many observers assert that authoritarian regimes are better at mobilizing resources for rapid economic progress through the extraction and disposition of (forced) savings from a relatively pliant population. Dissent, where allowed, can be muted and political debate censored at the whim of the ruling regime. Such an approach to governing bears troubling and striking similarities to fascism.[10] Creeping fascism can therefore insidiously supplant the despotism of socialism.

In reality, the combination of competitive capitalism and liberal democracy (liberal capitalism) provides a more compelling set of incentives. By insuring that individuals are personally rewarded with the fruits of their labor, this system creates stakeholders across a broader constituency. In turn, by allowing the 'invisible hand' of personal self-interest to motivate individual effort, liberal capitalism provides a self-sustaining incentive system for economic growth that offsets the presumed advantages of coerced accumulation under authoritarian capitalism.

Most importantly, liberal capitalism provides the best guarantee for private property rights, which are an essential sustained economic growth. Liberal capitalism also provides the poor with individual freedoms allowing social and economic mobility as a means for self-empowerment. Clearly, the middle class is not the only social segment interested in promoting democracy.

Ultimately, the advances of liberal capitalism depend upon the evolving characteristics and role of genuine entrepreneurs. The growth-promoting innovations of 'real' entrepreneurs go beyond merely seizing opportunities to 'buy low, sell high.' Entrepreneurs are by nature iconoclastic. As strong individualists, they challenge the status quo, whether it be the competitive structure of a market or authority frameworks. More specifically, this includes opposing government policies that impede their quest for monetary gain. Authoritarian regimes control economic activities, often by creating pseudo-entrepreneurs through the provision of special privileges. However, only 'real' entrepreneurs can generate sustained growth. Their counterfeit cousins focus upon restricting competition and in maintaining the political status quo. Authoritarian capitalism depends upon obedient bureaucrats, compliant party cadres, select business interests and other sycophants of the ruling regimes.

While it may be obvious, it is worth noting that many authoritarian regimes are incapable of delivering economic progress, e.g., Cuba, Zimbabwe, Burma-Myanmar, Bangladesh, Pakistan, Afghanistan, Iraq, and Iran. Thus, the visible hand of the interventionist state does not guarantee successful economic development. Government bureaucrats can be just as fallible as the private decision makers they seek to replace. This fallibility is not limited to decision makers guided by ideologies, like communism. It also arises out of Confucian paternalism.

Even Japan's Ministry of International Trade and Industry (MITI) is known to have picked as many losers as winners in the decades of interventionist promotion.[11] MITI's mediocre track record demonstrates the long-run deficiency of neo-mercantilism disguised as the export-oriented development strategies common to many of the newly industrialized countries (NICs). China's economic policies reflect a neo-mercantilist logic. In China, as in most authoritarian regimes, the primary purpose of extensive controls over the economy is to maintain and protect the existing structure of political and economic interests. Such attempted controls proved to be abject failures when implemented as a component of central planning.

In the end, the 'cruel choice' associated with the sacrifice of freedoms to repressive government interventions is merely a 'quick fix' that provides short-run gains. In the long run, stunted growth potential inevitably leads to social and political instability. This being the case, civil liberties and individual freedoms are not mere abstractions, but integral components of sustainable economic growth. As such, self-interested leaders and their economic advisers would be well advised to include them in their macroeconomic calculus.

Survival and success in the increasingly open and highly competitive international economic order require efficient institutions that are flexible and that encourage innovative, risk-taking entrepreneurs. Authoritarian capitalism is unlikely to meet these requirements. Beware of those who claim that pluralism and prosperity are incompatible. In reality, political freedom and high-paced economic growth are not mutually exclusive, but combine to insure that short-run gains are translated into long-run progress.

The media in Asia

Operating in an authoritarian environment makes members of the Asian media, like their fellow citizens, heavily dependent upon the approval of their government. Consequently, media reports often tend to reflect a government-enforced orthodoxy. Banal reports on cultural events and non-controversial activities replace hard news and critical analysis. Journalists fear that a 'real' story might cause local or regional governments to 'lose face.' Granted, part of the reticence of the Asian media is based upon cultural traditions that are less supportive of the sort of confrontation that much of the Western media prides itself upon. However, the restraint evident even among international journalists suggests something more sinister. Self-imposed censorship allows events like the Dili Massacre, the devastating effects of regional deforestation, and periodic culling of indigenous tribes to proceed unabated and without the public debate that would be sparked by widespread media reporting. When the local media attempt to assert any independence from East Asia's authoritarian regimes, they do so under the threat of ruthless prosecution and possible ruin by state watchdogs. The international media is treated with scarcely less contempt if they offer critical analysis.

There is one area, however, where the media is granted total license. In keeping with the promotion of the concept of 'Asian values' by incumbent regimes, articles are carefully selected from international wire services to illustrate the decadence, moral inferiority and imminent collapse of the West. Meanwhile, Western media sources that comment critically upon certain Asian regimes face the prospects of having their circulation curtailed or being sued for 'interfering in domestic politics.'

Consequently, much of the media in Asia is preoccupied with reports on the approaching Asian century based upon Asian economic growth and upon allusions to an emerging Pan-Asianism. This view is often presented as a Darwinian struggle where the West is portrayed as being on its last legs, engaged in a zero-sum battle with the East, where winners eliminate losers. By virtue of its presumed economic and moral superiority, the next Reich must obviously be an Asian one. Yet this view neglects one of the fundamental lessons of Western economic development, that free trade based on comparative advantage tends to be a win-win arrangement. With most Asian countries producing a relatively homogeneous line of low value-added goods for export, regional competition must give way to an outward-looking global view.

Singapore's media policy: An Asian model?

Singapore's regime has taken a heretofore highly-effective, two-pronged approach to achieving control of the media, both inside and outside its borders. The first prong consists of censorship and control. On the one hand, this is implemented directly through regulations that act as a prior restraint on speech content (e.g., Internet prohibitions, to be discussed further below). Similarly, Singapore's Newspaper and Printing Presses Act amounts to a *de facto* nationalization of the media that, contrary to First Amendment guarantees of individual free speech for American citizens, provides protections for government speech. On the other hand, media censorship and control are achieved indirectly through the strategic application of libel laws to harass those who speak their political mind (e.g., this author's personal experience with an op-ed piece published in the *International Herald Tribune*, also discussed below).

The second prong consists of media manipulation. The government deliberately publicizes contrived prosecutions of individuals portrayed as decadent outsiders in stark contrast to the regime's virtuous rulers who steadfastly protect community welfare. While these cases make a mockery of due process in the civil liberties arena, the regime cleverly maintains a reputation for legal integrity by scrupulously administering commercial law. Finally, the contrivance of 'Asian values' is deftly applied as the ultimate refuge from outside criticism, which is viewed as an unwelcome cultural intrusion or inappropriate interference with Singapore's domestic affairs.

An increasing number of sacrificial lambs have suffered under the pretense of protecting the integrity of Singapore's political institutions. A number of recent prosecutions suggest that the judges' loyalty to the regime is stronger than their dedication to the rule of law. For example, in January 1995 I was tried *in absentia* and found that I had expressed contempt for Singapore's judicial system in a newspaper article that did not mention Singapore by name. Four other defendants were named and found guilty, including the editor and the publisher of the *International Herald Tribune* (IHT) where my article appeared ('The Smoke over Parts of Asia Obscures Some Profound Concerns,' 7 October 1994). The government also held the printer and distributor of the paper accountable for their role in facilitating the appearance of my offending words. All defendants were fined and ordered to pay court costs.

The passage that was said to have caused offense was a single sentence that suggested that some East Asian regimes relied upon subtle techniques to quell political dissent, including reliance 'upon a compliant judiciary to bankrupt opposition politicians.' Ironically, in stating the Government's case against me before the High Court of Singapore, eleven cases were cited where political opponents were sued by members of the regime. In most of these cases, the awards resulted in the personal bankruptcy of the defendants. Seven of these lawsuits were filed by Mr Lee Kuan Yew, Singapore's Senior Minister and former prime minister.

Singapore's Attorney General, Chan Sek Keong, said it was 'common knowledge to anyone familiar with Singapore that the government had a track record of suing opposition politicians.' In turn, he was unable to cite any other country where this had happened. Ironically, in attempting to offer evidence to convict me, the prosecutor proved that my claims were true. Nonetheless, my statements were deemed to have 'scandalized' Singapore's judiciary and so, along with the other defendants, I was found guilty of contempt of court.

In response to a subsequent civil lawsuit for libel filed by Mr Lee arising out of my article, the IHT reached an out-of-court settlement for 300,000 Singapore dollars (about $210,000) in December 1995. As I was not consulted or represented during those negotiations, Mr Lee Kuan Yew reserved the right to seek damages from me at a later date, a threat that was carried out at the end of March 1996. In papers filed before the courts in Singapore, Mr Lee asserted that my comments constituted a 'vicious' and 'malicious' attack on him that 'hurt' him deeply. He insisted that my 'lack of remorse' was an aggravating factor that justified making the award 'substantially larger' than the amount agreed to in the out-of-court settlement with the IHT. As evidence of my remorseless attacks on his integrity, Mr Lee cited the recent publication of my book, *Singapore's Authoritarian Capitalism*.

In early April 1996, High Court Judge S. Rajendran said that I had repeated the libel in another article and had refused to apologize, showing that I 'was motivated by malice and was intent on injuring (Mr Lee) as widely and gravely as possible.' Further, I 'was jointly liable with the other defendants for the 300,000 Singapore dollars and solely liable to the plaintiff for the additional 100,000 Singapore dollars ($71,000).' Obviously, Judge Rajendran accepted Mr Lee's contention that I had libeled him by 'innuendo.'

These actions by Mr Lee and the PAP regime were intentional, well-orchestrated and successful at achieving their desired result: the intimidation of the international media. Smarting from previous reductions in the circulation numbers of their publications, many newspapers and magazines are increasingly timid about publishing criticisms of Singapore's regime. During less than nine months of 1994, the IHT faced two lawsuits for defamation filed by Mr Lee.

For its part, the IHT, published in Paris and co-owned in equal shares by the *Washington Post* and the *New York Times*, took a futile line of defense. Public apologies by the IHT, intended to mollify the plaintiffs, instead sealed their fate by admitting fault for publishing injurious remarks. After my article appeared and before our trial, the IHT published a 'clarification' that apologized unreservedly for their role in the affair. I was neither consulted nor advised of this deplorable decision. Their reward was Mr Lee's lawsuit, despite their good faith effort to meet his requirements.

In a separate court appearance in 1995, the IHT was ordered to pay nearly $650,000 to settle another lawsuit stemming from an article penned by Philip Bowring, wherein he referred explicitly to Singapore and its 'dynastic politics.'[12] The plaintiffs in the suit included Lee Kuan Yew and his eldest son, Lee Hsien Loong, along with the current prime minister, Goh Chok Tong.

By going after the pocketbooks of newspaper publishers and owners, Mr Lee is able to project a benign image as a law-abiding victim seeking civilized redress through the courts. In so doing, the righteously indignant Mr Lee avoids the negative press associated with a strong-arm tactics like banning publications or arresting editors. In addition, sympathetic coverage of these trials by the local media provides the world with another *infomercial* extolling the rectitude and efficiency of the Singapore justice system.

The regime in Singapore has created an impression of integrity for their legal system by adopting the words of Anglo-American justice, yet subverting its substance. This has been accomplished through a clever use of semantics that have provided a misleading perception of 'due process.' In the US and Great Britain, due process is imbued with the sense of a good faith search for the truth before independent judges. However, in my own trial this was reduced to a superficial procedure toward what most observers considered a predetermined outcome.

Stung by these costly attacks, the IHT subsequently left out a spate of biting critiques of Singapore's regime by syndicated writers whose columns routinely appear when they address other issues. Most notable in this regard were columns by William Safire, who has been embroiled in a war of words with various members of the ruling clique. Ironically, some of the most confrontational articles by Mr Safire have appeared in the principal English language newspaper in Singapore, the *Straits Times*. In contrast, the IHT refrained from publishing those essays of Mr Safire's that involve criticism of Singapore, even though his column appears regularly in those pages.

After my own experience, Singapore introduced another measure designed to restrict the free flow of information. Visiting journalists must now have special visas, unlike lawyers or businessmen who visit to hold business meetings or make business contacts. This double standard will make it easy to keep out those journalists whose reporting offends the regime.

The tactic of harassing individual members of the media, combined with costly lawsuits and circulation restrictions aimed at publishers, are having the desired chilling effect on political speech. Self-censorship is becoming much more common among the previously outspoken English language press in Asia. An increasing number of editors advise writers that articles concerning Singapore must be vetted by their lawyers. Needless to say, few opinion pieces critical of the repressive tactics of the regime are able to clear such formidable hurdles.[13]

Reining in the Internet

Many commentators envision the Internet as a powerful influence in liberalizing authoritarian regimes. The basis for this wishful thinking is the role that fax machines and satellite television were said to have played in providing linkage to the outside world for the students who occupied Tiananmen Square. Unfortunately, many countries in East Asia have exhibited the intent and the capacity to obstruct the free flow of ideas across the Internet and other forms of electronic media.

While many of their neighbors prepare to be buoyed up by the rising tide of the 'Information Age,' authoritarian regimes are tossing out an anchor that will eventually cause their ship to run aground. Although many of these countries are swiftly becoming empowered by their participation in the global economy, their leaders feel increasingly threatened by changes to the social contract demanded by a citizenry that is becoming increasingly cosmopolitan and restive.

Perhaps the most menacing outside influence that might 'contaminate' Asia is the concept of multiparty governance. In response, insecure autocrats have resorted to censoring the Internet to insure that political conversation remains a monologue by the rulers.

At the end of August 1996, China's authorities announced one of the most aggressive plans for restricting access to the Internet in Asia. China's system entails the installation of a filtering mechanism designed to sift through the various web sites in search of objectionable material. Access to those sites deemed offensive could then be blocked. The test for blocking access to a site is based upon whether its contents might lead to 'spiritual pollution.' Thus far, about 100 purveyors of information have been identified as injurious to the public spirit.

Because the notion of 'spiritual pollution' is vague and excessively broad, the Internet censors can find objectionable material just about anywhere. Some web sites are blocked because of sexually explicit content. However, others are shut out for their political views, such as the page for Tibetan exiles or for the Democratic Alliance in Hong Kong. Likewise, a large number of commercial news services that are available on the Internet are also affected. Among these are web sites for CNN, the *Economist*, the *South China Morning Post*, *Time*, the *Wall Street Journal*, and the *Washington Post*.

These censorial steps in China are facilitated by the fact that there are few providers of Internet services. Although another is scheduled to begin operation by the end of 1996, there is presently only one commercial server with about 20,000 customers. Another 200,000 users access the Internet through their connections on two academic networks. This number is a tiny fraction of the Chinese population, even after allowing that there are multiple users for almost every account.

In light of its reputation for tight control over the print and broadcast media, it is not surprising that Singapore leads the way in implementing restrictions on the electronic media. Given that Singapore is one of the most highly 'wired' communities in the world, its leaders seemingly face insurmountable obstacles in mediating Internet transmissions.[14] However, this single-party regime can be very effective in marshaling sophisticated electronic information technologies to achieve its political goals. Electronic media control will be accomplished by limiting users to a single provider controlled by Singapore Telecom, a government monopoly headed by the youngest son of Lee Kuan Yew, Lee Hsien Yang. This will facilitate comprehensive monitoring and allow the government to sever consumer access to specific news groups at its discretion. At the same time, software can search for key words and filter out targeted material.

In addition, new laws impose legal sanctions on users and servers for any information they provide or receive. Singapore has a number of 'Cybernet cafés' where customers buy access time for connection to computer terminals. Legal action was taken against one of these innovative cafés for the transmission of an allegedly libelous statement by one of its patrons. Subsequently, most others have reconfigured their systems so that clients can only browse the Internet and not post material on news groups.

Another innovative mechanism aimed at policing cyberspace are 'proxy servers.' These are part of a special computer system that has been installed to monitor sites that Singapore's government deem objectionable. Thus, virtually all of Singapore's 130,000 subscribers must pass through a gateway guarded by these proxy servers in order to access the Internet.

Forms of expression that would arouse the ire of the authorities include criticisms of the government, pornographic images, or discussions that might inflame racial or religious passions. However, the government's guidelines are so vague that it is difficult, if not impossible, to know what may constitute prohibited conduct.

Net aficionados may scoff that these measures can be skirted by an innovative and devious mind. However, the government holds several cards that give it the upper hand. First, most users are required to use SingNet, a commercial server that is controlled by Singapore Telecom, the government's telephone monopoly. This makes it easier, in principle, to monitor Internet traffic. Second, the regime clearly intends to prosecute violators to the full extent of the law to meet their ends. Therefore, aggressive legal action will be taken to railroad individuals whose remarks or actions offend or threaten the censormeisters.

Vietnam's government is taking steps that are similar to those taken by the autocrats in Singapore and China. Those Vietnamese hoping to have unrestricted access to the Net will have to wait. Although Vietnam has at least 5 different service providers, 4 of them come under direct government control and none offers access to the full array of Internet services. Interestingly, American firms, including Sun Microsystems, are actively marketing security software in Vietnam to stop the 'chaos' of unfettered information flows. Clearly, these steps are being taken by the Vietnamese communist leaders because they fear that foreign influences will jeopardize their grip upon single-party rule.

Although these controls are justified by authoritarian Asian regimes as a mechanism for protecting cultural values, they are actually tools designed to maintain power in the hands of the ruling parties.

Media freedoms in East Asia: An endangered species?

Singapore's successes in routing its media critics set a negative example for other regimes that hold individual rights in contempt. Under the guise of preserving national security or protecting public morals, leaders in other countries, including Pakistan and South Korea, are beginning to use the courts to silence their most nettlesome opponents. Following the examples of China and Singapore, Vietnam has warned domestic journalists not to report 'sensitive economic or defense issues.' In July 1996, the Interior Ministry sent police to investigate three newspapers because of business stories involving alleged violations of national security laws. No longer fearful of outside pressures or trade sanctions, Indonesian authorities will be able to continue their ruthless crackdown in East Timor. Beijing can continue to rely upon forced labor to gain a truly unfair competitive advantage in trade while intimidating democrats in Hong Kong and threatening Taiwan. Forces of conservative nationalism in Japan are shaping public opinion against further acts of contrition for their actions in World War II.

And why should they act otherwise? Authoritarian regimes no longer have to contend with substantive diplomatic pressures owing to the Clinton administration's decision to renew China's MFN status despite a dismal human rights record. Even a small country as Singapore feels empowered to harass American citizens, flout the UN Convention Against Torture, and aggressively attack the international media. Whatever the arguments used by apologists for the American policy of 'commercial diplomacy,' the resulting moral vacuum in international affairs emboldens despots.

In capitulating to the demands of authoritarian governments and restraining its coverage of controversial issues in Asia, the media is choosing to renounce its role as a forum for and guarantor of free expression. Amidst censorship, self-imposed and otherwise, legitimate voices of political opposition are denied a necessary outlet for their views. Worse yet, with the press muzzled, dissenters are increasingly subjected to the oppression that they would denounce in a truly free press, while the rest of the world is kept unawares.

Obsessive control over the media is consistent with the core values of filial piety and unquestioning obedience to authority that Asian autocrats seek to impose on their citizenry. While the image of authority figures as the ultimate source of knowledge was jettisoned in the West during the Renaissance, this notion is alive and well in Asia. Supporters of the 'Asian Model' insist that citizens exhibit unqualified loyalty and subservience to government officials. To promote this end, a subdued press provides some assurance that response to dissent shall be on the terms of the regime. Thus, reinforcement of traditions of respect for authority as a key 'Asian value' provides a convenient credo to legitimate one-party rule, dynastic and otherwise.

Media control comes in various forms. For example, Rupert Murdoch's agreement to exclude the BBC from Star TV transmissions is a kow-towing gesture to China's regime that has been praised as sound business judgment. Much of the rest of Hong Kong's media, known previously for fierce independence, is beginning to toe the line to ward off the wrath of the impending new rulers. In addition to the restrictions mentioned previously, Singapore encourages self-censorship through legislation making retailers liable for selling publications that are eventually found to contain libelous material. Likewise, publishers can be held equally accountable for broadcasting the censurable statements of those whose views they air. The international media is cowed from discussing Singapore's domestic politics by threats from the regime. Uncooperative publications may be 'gazetted' (a costly procedure of placing a numbered, government-provided stamp on each copy) or strict restrictions may be placed on the copies available for sale in Singapore.

Apologists for the restraints on freedom of the press offer arguments that fall into two categories. First, the decline of the West, as epitomized by exaggerated images of crime-ridden and impoverished inner cities inhabited by crack-addicted and unwed mothers, is somehow traced to the protection of individual civil liberties. However, Asian authoritarian regimes merely assert, but fail to substantiate, the alleged causal link between Western moral decline and individual freedoms. In all events, it is spurious to equate the excessive behavior of some individuals with the failure of individualism and self determination. The second set of arguments asserts that press freedom is either irrelevant or intolerably irreverent because Asians are purported to defer traditionally to authority. In sum, both arguments conclude that open debate and the promotion of individual freedom generate only costs, and convey no benefits to society.

History shows that kid glove treatment by media moguls reinforced the respectability of Mussolini and Hitler. Doubtless such appeasement aided them in their quest for an authoritarian grip on power that led to the devastation of Europe. Likewise, in the case of the 'Asian Model,' Asian autocrats do not deserve unqualified praise for overseeing improvements in the material position of their citizenry or for making the trains run on time. Intellectual freedom and dignified dissent by the individual are also laudable goals to be promoted. Interestingly, India's former Prime Minister Rao, certainly a prominent Asian leader, declared that continued prosperity demanded more democracy, not less. This view is also echoed by President Fidel Ramos of the Philippines, President Lee Teng-hui of Taiwan, Mr Martin Lee and members of his Democratic Alliance in Hong Kong, and Kim Dae Jung of South Korea, just to name a few. Similarly, Deputy Prime Minister of Malaysia, Anwar Ibrahim, accepts the political patronage of Dr Mahathir Mohamad, but he rejects the latter's strident expressions of Asian nationalism. Unlike their authoritarian counterparts, Asian pro-democracy forces can substantiate their stance by citing West's long track record of generally sustained economic growth, productivity increases, and innovation.

Ultimately, the viability and success of a sociopolitical order cannot be achieved merely by political fiat. Instead, success of the 'Asian Model' will best be measured in terms of its longevity and emulation by other communities. It will be interesting to see if the 'Asian Model will stand up to the challenges of the 'Information Age,' and the natural yearning of people to free themselves of economic and political fetters.

Conclusion

It appears that much of the strident rhetoric associated with the promoters of 'Asian values' is driven by a lingering resentment toward European colonialism and American military dominance. Identification of social and cultural values have become an effective weapon in the arsenal of leaders with a loaded political agenda.

The ideals typically associated with modern Western society are often identified as so-called 'middle class values.' These include the promotion of diversity and freedom of individual choice. Such values are expected to promote merit-based compensation while maintaining an effective check on the reach of government. In addition, and a reasonable distribution of income and wealth is expected to ensue.

In seeking to provide the greatest amount of satisfaction to the greatest number of people, Western middle-class values are quite compatible with the goals expressed by newly industrializing Asian countries. Indeed, the search by independent individuals for a comfortable environment through cooperative behavior is perhaps the most universal of all values.

As economies develop, social and political institutions tend to lag behind and cause internal friction. The intensity of these conflicts is softened by modernizing forces whereby revolutions are replaced by less radical movements.

International economic policy and foreign relations should be predicated on the notion that differences in the interpretations of cultural values are transitory. Greater focus should be put upon the mutual economic development of all countries. Asian economic development will remain quite fragile until growth becomes less dependent upon foreign demand.

Notes

1   The so-called 'Singapore School' has been particularly aggressive in promoting 'Asian values' as a mobilizing myth of its own nation-building process. For example, see K. Mahbubani, 'The Dangers of Decadence – What the Rest Can Teach the West', *Foreign Affairs* (1992, Vol. 72, No. 4,); 'The West and the Rest', *The National Interest* (Summer 1992); 'The United States: Go East, Young Man', *Washington Quarterly* (17, No. 2, Spring 1994) and 'Live and Let Live – Allow Asians to Choose Their Own Course', *Far Eastern Economic Review* (17 June 1994). Also, see B. Kausikan, 'Asia's Different Standard', *Foreign Policy* (No. 92, Fall 1993), and F. Zakaria, 'Culture is Destiny: A Conversation with Lee Kuan Yew', *Foreign Affairs* (1994, Vol. 73, No. 2). See also E. Jones, 'Asia's Fate: A Response to the Singapore School', *The National Interest* (Spring 1994), pp. 18-28.

2   A particularly adversarial tone is evident in the work by two ardent Asian nationalists, Dr Mahathir Mohamad and Ishihara Shintaro (*The Voice of Asia: Two Leaders Discuss the Coming Century*, New York: Kondansha International, 1995). In its original Japanese version, its title was rendered as *The Asia that Can Say No*.

3   Satellite dish licenses in Singapore are restricted to financial institutions whose applications are supported by the Monetary Authority of Singapore or commercial institutions supported by the Economic Development Board or media organizations with the support of the Ministry of Information and the Arts. Other eligible licensees are foreign embassies and government ministries and statutory boards.

4   There is considerable ambivalence and some hostility among Asians about the supposition that there are distinct Asian values. See D. I. Hitchcock, *Asian Values and the United States: How Much Conflict?*, Washington, DC: Center for Strategic and International Studies, 1994. Also, see Kim Dae Jung, 'Is Culture Destiny?', *Foreign Affairs* (1994, Vol. 74, No. 4) pp. 189-94 and E. Jones, 'Asia's Fate', op. cit.

5   Hitchcock's report was based upon interviews with 100 Asian academics, think tank experts, officials, businessmen, journalists, as well as religious and cultural leaders. N. Vittachi conducted a survey of readers of the *Far Eastern Economic Review* (7 September 1996). Most of the respondents fit into the same categories as those listed by Hitchcock.

6   In August 1996, Chun Doo Hwan was sentenced to death, while Roh Tae Woo was sentenced to 22 ½ years in prison. Both men were former presidents and army generals. Along with them, dozen senior officials in their governments and nine leaders of major Korean conglomerates were also convicted.

7   C. Lingle, *Singapore's Authoritarian Capitalism: Asian Values, Free Market Illusions, and Political Dependency*, Fairfax, VA: The Locke Institute, 1996.

8   D. Jones and D. Brown, 'Singapore and the Myth of the Liberalizing Middle Class', *The Pacific Review*, Vol. 7, No. 1, 1994, pp. 79-87; and D. A. Bell, D. Brown, Kanishka Jayasuriya, and D. M. Jones, *Toward Illiberal Democracy in Pacific Asia*, London: St. Martin's Press, 1995.

9   E. T. Gomez, *Political Business: Corporate Involvement of Malaysian Political Parties*, Townsville, Aus.: James Cook University, 1994.

10   Attraction to this approach might not be limited to East Asians. For example, the frustration in Europe over current economic problems might enhance the appeal of authoritarian capitalism and boost the political fortunes of neo-fascist and ultra-nationalist political parties there.

11   R. Beason and D. Weinstein, 'Growth, Economies of Scale, and Targeting in Japan (1955-90)', Harvard Institute of Economic Research, Discussion Paper 1644, 1993.

12   The offending article raised the issue of dynastic politics in Asia and 'the battle between the corporatist needs of the state and the interests of the families who operate it.'

13   In my own case, the acceptance rate for my articles submitted to newspapers in the region fell dramatically. Another instance of self-censorship is that articles about my book on Singapore or me were killed by editors of two magazines that have substantial presence in East Asia. In both instances, the reporters assured me from the outset that they had clearance from their editors for the respective stories. In the end, the editors decided that there were too many risks in reporting the truth.

14   An action plan to 'wire' Singapore appeared in 1992. *IT2000 – A Vision of an Intelligent Island* is a compulsory pan to connect all 750,000 households to a centralized computer network. This system will electronically inter-link households with government organizations, businesses, schools, and libraries.

7 Geo-politics and the 'Asian Century': Political hazards and strategic uncertainty

Just as in other regions of the world, East Asia is susceptible to a variety of domestic, regional, and global upsets that could lead to military action. For example, many East Asian regimes face challenges to the existing social contract, or uncertainty over the succession of long-serving rulers. Despite official reassurances to the contrary, there continue to be concerns about who will lead China, Indonesia, Malaysia, Singapore, and Vietnam into the twenty-first century.

An important factor inhibiting the cohesion of the Asian-Pacific community is the continued enmity among some of the largest players in the region (e.g., China and Russia; China and Japan; North and South Korea), exacerbated by irredentist claims in the South China Sea (e.g., Natuna, Paracel and, Spratly Islands) or territorial disputes associated with separatist or independence movements (e.g., East Timor, Mindanao, Taiwan, and Tibet). In addition, there are global concerns (e.g., trade disputes) arising from international grievances in the post-Cold War period. Finally, there is the risk of nuclear crises that could emerge between China and America, North Korea and Japan, China and India, and India and Pakistan. Besides regional conflicts, there is the danger that nuclear weapons may be used by terrorists or by separatist forces.

Pacific Asia is not immune to ethno-religious aggression, or nationalist aspirations that might lead to the break-up of various nation states. Violent incidents in trouble spots like East Timor, Mindanao, Kashmir, Tibet, and Xianjiang are trouble spots that have reverberations throughout the region.

Infrastructure investment represents public expenditures necessary for the development of a modern economy that can operate in the globalized market. Military spending ought to be considered an important element of this infrastructure budget. East Asian economies can be expected to protect their increased economic prominence on the world stage by expanding their capacity to control their own destiny. This will be accomplished through military and strategic alliances, as well as through the development of their own defense capability.

The easing of bipolar anxieties related to the end of the Cold War has increased the need for East Asia to provide its own self-defense. On the one hand, there has been a continual, if gradual, disengagement of the US from the area. With the withdrawal from Philippine military bases, there are increasing pressures at home and in the host countries to reduce commitments of American armed forces to both Japan and South Korea.

On the other hand, sophisticated weaponry has become available at bargain basement prices through the highly competitive global arms bazaar. In 1995, Southeast Asia overtook the Middle East, after the US and Europe, as the third largest weapons market by purchasing over $9 billion, or 22 percent, of world arms sales. From 1990 to 1994, every major East Asian country except Vietnam and North Korea increased their annual spending on defense by more that 25 percent.[1] An increased proportion of these purchases has involved high-tech components with long range aerial and naval capabilities. Taiwan alone has committed $40 billion to weapons procurement, and Indonesia purchased the entire fleet of the former German Democratic Republic. Most countries are investing in procuring or expanding submarine fleets.

With many of the East Asian countries well-advanced in their capability to produce sophisticated electronics components, they will inevitably attempt to leapfrog into high-tech weapons production. Certainly, Japan, Singapore, South Korea, and Taiwan possess the necessary scientific and technological infrastructure to produce advanced armaments and to engage in electronic warfare.

There is some dispute over whether these purchases diverge enough from normal spending to constitute an arms race. Many of the acquisitions are merely replacement of outdated equipment with more modern weaponry. Nonetheless, nearly every country in East Asia has increased its defense spending by about a third over the previous decade, while several in Northeast Asia have done so in the past five years.

Smoldering rivalries and territorial squabbles (including unresolved border disputes) have been revived by the anticipated removal of the American security umbrella.[2] At the same time, rapid economic growth has provided an increasing number of countries with the means to be regional actors in the security game. With higher income and more advanced industrial development, countries in the region are able to acquire or to produce more sophisticated armaments. On balance, the exit of the world's sole remaining superpower, combined with a regional arms buildup, can be expected to increase the probability of strategic instability in East Asia. It appears that East Asia may soon eclipse the Middle East as the most rancorous regional security challenge.

An obvious hurdle for Asians is the cost of providing their own collective or individual security umbrella to replace that offered by America. Even if East Asian countries can afford to internally fund their own defense, it is difficult to imagine that China or the ASEAN countries could provide the necessary moral leadership, given their refusal to be involved with their neighbors' internal affairs, and especially since enmity runs so deep among the largest players in the region. At the present time, peace in their own neighborhood depends more on the presence of the American Seventh Fleet than on any internally generated sense of accord.

Bright spots of cooperation in an unsettled region?

All signs do not necessarily point to heightened conflict in East Asia. Most of the major players participate in either regional or global associations. The notable progress arising out of summit meetings held by the Asian-Pacific Economic Cooperation forum (APEC) and the Association of Southeast Asian Nations (ASEAN) provides evidence that a credible search for cooperative agreements is under way. More narrowly defined groupings such as the East Asian Economic Caucus (EAEC) and the ASEAN Regional Forum (ARF), a security deliberation body, are also cited as evidence of growing regional cooperation. Similarly, participation in and applications to the World Trade Association (WTO) indicate a commitment to global cooperation.

However, the scope of these organizations is quite limited and attempts to influence other members on non-economic matters are generally frowned upon by the participants. Consequently, most observers believe that, by comparison to North America or Europe, East Asia is 'underinstitutionalized' in having too few formalized mechanisms to defuse political or military tensions. In bilateral talks, Australia and Indonesia were able to reach an agreement that promised mutual access to disputed seas that lie between them. This formula for sharing of the seabed minerals and fishing grounds might serve as a model for other countries in the region.

'Asian values' and ASEAN dilemmas

It is often remarked that the strength of the Association of Southeast Asian Nations is in its 'summitry.' ASEAN summit meetings are harmonious affairs that abound with press releases that predictably proclaim unanimous agreement. However, outwardly calm interpersonal dealings in Asia that project a superficial sense of harmony often mask deep divisions.

The steadfast refusal to comment on the internal affairs of their partners is a defining characteristic of ASEAN relations. Internal problems in many East Asian countries are concealed by an elaborate set of controls implemented by authoritarian regimes. Thus, it is more than a deferential nod to Asian tradition that ASEAN members so seldom criticize their neighbors. Most leaders dare not point accusing fingers at their peers for fear of having their own domestic problems placed under more intense scrutiny. The 'glass houses' constructed by authoritarian rulers obviously cannot withstand internecine stone-throwing. It is not surprising that most ASEAN governments consider allowing other regimes to save face as more important than protecting the interests of individual citizens.

The brittle nature of authoritarian regimes in the region engenders a hypersensitivity that makes it difficult for citizens or outsiders to offer even the mildest criticism. In this situation, posturing over 'Asian values' is a device for justifying opportunistic political arrangements as though they represent *bona fide* moral values based upon Asian traditions. The handling of two high profile criminal cases in Singapore illustrates both the fundamental fallacy of 'Asian values,' as well as the deft manipulation of this concept for political expediency.

The swift and certain administration of justice is often touted by the Singapore government as a core Asian value. An oft-cited corollary is that the welfare of the community outweighs any one citizen's individual rights. Thus, in order to establish and maintain a reputation for being a law and order state that it tough on crime, prosecutions must have a high success ratio, and punishment must be severe and well-publicized. In addition, it is critical that the public view convicted defendants as guilty interlopers who threaten the social fabric, and not as victims of the judicial system.

The prosecutions of American student Michael Fay and Philippine housemaid Flor Contemplacion reflect the recipe described above. Neither individual could reasonably be expected to arouse much sympathy on the part of the general public. In both cases, the defendants were foreigners and their alleged crimes were sure to resonate with the public. Vandalism on Mr Fay's part was portrayed as a breach of the peace by a Western barbarian, while Ms Contemplacion's alleged murder of her male Singaporean employer threatened the country's sense of public safety.

In both cases, the defendants were convicted as charged, with guilt predicated largely on confessions obtained after a significant period of confinement.[3] In contrast, it is important to note that confessions are considered to be inherently suspect in American jurisprudence, and so cannot be used to convict a defendant unless accompanied by compelling corroborative evidence. By allowing prosecutors to secure convictions without having to do any homework on their own, the Singapore system relieves the state of the burden of proof routinely carried by their American counterparts. With this advantage, prosecutors are sure to have a high ratio of convictions that can be used to illustrate the superior 'effectiveness' of Singapore justice.

Punishment in both cases was severe, well-publicized, and carried out expeditiously. Mr Fay was denied an exemption under Singapore's 'first-time offender rule' and flogged, while Ms Contemplacion was hanged. These harsh sentences were carried out despite presidential pleas for clemency in both cases. Furthermore, the Singapore authorities were unwilling to consider subsequent evidence that might have exonerated Ms Contemplacion, as well as suggestions that Mr Fay's confession had been coerced.

Sensational media coverage in America, combined with the unsympathetic nature of the defendant, made the Michael Fay case a propaganda victory for Lee Kuan Yew. Singapore was indeed viewed by many Americans as a no-nonsense, law and order state, thanks to a strong central government able to implement the Asian value of swift, firm justice. Thus, rigid authoritarian control was ostensibly justified as a necessary condition for the preservation of Asian values, specifically against decadent Western influences like democracy and individual rights.

However, Singapore's ploy backfired with fellow Asians in the Philippines. The execution of Flor Contemplacion generated widespread outrage and severely strained diplomatic ties between Singapore and the Philippines. Ironically, however, it was the Filipinos, and not American citizens, who challenged the substance of Singapore's oft-repeated claim that 'due process' is observed in all their legal proceedings.

Similarly, with the aim of creating a misleading image of tranquillity, one East Asian pundit has asserted that 'more lives are lost daily on the periphery of Europe than in the entire Asia-Pacific region.' The truthfulness of this statement cannot be verified, however, because independent corroboration for what happens in much of Asia is simply not possible due to onerous restrictions upon all forms of media. Consequently, many of Asia's citizens receive diluted and distorted information, or remain completely uninformed save for access to self-serving government communications. Control of information by authoritarian rulers allows them to release news on their own terms, trumpeting their successes while concealing their failings. For example, the misleading comparison of lives lost in conflicts mentioned above is deeply flawed. Whereas the world's media provide vivid coverage of Chechnya and Sarajevo, questions about the number of civilian lives lost in political struggles in Burma-Myanmar, East Timor, or Tibet remain unresolved. Likewise, despite the presence of numerous foreign journalists and other eye witnesses, the number of casualties in Tiananmen Square remains open to controversy thanks to tight media control by the Chinese government.

Unfortunately, the indifference of many East Asian regimes to such outrages and crises reinforces the perception that governments in the region place a low value upon human life. This observation must be tempered by an understanding of governments ruled by technocrats who impose patriarchal, collectivist ideals wherein the interests of the wider community always trump those of the individual.

Until recently, many ASEAN regimes relied upon the specter of a communist menace to justify repressive means for maintaining power. With communism consigned to the dustbin of history, some Asian regimes now justify their rigid authoritarian control by portraying 'decadent' Western influences like democracy and individual rights as a threat to their communities. Surely, the only parties threatened by the expansion of democratic institutions to authoritarian Asian governments are one-party or single-family regimes.

Hypocrisy as an Asian value?

Singapore's elder statesman, Lee Kuan Yew, has commented to the effect that pro-democracy leader Aung San Suu Kyi of Burma-Myanmar may be unsuited to govern. He suggested that Ms Suu Kyi should content herself with serving as a behind-the-scenes symbol of national unity and leave the tough choices of governing to the military junta that currently rules Burma-Myanmar. This same military dictatorship refused to honor the 1990 general election results, despite the fact that opposition groups led by Ms Suu Kyi won 82 percent of the vote.

Mr Lee is purportedly an ardent supporter of ASEAN's policies of 'noninterference' and 'constructive engagement' with respect to dealings with Burma-Myanmar. He has often insisted that outsiders should not comment on any other country's domestic policies. Consistent with this position, he demands that critics steer clear of Singapore. Likewise, he has admonished those who criticize human rights abuses in China, or who challenge its claim of sovereignty over Tibet and Taiwan. Therefore, it is strange that Mr Lee saw no inconsistency in his suggestions that Aung San Suu Kyi, the democratically elected leader of the majority party of Burma-Myanmar, should give up her quest to fulfill her mandate. Mr Lee's apparent hypocrisy may stem from his intimacy with former Burmese dictator Ne Win and with many members of the military junta that illegally rules Burma-Myanmar. He may also be seeking to protect the extensive investments undertaken by Singaporean firms there.[4]

In asserting that the only effective instrument of government in Burma-Myanmar is the military, Mr Lee insisted that the absence of strong-armed, centralized control could cause Burma-Myanmar to disintegrate 'like Bosnia.' Extending his grim analogy, he challenged those outsiders who would support ousting the military regime to stand prepared to assume responsibility for running Burma-Myanmar and keep it intact.

Clearly, Mr Lee's statements violate his own guidelines against outsiders' interference with the domestic politics of others. His remarks also ignore the overwhelming popular support for Ms Suu Kyi, as clearly expressed in the

131

1990 election, and evident now in the increasingly large regular gatherings in front of her residence despite aggressive government interference. By intimating that Ms Suu Kyi was unfit to govern, Mr Lee insulted those Burmese citizens who voted for her, as well as those who have risked their lives and freedoms to support democracy.

As a result, dissident Burmese student groups condemned Mr Lee for 'an insult to the Burmese people' and demanded a public apology from him. The students emphasized that Lee's comments were a 'preposterous contradiction,' for while he openly voices his negative opinion on Ms Suu Kyi, the Singapore government refrains from critical comment on human rights in Burma-Myanmar. Indeed, it is the height of hypocrisy when Burma's ASEAN neighbors sell offensive weapons to Burma's ruling party (known as the State Law and Order Restoration Council or Slorc) so that it can remain in power and these sales are not viewed as 'interference.'[5] Singapore, in particular, has apparently been providing arms and training to the Burmese junta since it came to power in 1988.

These arms sales and other commercial dealings with Burma-Myanmar are justified under the ASEAN policy of 'constructive engagement' which argues that increased economic contact is the best road to democracy. The collective view of current ASEAN members is that interference in the internal affairs of other countries will impede economic progress and political stability. Implicit in this approach is a thinly veiled mistrust for citizens choosing their own destiny. In any event, many governments in the region and their cronies are directly involved in business ventures in Burma-Myanmar. The net effect in these cases is that private interests of foreign rulers help to reinforce Burma's repressive political status quo. Thus, it appears that hypocrisy fits well alongside nepotism, corruption, and the other less savory values exhibited by East Asia's authoritarian rulers.

Besides the obvious hypocrisy about not dabbling in the domestic politics of other countries, ASEAN's constructive engagement policy toward Burma-Myanmar may be based upon the erroneous notion that there is a tradeoff between high-paced economic growth and political freedom. Such a view presumes that democracies are at a distinct economic disadvantage relative to authoritarian, even totalitarian regimes. Thus, while economic freedom may be required for the emergence of political freedoms, the reverse may not be true. Indeed, political freedom is portrayed as an obstruction in the early stages of economic progress. The problem with this assertion is twofold. First, it runs counter to the experience of the US as the world's only economic superpower. Second, when authoritarian regimes generate rapid economic progress, it comes at a high social cost and is ultimately unsustainable, as in the former USSR. Dissent, where allowed, tends to be muted and political debate subject to the whims of the ruling regime.

Fortunately, the negative attitude toward democracy that Mr Lee shares with Burma's current military leaders is rejected by the citizens and rulers of Japan, the Philippines, South Korea, Taiwan, and Thailand. In their capitals, harsh limits upon political dissent are *not* seen as a necessary evil underpinning economic advance. On the contrary, the advancement of these high-growth Asian economies is a testament to the symbiosis of political and economic freedom.

Meanwhile, analysts and Burmese exiles point out that while Asian leaders may be averse to directly influencing Burma's junta for cultural reasons, they are also reluctant to assist the US in applying coordinated economic pressure on Burma's military rulers to ease their crackdown on anti-government activists. For example, despite regular entreaties to Burma's rulers to soften their stance against dissidents, Japan has not used its aid of about $140 million a year as a lever to influence the junta. Thus, American attempts to seek regional support for an end to the campaign against democracy leader Aung San Suu Kyi are hampered partly by Washington's perceived lack of leverage in the region. More crucial is ASEAN's double-edged policy of diplomatic non-interference coupled with tacit economic support for the repressive political establishment.

Encouraged by the lack of moral condemnation from the world community, Burma's hard line rulers have not hesitated to enact tough new legislation to suppress their political opponents. In effect, Ms Suu Kyi and her party are banned from saying or doing anything contrary to the government's planned new constitution, even though the content of this document has not yet been determined. Over 230 members of the opposition National League for Democracy were detained by Burmese military police while attempting to attend a meeting convened by Ms Suu Kyi to commemorate the sixth anniversary of the annulment of their election as the majority party in the parliament. In spite of this reprehensible behavior, it became clear at an ASEAN ministerial meeting in July 1996 that Burma-Myanmar would join the regional trade group by the year 2000. In the meantime, it has been allowed membership in the ASEAN Regional Forum (ARF), which is a regional security deliberation body.

A similar situation has developed in Indonesia, with the ruling Golkar party actively seeking to thwart the political ambitions of Megawati Sukarnoputri. Attempts by the Golkar party to oust her from the leadership of one of the three legal political parties reveal the insecurity of the current regime. Like Suu Kyi, Megawati's father was an anti-colonial freedom fighter, but he was deposed by the current regime in 1967. Beginning in 1996, civil disturbances in support of Megawati have rocked the fragile facade of calm in Indonesia's capital, Jakarta. Unfortunately, because many other ASEAN member countries are also ruled by autocratic regimes, these events will only tighten their collective resolve to keep quiet about their neighbors' problems.

Because of its perceived effectiveness in inhibiting the spread of communism, authoritarianism was accepted as the dominant political arrangement in most of East Asia after World War II. In the post-Cold War world, however, freedom of thought will be an increasingly essential prerequisite for the entrepreneurial activity that is the basis of economic advance. In the new global economy, oppressive actions taken by the regimes in Burma-Myanmar and Indonesia are as outmoded and self-defeating as is economic protectionism.

Illusions of a peaceful pacific

In theory, increased economic interdependence should lead to greater trust and diminished hostility among East Asia's historical rivals. In practice, unfortunately, a shared economic destiny is unlikely to be enough to insure tranquillity in the region.

Wishful thinking, political opportunism, and superficial cooperation agreements generated by highly publicized summit meetings combine to create a false sense of optimism about continued peace and stability. Certain Asian analysts claim that the commitment to economic growth provides a sufficient impetus for peace to be maintained.[6] Indeed, economic and political self-interest motivates various groups to downplay sources of regional geopolitical instability. This being the case, diplomats, politicians, and bureaucrats tend to avoid discussing the tough issues in public. Similarly, corporations with investment interests in East Asia can be expected to maintain an upbeat outlook in order to set their shareholders at ease. Meanwhile, lobbyists for governments in the region will burnish their public relations images and offer reassurances that all is well.

Unfortunately, presumably independent academic researchers may face clear incentives to follow the party line. Many of those working outside of Asia will be funded by grants from Asian governments. Similarly, those working in Asian universities are vulnerable to pressure not to 'rock the boat' by stirring up controversy. In both instances, these scholars can retain a sense of integrity only by limiting their inquiry to less controversial subjects. In sum, the message here is that many of those who comment on the state of geopolitics in East Asia may have serious conflicts of interest that are not readily apparent. Their comments may therefore convey a false impression of objectivity, and may actually be more effective than the outright propaganda of their foreign patrons.

China as a loose cannon

China's impressive economic performance has been a mixed blessing for its neighbors. On the one hand, China's growth has served as a locomotive underpinning the economic vitality of East Asia, both by providing a source of inputs and by serving as a market for outputs. On the other hand, China's newfound strength, when combined with potential domestic political instability, poses a military threat to its neighbors. With the central government weakened by dramatic social change and uneven economic development, there is the constant fear that a vacuum of power might lead to chaos that would have a disastrous effect on the security of other countries in the region.

Along with the modernization of its economy, China has dramatically upgraded its military capabilities. Overall, China's defense expenditures increased by over 60 percent from 1989 to the mid-1990s. It is often pointed out that the real increase is only about three percent when adjusted for price level changes. However, it is widely know that China's published figures often substantially understate its defense spending. A noteworthy example of the modernization of China's military is the extension of its navy's reach beyond the defense of near-offshore and coastal boundaries.[7] This increase in China's offensive capabilities through the development of a 'blue-sea,' deep water navy has been coordinated with closer ties to the rogue regime in Burma-Myanmar. This unholy alliance ominously provides China with access to more remote deep water ports.

The modernization process of China's military is marked by a distinctive feature: the commercialization of the People's Liberation Army (PLA). From a fiscal policy point of view, it might seem beneficial that the PLA has developed its own non-governmental sources of funds through the ownership and operation of over 10,000 different business enterprises. These commercial ventures range from tourist hotels and restaurants to factories producing a variety of consumer goods. However, serious questions ought to be raised when a financially independent military no longer has to answer to civilian authorities.

The changing character of China's military has had a negative impact on internal and external security. For example, reports suggest that the increased frequency of piracy along China's coastal waterways is attributable to members of the PLA and their own naval vessels. One especially dramatic incident involved the seizure by American federal agents of over 2,000 assault rifles that had been imported by companies affiliated with the PLA. Barring active complicity by the Chinese government, it appears that military commanders are too preoccupied with making money to exercise responsible oversight of the armed forces under their command. Similarly, the involvement of the PLA in a business venture may make it difficult for judges and other officers of the law to bring their activities under proper scrutiny due to intimidation or lack of jurisdiction, or interference by the ruling party.

China's expanded military capability is one of the causal factors behind what may be shaping up to be a destabilizing regional arms race. In addition, China's irredentist tendency, as evidenced by its numerous and contentious territorial claims, puts it on an accelerated collision course with its East Asian neighbors. For example, China lays claim to about 80 percent of the entire area covered by the South China Sea. This disputed area includes islands such as the Natuna islands group, the Spratlys, and the Paracels, which lie along a broad plateau that stretches outward from China's eastern coastline for as much as a thousand miles. In addition, China has laid claim to a 200 nautical-mile economic exclusion zone around the Paracel Islands. This assertion of sovereignty is based upon Beijing's loose interpretation of the Law of the Sea Convention that China signed in June 1996. China's claims are likely to be rejected by most signatory parties because the provisions upon which China relies were intended to apply to archipelagic states, such as Indonesia or the Philippines.

There are also conflicting claims to islands situated among oil and gas reserves under the East China Sea that stretch from Shanghai to Okinawa. One particularly contentious dispute has been over a largely uninhabited archipelago known as the Diaoyu Islands by the Chinese and the Senkaku Islands by the Japanese. Despite contradictory historical claims to sovereignty, these islands along with Okinawa were handed over to Japan by the American government after World War II. In 1996, protests erupted in China, Hong Kong, and Taiwan when a rightist student group with ties to the *yakuza* (Japanese organized crime syndicates) constructed a lighthouse on two of the islands.

All these claims potentially compromise the integrity and security of vital international sea lanes that are the conduit for an increasing proportion of the world's commerce. A related concern is the continued security of international commercial flows through the Taiwan Strait, once Hong comes under the jurisdiction of the Beijing authorities.

A basic sense of national insecurity underlies China's intractable obsession with repatriating all land claimed by them. In addition, many of these territorial disputes stem from a desire to exploit the natural resources of these areas, such as petroleum and other minerals, or to protect fishing grounds. These resources are seen as vital inputs for feeding China's expanding population and for sustaining the engines of economic growth. Indeed, the continuing struggle to control offshore oil supplies in East Asia may be the most significant source of regional instability.

Just as transparency in financial markets serves to build mutual trust, China needs to recognize the need for military transparency. As a gesture of confidence building, the authorities in Beijing ought to make clear statements of policy and purpose for its military, along with assurances of its accountability to political authorities. By taking such steps, it might offer some reassurance to nervous neighbors that military force will not be used to seize disputed territory.

Apparently, there are two categories of non-Western countries that have become rich. One group consists of oil-rich monarchies whose stability depends upon an ability to buy favor from their citizens and, if necessary, the use of force to curb political opposition.[8] Others, like Japan, faced the long and arduous task of modernizing their legal, political, and economic institutions. Beijing's attempt to gain control over an enlarged segment of the East and South China Seas may buy some time. However, in the long run this tactic will divert Beijing's attention away from the unavoidable need to accept the admittedly disruptive changes that come with modernization.

Fervent nationalism coupled with an aggressive military approach may have once defined power politics for countries seeking to be global players. But that was yesterday. On all the above counts, China's best hopes for the future are to remain fully engaged in peaceful discourse and mutually-beneficial trade arrangements.

Nationalism hates a vacuum: China's risky return to xenophobia

It would be bad enough if China's Communist Party leadership faced only a moribund state ideology while trying to cope with wrenching economic and social change. Added to their woes is the increasing uncertainty about the passing of 'paramount leader,' Deng Xiaoping. The repeated insistence that a seamless succession to power has been put in place has done nothing to reassure outside observers.

Faced with these unsettling circumstances, the Chinese leadership has dusted off the nationalist card. Apparently, nationalism hates an ideological vacuum. It is perplexing that the sort of venom offered by nationalists gets such a sympathetic hearing from the general populace. Their basic objection is that 'barbarians' or outsiders of lesser worth are to blame for some regrettable state of affairs that has befallen their nation. This is the sort of demonizing that Hitler did so effectively, that Milosevic and Tudjman initiated in the Balkans, and that Chinese nationalists are now offering. Nationalism is a dangerous game that has too often led to disastrous consequences.

The possibility that nationalism will supplant making money as the national focus may seem unlikely to many observers, especially after Deng Xiaoping announced that 'to be rich is glorious!' However, a distinct and dangerous momentum suggests otherwise. Heaving missiles at Taiwan is one poignant demonstration of militant Chinese nationalism.

A book entitled, 'China Can Say No!' became a bestseller in China during 1996. Interestingly, its authors are nominally pro-democracy activists. Though weak on thoughtful political analysis and uninformed about foreign policy, this book contributes to the surge of Chinese nationalism by offering a litany of anti-American slogans. Its authors reduce international relations to an adversarial game wherein the sole end of other countries is to thwart the legitimate ambitions of the Chinese people and to frustrate their long march to prosperity.

Some elements of increasing national consciousness in China are understandable, even laudable. Recent modernization of the armed forces and impressively high rates of economic growth are coincidental with the removal of the last remaining foreign power on Chinese soil. It is natural that these factors inspire a resurgence in national pride and patriotism. Chinese everywhere have good cause to identify positively with their rich culture and noble history. However, they should be alert lest their virtuous patriotic impulses become subverted into xenophobic jingoism.

While patriotism can be a positive force, other manifestations of nationalism have an ugly side. Divisive and exclusionary images of 'them versus us' create unnecessary tensions that are counterproductive to long-term prosperity. Nationalism may buy a bit of time for China's communist leaders. But the cost may be an unintended return to the sort of isolation that the post-Mao leadership has been trying to remedy. This would surely bring an end to the momentum of reform and modernization that has provided benefits to so many Chinese citizens.

The greatest risk is that nationalistic maneuvering will undo economic progress in China. One of the immediate costs arising from the show of force over the Taiwan Strait was to frighten off some international investors. Herein lies one of the crucial contradictions of the path chosen by China's leadership. Continued economic growth is heavily dependent upon access to foreign markets and investment capital. In any case, the exclusionary tendencies related to nationalism will almost certainly impede China's ability to serve as an honest broker in international trade dealings, thereby jeopardizing their application for WTO membership.

In practical terms, the isolationist elements inherent in a nationalist foreign policy make it extremely difficult, if not impossible, for the Chinese government to achieve the economic goals stated in its Five Year Plan. This includes a commitment to sustain an average annual eight percent growth rate in Gross Domestic Product (GDP) while limiting inflation, to right-size the SOEs, to improve global economic relations, to narrow the disparity in development between the coastal and inland provinces, and to hold urban unemployment to four percent. Unfortunately, data released for the first half of 1996 indicate that China will have a hard time achieving these targets. After excluding inventory buildup, GDP growth was only seven percent while domestic consumer demand has been flat. Unemployment has risen to 10 percent nationwide and is 20 percent in the industrialized northeast. In addition, SOE losses were at a record high by the end of 1996.

Setting aside nationalist rhetoric, objective economic analysis leads to one inescapable conclusion: continued economic engagement with the West is the *sine qua non* for China's economic progress. More specifically, economic engagement with the West essentially means three things. First, China needs to have access to international capital markets in order to fund the expenditures required for modernization. Second, China must maintain and seek to expand its lucrative export markets. Third, China needs to import the advanced technologies that it has been unable to develop internally.

Access to long-term capital markets of the West is necessary to fund the huge physical infrastructure projects that China so desperately needs. There must be substantial expansion of China's road network, improvement of its ports, and increased energy production facilities or commercial activities will fall short of their goals. At the same time, there is a need to commit an enormous amount of financial capital to the matter of flood control to protect cities and farmland.

Foreign investors are also needed to play a key role in helping China reform its ailing SOE sector. Nearly a third of China's 11,000 SOEs are unprofitable, and they employ nearly 100 million workers. Plans to rationalize this sector through consolidation could displace upwards of 7.25 million workers officially designated as 'redundant.' China's notoriously inefficient tax system and profligate public expenditures mean that it is practically impossible to provide sufficient internal funding for social security and medical insurance expenditures for displaced workers. Infusions of foreign capital will be a necessary source of the additional funds needed to mitigate the socially disruptive impact of such massive layoffs.

Similarly, foreign investors will play an integral role in reforming the banking sector. About one-third of all bank loans in China are 'non-performing,' i.e., interest and principal payments are overdue. Such questionable loans could be repackaged and sold at a discount to willing buyers. However, given the magnitude of the problem, plans to 'securitize' these loans by transforming them into tradable assets, will require the active participation of foreigners.

Being an export-driven economy, China's ambitious GDP growth rate targets require the maintenance and expansion of its non-Asian export markets. Accurate measures of Chinese exports to the US are obscured by re-directing goods through Hong Kong or from fraudulent re-labeling of certificates of origin. Nonetheless, it is estimated that trade with China accounts for about 40 percent of America's total trade deficit as of June 1996. Furthermore, as an exporter of mostly low value-added products, China is vulnerable to competition from other newly industrializing countries. Rising costs in China's two principal export production areas, Shanghai and Guangzhou, place them among the highest in the world.

In particular, China has not been able to keep up with the changes wrought by the formation of NAFTA. It has fallen from first to third in terms of textile exports to America, having been displaced by NAFTA partners, Canada and Mexico. In order to maintain its foothold in world export markets, China will require more sophisticated manufacturing technology to upgrade toward higher value-added production. Being a technologically parasitic economy, however, China is dependent upon imported technology to make this transition.

Heightening tensions associated with nationalism pose the risk of setting off 'Cold War II' discussed in Chapter Five. A newly reinforced sense of xenophobia could result in an increasingly intransigent China squaring off against an imagined group of hostile outsiders. Nationalistic paranoia supports an impression that foreigners are attempting to weaken China by partitioning it. This explains the hypersensitivity of Beijing to questions over Taiwan and Tibet. Sober reflection suggests that increased interaction with the West has combined with China's own internal modernizing forces to encourage moves toward greater political decentralization in China.

China's erstwhile communist leaders appear to be unable to resist the temptation to turn to nationalism as a mobilizing theme. This can be done with relative ease since the communist leaders have intimate knowledge of the extensive bureaucracy of the outgoing regime. This institutional structure can be readily adapted with nationalism replacing class struggle as the mobilizing ideology. Thus, economies undergoing transition from communism already possess an infrastructure that readily accommodates the sort of intervention and favoritism associated with nationalist governance.

In addition, the nature of the residual political and economic structures makes the move toward nationalism an easier political play than moving toward full-blown democracy. Indeed nationalism is nurtured under the sort of Leninist one-party state that existed in China. Such a closed and insular society provides little opportunity to interact with outsiders, thereby instilling a sense of skepticism and distrust of 'foreign' things and persons. These conditions reinforced the xenophobia exhibited by Chinese rulers for centuries. These structures and traditions of political domination, left intact despite the decline of communism, are well placed to nurture nationalist sentiments.

And so it is in China, that while the logic of the centralized state is swept away by the decentralizing logic of a market economy, it grasps desperately for the straw of nationalism to keep it afloat. This move toward nationalism is inconsistent with Deng's ideological commitment to non-ideology. Rephrasing his famous dictum, 'it does not matter if the cat is black or white, but the one that catches the mouse should be a Chinese cat.'

Nationalism and accompanying chauvinistic rhetoric may have various benefits such as assisting in social cohesion. However, these are likely to be short lived. Behind every declaration is the implicit justification that it serves to bind the country together and hold chaos at bay. The most immediate benefit to the ruling party resides in the hopeful outcome of maintaining the political status quo.

With the stakes so high, it is too easy to overlook the costs of such ventures. Part of this myopia results from those apparent benefits that have immediate impact, while costs arising out of nationalism may be less tangible and appear at some later date. The costs can be considerable since a successful movement to stir up nationalist sentiments may only delay inevitable economic and political transformations.

What is puzzling is that the Chinese have never held their rulers accountable for the humiliations heaped upon them as a nation. Disinterested reflection confirms that there are serious questions about the apportionment of blame for the outcome of the Opium Wars. Surely the Emperors of the Qing dynasty bear some blame for weakening this inherently prosperous country to the point where a few gunboats could humble it. More recently, it would appear that the privations and atrocities experienced during the Civil War, the Great Leap Forward and the Cultural Revolution were human disasters of a magnitude much greater than having Hong Kong and other territories in the hands of foreigners. Presumably, the emergence of a mature civil society will engender more informed judgments about the quality of China's leaders, and lead toward a political meritocracy.

None of this excuses the rapacious attitudes exhibited by British imperialists and the tragedies that may have befallen those sucked into the addictive vortex of opium. However, nationalists tend to rewrite history so that only the negative aspects of international relations are highlighted. Those who would assign such one-sided blame upon outsiders doom themselves to forever play the victim. Unless there is considerable introspection and soul-searching into what cultural conditions lead to the cycles of China's destructive leadership, similar outcomes will plague China yet again. Despite their intentions, pursuing the path toward rigid nationalism is likely to ensure that history will remember the current generation of leaders as those who 'lost China.'

Unsteady hands at the tillers?

For all the advances of democracy in the Philippines, Taiwan, Thailand, and South Korea, much of East and Southeast Asia remains in the grip of some form of authoritarian regime. At the same time, there is an emergence of 'weak states' where the central authority of the nation-state is weakened as in China or nonexistent as in Cambodia. The region's diverse political arrangements, coupled with the immaturity of Asian transnational organizations, leaves considerable room for conflict and misunderstanding.

East Asian authoritarian regimes are characterized by a patriarchal hierarchy that is often dominated by one party or one family. In such a setting, initiative is discouraged and dissent is suppressed. Ministers and mid-level bureaucrats, like the compliant citizenry, await instructions from above. Because challenging the consensus can be a career-threatening move, problems are not addressed, even when the means to resolve them might be at hand. Overt and tacit threats of retaliation from a vengeful authoritarian regime tend to muzzle the press. If the regime in involved in negotiations of some kind, the populace is deliberately kept in the dark until a successful formulation emerges. This allows the leadership to cover up interim missteps and mistakes that they fear would result in a loss of credibility.

While the supposed benefits of consensus and cooperation are emphasized, the costs of enforcing the consensus and creating a fiction of cooperation are overlooked. One immediate drawback is a bureaucracy that lacks the agility and flexibility to respond quickly or creatively in a crisis, as was sadly illustrated by the inaction of the Japanese government in dealing with the Kobe earthquake disaster in 1995. Longer-term costs can include major social upheaval, owing to the government's intolerance of views outside the mainstream, or failure to consider the input of the affected citizenry.

The failure of many regimes to come to grips with a variety of problems is also partly due to the well-known Asian institution of 'saving face.' As evident in the excessively cautious interactions of ASEAN countries, this phenomenon is not limited to Northeast Asia. ASEAN countries are well known for keeping silent on the internal affairs of their partners and neighbors. With their own dubious human rights records, many of these countries choose not to cast stones whilst living in a veritable glass house. This mutual pact of critical non-aggression prevents Asian countries from effectively using peer pressure to correct the aberrant behavior of rogue states. It would appear that the chore of conserving 'face' by the authoritarian governments of the region can be a time-consuming activity.

Worse yet, a preoccupation with 'saving face' precludes dispute resolution through compromise. In such instances of unyielding national pride, confrontation may too readily give way to conflict. These institutionalized rigidities, combined with the widened availability of offensive weaponry, therefore reduce the likelihood that peaceful interdependence will develop further.

Intra-regional relations in East Asia appear to be guided by a sense of pragmatism that may leave the impression that practical collaboration will win the day. Unfortunately, the region faces considerable internal volatility due to an increasing number of power rivalries. The likely turbulence in East Asia will be fueled by economic competition, combined with the spread of military prowess in an area plagued by disputes over resources. While pragmatism may mitigate some disputes, it is unlikely to provide the basis for long-term strategic planning. Reliance upon crisis management and the current institutional arrangements offer little confidence in the capacity of the leaders of the region to maintain stability. Only when these regional rulers are truly accountable to the citizenry, can greater stability be expected.

One of the areas where there is a gross lack of accountability on the part of many East Asian rulers to their citizens is environmental management. Unfortunately, the costs arising from the neglect of impending and existing environmental problems will be paid by future generations. The next chapter examines these issues and offers some suggestions for change.

Notes

1   K. Calder, *Pacific Defense: Arms, Energy, and America's future in Asia,* New York: William Morrow and Company, 1996.
2   The Japanese are locked in disputes with a variety of other neighbors including Korea over a small group of islets in the Sea of Japan known as Tokdo by Koreans and Takeshima by the Japanese. A long standing sovereignty dispute with Russia continues to simmer over an archipelago of volcano islands known as the Kuriles.
3   Although Ms Contemplacion is said to have confessed, there are other incidents in Singapore where confessed murderers have been proven innocent. In one instance, a Malay laborer 'confessed' to murder and awaited trial for four years awaiting certain death by hanging. He was eventually released when he presented his passport with exit and entry stamps that proved he was not even in Singapore when the crime was committed. See F. Seow, *To Catch a Tartar,* New Haven: Yale University Press, 1994, pp. 229-30.
4   Singapore is the largest investor from Southeast Asia in Burma-Myanmar. As of 1995, Singaporean investments of $548 million are second only to the $643 million investments from Burma's former colonial master, Great Britain.
5   Aung Zaw, 'A Strange Kind of Non-Interference', *The Nation* (Bangkok: 22 June 1996).
6   K. Mahbubani, 'The Pacific Way', *Foreign Affairs* (1995, Vol. 75, No. 1).

7   The acquisition of modern submarines from Russia and Exocet missiles from France has allowed the Chinese to 'reverse-engineer' some high tech equipment for use in their own navy.

8   R. Pipes, 'Russia's Future, Russia's Past', *Commentary* (June 1996).

8 Burdens of nature: The environment and sustaining growth in East Asia

As we approach the millennium, one of the most compelling political debates will be how best to address the degraded state of the natural environment. Nowhere on earth are these problems more conspicuous than in those parts of Asia otherwise blessed with rapid economic growth. There is some irony in this observation, in that many East Asian governments implement programs that are ostensibly designed to serve social aims, at least those aims selected by rulers or bureaucrats. It is equally tragic that the exercise of authoritarian rule is unable or perhaps unwilling to stem the unabated decline in the environment. While the inability of domestic institutions or the unwillingness of many East Asian regimes to undertake reform leads to a continuation of such problems within their own borders, the weakness of the regional associations make them even less capable of coping with pollution on a cross-border basis.

The alarming environmental decay in East Asia contradicts the presumed philosophical underpinning for recent advances in the region. It is widely believed that the political commitment of Asian governments to communal well-being at the expense of individual rights is their great secret of 'success.' However, the estimated annual health costs arising from pollution in East Asia are staggering, and a detriment to the quality of life in the region.

The authoritarian socialist experience of East and Central Europe provides considerable evidence that extensive governmental control over an economy can have catastrophic environmental consequences. Impoverished and misled by communist planning, these countries had a dismal record even when compared to the most brazen extremes of capitalism. In all events, environmental preservation was not a priority of central planning dedicated to boosting industrial output. What remains to be seen is whether East Asian authoritarian governments that recognize private property rights and heed the signals of the market can do better than those communist regimes that did not. Needless to say, the jury is still out on that question.

145

Choking on its own success?

Although many environmentalists may assert that the environmental problems in East Asia are the consequence of unbridled capitalism, there is another angle that explains this peculiar pairing of boom with gloom. Indeed, the fault may well lie in some of the political institutions common to East Asia. While the supporters of 'Asian values' point to the merits of a collectivist approach to governance, many East Asian regimes have accomplished little in correcting environmental problems. The argument considered here is that East Asia's collectivist approach to environmental management may be the source of problems both now and in the future.

In treating the environment as a common or open access resource, there is a tendency for abuse as air or water pollution. Since no one person or community can claim title to the future value of such a commonly held resource, the only way to draw benefits from it is to use it before someone else does. Thus, there is no immediate payoff for husbanding the resource efficiently so that it is available in a future time period. Such predictable behavior constitutes what is known as 'the tragedy of the commons.'[1] When ownership rights are in suspense or are shared by all, incentives are distorted in that individual gains from conservation are relatively small. In other words, the impact of the losses from environmental waste is dispersed over the wider community, and therefore has a small impact upon any one person. Thus, there will be a tendency for individuals to abuse or overuse commonly held property such as the atmosphere, or those resources found in international waters.

Most of the measures of economic success recorded in East Asia to date overlook the offsetting environmental costs of expansion. Beijing's air is 35 times dirtier than London's and 16 times more contaminated than Tokyo's. Between 1991 and 2000, the level of air pollution is supposed to triple in Seoul and Bangkok and is expected to double in Taipei, Jakarta, and Kuala Lumpur.

The bad news is that in the near-term, rising incomes will exacerbate the already worsening air pollution problem by increasing the level of construction activity. As more individuals and families reach middle income status, the need for adequate transportation facilities and infrastructure will increase dramatically. Presently, most urban air pollution is generated by road transport vehicles. These vehicles are responsible for 75 percent of the air pollution in Beijing, 86 percent in Kuala Lumpur, and 95 percent in Taipei. Rising incomes will mean dirtier air, thanks to ever-increasing numbers of privately-owned vehicles on Asia's roads. To ease traffic congestion and avoid gridlock, Asia must dramatically pick up the pace of road construction. A UN report in 1995 pointed out that Asian countries face the impossible task of building an additional 1.2 million miles (2 million kilometers) of roadways by the year 2000. Such frantic, large-scale construction will emit an enormous amount of suspended particulates into Asia's urban air.

Costs to China for environmental degradation are estimated at 8.5 to 15 percent of its gross domestic product.[2] Some of these costs are simply being deferred and will be paid by future generations in terms of health effects. Others, like water pollution and damage to agricultural land, can be expected to have an immediate impact on China's capacity for growth.

The economic costs of East Asian pollution are already beginning to take their toll. Development in the region is likely to mean a continued shrinking of wilderness areas and disappearance of pristine coasts.[3] East Asia's tourism industry will therefore suffer. In Jakarta alone, the cost associated with industrial contamination of the air is calculated to be between $110 and $455 million. If pollution levels in Kuala Lumpur were reduced to comply with OECD standards, improvements in health would be worth $1.2 billion a year. Soil erosion in just the grassland areas of the Philippines leads to productivity losses of $100 million each year. Bangkok's infamous traffic jams cost not only in terms of pollution, but also in time lost from productive activities. With 40 percent of urban China unserved by sewers, most waste water goes directly into lakes and rivers. Only 4.5 percent of China's municipal waste water receives any treatment.[4]

Pollution of the Mekong River poses an especially difficult problem. There are six countries – Burma-Myanmar, Cambodia, China, Laos, Thailand, and Vietnam – that share its banks and draw from its waters. Increasing population and migration in these riparian countries, along with speedy industrialization, have placed enormous pressure on the capacity of the Mekong to absorb polluted water. As the world's twelfth largest river, it traverses about 2,500 miles (4,200 kilometers), beginning in the hinterlands of China and emptying into a massive delta at the South China Sea. At present, about 325 million inhabitants live along the river as it stretches across the various borders. In addition to sewage and industrial contaminants, changing cultivation patterns, including substantial areas of deforestation, have caused increased soil erosion and problems with sedimentation that obstruct the river's flow. An Asian Development Bank (ADB) report notes that forests in the region are declining by about 500,000 hectares per annum.[5]

To date, there has been no discernible cooperative effort to address the problems associated with the degradation of the Mekong. China's plans to build some 15 hydroelectric dams along the Mekong and its tributaries are causing great concern for the downstream countries. Either they will be deprived of much of the water held upstream in reservoirs, or they will be inundated by flood waters if the dams experience structural failures.

Immense forest fires frequently burn out of control in parts of Indonesia. These occur in rural areas where slash-and-burn farming techniques are prevalent. The resulting erosion has exposed seams of peat and coal that readily catch fire without protective ground cover. Once lit, these fires are difficult to control, and they spread relentlessly into adjacent forested areas.

In late 1994, the sky over much of the Malaysian peninsula was choked with the smoke from such a fire that burned thousands of acres of precious rain forest. It was so severe that Singaporean authorities issued health warnings for the elderly and infirm to remain indoors. Transportation links were interrupted by the closing of some airports, and even agricultural harvests were imperiled in the most fertile region of Malaysia. After nearly six weeks of smoke-shrouded skies, it was announced that a meeting of affected countries would only take place several weeks later. Instead of offering a plan to undertake some concerted remedial action, officials were merely quoted as stating that the problem would be cleared up in the rainy season.

Obviously, an ASEAN version of the code of silence, promulgated by authoritarian regimes as a tool for mutual political survival, does not allow for aggressive action on the part of member countries. Neighboring governments were reluctant to offer aid, or to criticize the handling of the fires, so as not to embarrass the Indonesian authorities. Consequently, there was almost no public discussion about the causes or questions about the application of remedies for the choking pollution. Allowing the Indonesian government to 'save face' was apparently more important than protecting their citizens or the region's environment.

While posted to the Shanghai University of Finance and Economics in the late 1980s, I read beautiful lyrical poetry about the stream that flanked its campus. The poet spoke gracefully about blooming trees that lined its bank and crystalline water that was brimming with fish. Alas, the words were penned in the previous century and bore no resemblance to the turgid flow that could have easily been mistaken for an asphalt byway. The banks were a barren wasteland dotted with smoldering garbage heaps. Farther afield during my travels in the nearby countryside just outside Shanghai, I found peasant shanties sitting cheek-to-jowl with industrial waste sites. Ground water mixed freely with the fluid from chemical waste dumps. Clearly, all was not well in the 'workers' paradise,' nor were the interests of all citizens taken into account.

Now in northern China, the Three Gorges dam project is underway to tame the mighty Yangtze River. It is unquestionably a marvel of engineering. Nonetheless, many believe that it will be an environmental nightmare, and so may be economically ill-advised. Criticisms of this Soviet-style project should not be dismissed as environmental alarmism. No plans have been made to solve the problems posed by the expected annual inflow of 265 billion gallons of raw sewage into the massive reservoir. Neither has there been any preparation to deal with the toxic waste dumps that will be covered by the rising waters. Critics point out that massive silting behind the dam is likely to cancel the presumed navigational benefits that are meant to transform Chongqing into a major inland port. Other objections have been raised over the expected loss of archeological sites. However, public discussion has been so muted that neither economic merit nor scientific accuracy can be questioned. One critic, summarily dismissed from the Communist Party for his objections, put it succinctly. 'If there aren't any problems, why are they afraid of open debate on the project?' In this restrictive setting, only benefits of projects can be discussed while questions about the costs or complications cannot be aired.

Deforestation is occurring more quickly in East Asia than anywhere else in the world. For example, rain forests covered about 70 percent of Cambodia's land area twenty years ago. Today the portion of forested land is 41 percent. Massive clearing of rainforest in preparation for the Bakun dam in Malaysia is also the cause of considerable anxiety. Nonetheless, Malaysian journalists have been conspicuously silent about reporting these concerns to the wider public. It might well be that the economic value of maintaining much of the forested area could have greater long-term benefits than the present cash price. However, government officials readily able to enrich themselves through payoffs or by setting up their own logging companies can be expected to adopt a short-sighted position on these issues.

Extensive environmental damage is obvious to even the casual observer in the high-growth areas of Asia. However, several factors conspire to obstruct a careful measurement of environmental degradation. Outsiders who seek information on the source and extent of pollution have to rely upon data provided by the Asian governments. Since most of the governments in the region impose strict control over data dissemination, independent corroboration is often impossible. At the same time, due to a traditional respect for authority or from fear of reprisal for challenging the (often imposed) consensus, the Asian media seldom indulge in aggressive investigative reporting.

Illusions of quality of life in Asian economic statistics

The 1996 report by the UN Economic and Social Commission for Asia and the Pacific (ESCAP) indicates mixed results. Poverty remains a problem due to slow growth in some countries, with intra-regional income disparities becoming more apparent due to higher growth in the Tiger economies. In contrast to the vibrant growth recorded by most of the East and Southeast Asian countries, South Asian countries are only posting modest gains while Central Asian countries have made little progress.

Although Japan may have the highest reported per capita income in the region and one of the highest in the world, the standard of living experienced by most Japanese is not necessarily enviable.[6] At best, the impact of all the high-paced economic growth on the quality of life for East Asians is uncertain. For example, Japanese workers have considerably less leisure time than their Western counterparts. Only about 20 percent have two day weekends, most work overtime, and most receive less than half the number of paid vacation days that American workers enjoy. Worse yet, due to protectionism and cronyism, Japan's consumers must also pay some of the highest prices in the world for food and housing of dubious quality.

For all their efforts and sacrifices, Japanese citizens are burdened with an enormous public debt that arose out of wild binges of public sector spending. Collusion, price fixing, and corruption were the hallmark of Japanese public works, as revealed in numerous court cases and the eventual imprisonment of high ranking public officials. Fabulous wealth was amassed by many of those companies or individuals directly involved, but the costs fell heavily upon Japanese taxpayers. As of the end of 1994, Japanese government debt amounted to $300 trillion, most of which was accumulated during a public construction boom that began in the mid-1970s. The typical Japanese house is smaller than its American counterpart with fewer rooms and more people per room.[7] In light of the enormous stresses faced by Japan's typical 'salary man,' it is not clear that they have received good value for the money spent or the sacrifices made. Despite its strong macroeconomic performance over the past century, the common expression 'rich Japan, poor Japanese' seems an apt description of the situation in modern Japan.

There has been much critical discussion about deficiencies in the various methods used for calculating national income figures, both in Asia and elsewhere. However, the impact of these formulation flaws on the direction of Asia's economies pales in comparison to the potential damage caused by politicians who intentionally misuse these statistics to justify and further their political or social agendas. For example, authoritarian leaders seemingly place undue emphasis on GDP growth statistics as an unqualified barometer of their economic success. When used in this way, the data do not offer an unadulterated story because they are being opportunistically interpreted to describe phenomena they were not intended to measure. In this regard, it is instructive to note that GDP and national income estimates have a limited purpose in providing an estimate of a monetary value for annual economic activity. Their underlying purpose is to report the value of products or services as indicated by the willingness of people to spend money for them. It may sound crude, but the transfer of monetary assets is perhaps the only 'objective' indicator of the values of the community. Prices summarize many implicit values that are communicated by the actions of purchase and sale. If national income statistics fail to make these values explicit, it is because they were not designed to measure the intentions or motivations of buyer and seller, per se. The data are simply an objective record of the prices at which observed exchanges take place.

Proposals for improving measures of national income constitute an ongoing and informative project. Discussion of these alternatives is especially instructive in reminding non-economists what economists do *not* seek to measure. Obviously, some of the anomalies that lead to criticism arise from laymen using too wide an interpretation of what GDP is meant to measure. Nevertheless, whatever the sins of economists, it may be that the greatest damage is done by government officials who are too slavish in their reliance upon, or brazen in their manipulation, of GDP measures as a guide to policy.

There is considerable evidence to suggest that the speedy growth in several East Asian economies has been fueled by the rapid depletion of non-renewable resources, and excessive consumption of renewable ones. However, as was discovered in the case of the Philippines, this approach produces prosperity with a short life. Nevertheless, when virgin forests are clear cut for timber or to increase farm production, this activity is calculated as a net addition to national income. Thus, conventional estimates of economic growth tend to overstate real gains because the costs associated with lost natural habitat are not included.

Regarding the natural and the social environment

The familiar aspects of the decay of the natural environment are only part of the picture. While pollution provides stark evidence of the abuse of the *natural environment* in Asia, authoritarian regimes in the region exhibit profound disregard for the *social environment* by ignoring individual rights and democratic freedoms. Under their political arrangements, a vicious cycle replaces the virtuous circle that should exist between economic growth and environmental quality. In most instances, increased wealth should facilitate the discovery and application of technology for improving environmental infrastructure. By accelerating obsolescence, high growth should cause older technologies that are pollution-prone to be more energetically replaced by cleaner, greener production techniques.

The governments overseeing the East Asian 'miracle' economies are usually credited for 'getting the basics right.' This may have been correct if 'basics' is defined as the mobilization of resources as a precondition for East Asia's bursts of growth. However, if 'basics' are more broadly defined to encompass long-range fundamentals, then East Asia's authoritarian regimes have gotten it wrong. Indeed, much of the degradation being observed in Asia at present arises out of the same government institutions that are supposedly behind the region's envious growth record.

Many former and erstwhile communist states of East Asia have been following a modernization path with a Marxian bias toward industrial production as a measure of national wealth and power. This obsession with heavy industry has led authoritarian regimes to ignore environmental concerns and to pursue policies such as income transfers and subsidies that distort the price of many natural resources. For example, in order to appease powerful agricultural or manufacturing lobbies, prices for energy and water have been kept artificially low, thereby leading to overuse. In short, government control of markets and prices is generally a recipe for environmental disaster because users reap the full benefit, but do not have to pay the full cost, of consuming natural resources. Instead, the burden of these costs is shifted to the community at large.

By its nature, authoritarian rule perpetuates the problem in that it thwarts the spontaneous formation of those elements of civil society that enhance public awareness of controversial issues. There is a characteristic lack of openness and debate reinforced by intolerance of dissent. This is implemented by either forcefully muzzling the media, or through threats that induce self-censorship. When journalists steer away from politically sensitive issues en masse, a contrived sense of public well-being results that allows real problems to fester, undetected.

In a system where property rights are ambiguous, authoritarian leaders have an incentive to maximize gains in the short-run. State ownership results in the 'tragedy of the commons' that was described earlier. Current leaders realize that they can maximize their own well-being only if they sell off the natural resources in the present. This may involve outright sale, controlling access through regulation, or the sale of licensing agreements to the highest bidders/bribers. Current consumption therefore assumes priority over the judicious husbanding of resources. In other words, since the future may belong to another person or clique who will probably follow a similar course of action, it becomes individually 'logical' to oversee hasty depletion of timber or mineral resources. This was evident in the growth spurt in the Philippines during the 1970s, and in Thailand during the 1980s. In these countries, the quick enrichment of a few well-connected individuals through the rapid depletion of these countries' resources has also worsened income disparities between the rich and poor. A few families, mostly with political or military connections, became fabulously wealthy, while little of the money inflow trickled down to the masses. It is likely that similar developments will be observed in Burma-Myanmar, Cambodia, Laos, and Vietnam.

Economists identify a variety of situations where markets fail to correctly allocate the full costs of the purchase and sale of a good or service. For example, pollution is a case where the market price struck by buyers and sellers does not include 'external diseconomies,' i.e., those non-compensated social costs that spill over onto third parties. It is then asserted that the presence of these externalities provide grounds for corrective interventions by the state. Thus, while environmentalists focus upon the social impact of such market failures, they should also be concerned with publicly-imposed externalities or 'government failure.' For example, governments often undertake policies that impose costs on the greater community while conferring benefits to a small and vocal special interest group. Even well-intentioned efforts at cleaning up the environment may lead to unexpected costs in other areas, including the loss of jobs and declining living standards, or repression of market exchanges among willing participants. Indeed, government interventions inevitably involve some form of compulsion, including regulations or restrictions on freedom of exchange, and confiscation of property either through nationalization or taxation.

An alternative explanation suggests that externalities are frequently the result of public policy (government) failure. This view is based on the premise that one of the most important functions of the state is to establish and enforce a system of rules that effectively assigns responsibility to individuals for their action. One of the best means for instituting this accountability is a system of private property rights. If governments do not properly define and enforce property rights, then externalities emerge.

A few examples might be helpful. Compare the situations where ownership rights are clear, protected, and transferable, to those situations where ownership of property is either vested in the state, held in common, or is in suspense. In the first instance, the legal system would provide property owners with a means of redress against polluters. By virtue of well-defined and enforceable ownership, resource owners would have a vested interest in maintaining the value of their assets and would be less likely to allow it to diminish. The incentive structure, while it may be as imperfect as the humans who react to it, will tend to reward prudent uses of land and resources and mete out punishment (as diminished market value) for imprudence.

In contrast, government ownership of property lends itself to interest group pressures that will very likely result in sub-optimal property use. Being immune to market discipline, such interests will tend to overstate their 'demand,' or understate their willingness to pay. In this case, the incentive structure is not simply imperfect; it is defective to the point of ensuring imprudent behavior. If everyone is the owner and no one is able to realize an advantage from improving the value of the property, there is little incentive for any one person to protect and preserve. Indeed, many of the Asian countries with widespread ownership by the state have pollution problems far in excess of those in advanced industrial states where there are well-defined and well-enforced private property rights. Industrial pollution in China as well as in East and Central Europe provides stark examples of some of the worst cases of this type of public policy or government failure.[8]

Absurd results can occur in these circumstances. For example, pandas might be hunted to near extinction on commonly held lands or there may be 'too many' pandas if governments are lobbied by groups who do not acknowledge the costs of protecting them. However, a 'correct' number of pandas is more likely to exist and then thrive under the protection of self-interested owners who promote their survival to insure a steady flow of income just as for cattle or chickens. Similarly, the absence of private ownership rights over the air and water, while admittedly an abstract concept, is likely to insure that they will be overused and abused.

Besides ill-defined property rights, another cause of ecological externalities in many Asian countries are various government policies that inadvertently cause individuals to behave according to 'effective preferences' that diverge from the 'ideal preferences' stated by governments. For example, agricultural policies intended to increase production in developed and less-developed countries have unintentionally induced farmers to clear-cut indigenous forests, drain wetlands and destroy wilderness areas. Soil erosion, along with runoffs of agricultural pesticides and fertilizers, clog and pollute waterways. Thus, while the government ideally prefers that there be no environmental disruption, its policies effectively insure the opposite result. Government policies and regulations that attenuate property rights through regulation or takings, are perhaps as likely to worsen the situation as they are of resolving it.[9]

Another way of understanding the role of the state in causing conditions conducive to environmental decay, is to think in terms of proximate and fundamental causes. The proximate, or most immediate, cause of damage to the environment may appear to be private undertakings. However, the institutional structure establishing legal and economic constraints defines the fundamental incentive structure for most communities. Many of the proposals for addressing environmental problems are directed at the proximate source of the problem, i.e., private action. However, this is tantamount to treating symptoms rather than correcting root causes attributable to public policy interventions that failed to achieve their stated goals.

Among many of the regimes in Asia, problems of degradation in the natural environment are matched by declines in the social environment. For example, corruption and moral decay, rising crime, and crowding are unwanted byproducts of China's 'miracle' economy. These problems basically flow out of government-imposed institutions and constitute a form of 'policy pollution.' The rationale offered for the lack of democratic rights and freedoms in developing countries is merely a smoke screen for political opportunism.

While worshipping at the altar of GDP, many Asian governments offer up sacrifices of both the natural environment and the social environment. The suppression of personal freedom and the absence of guarantees for individual rights are aspects of these 'government failures' that are excused by an insistence that the collectivism emerging out of 'Asian values' renders such civil liberties unnecessary. Thus, as mentioned above, governments in the region defer to a mantra of 'growth first, rights later.' Perhaps the most cynical justification for authoritarian rule is the unproved assertion that Asians wish to be and must be ordered about by a strong-willed ruler.

Authoritarian leaders in Asia offer prosperity only in terms of stark tradeoffs. Personal liberty must be sacrificed for the greater good and economic advance. It appears that many of them also believe that a healthy and clean environment is an obstruction to continued growth. It is as though some East Asian leaders only interpret *yin* and *yang* as hapless cousins set at wide extremes.

Despite these perplexing problems, the remedy does not lie in government regulation and intervention alone. Indeed, there is ample evidence of the abject failure of government actions to remedy environmental damage. In fact, governments have often implemented programs that have unintentionally exacerbated the problem. Effective remedial action requires three steps. First, the public must recognize that although a certain amount of pollution may be necessary, even desirable for economic prosperity, wanton disregard for the environment is not. Second, institutional arrangements must be changed so that the government's ideal preferences are the product of an informed public consensus, and not merely reflective of the desires of a few special interest groups, like environmentalists or trade groups. Third, these same institutional arrangements must insure that government's ideal and effective preferences are synchronized so as to avoid unintended results.

Public passivity to the abuse of individual rights and freedoms in East Asia should be considered to be no more excusable than disregard for the natural environment. As implied by the preceding paragraph, a tradeoff arises in that increased protection of the environment may lead to unintentional, and in most cases undesired, substantial losses of individual freedom of choice or action. An unchecked enthusiasm for environmental protection may lead to as much injury to the sociopolitical, economic, and cultural environment as has abject neglect of the natural environment led to its debasement. This potential harm to the political and economic environment could emerge in the same sort of assaults upon individual freedom of action and private property rights as was evident during the tragically failed experiments with authoritarian socialism. Decentralized decisions of individual entities will tend to be challenged by centralized decrees. Voluntary, interpersonal interactions motivated by efficiency are likely to give way to coercive, politicized decisions prompted by political expediency and/or the exigencies of a 'scientific' order.

Protection and rehabilitation of the natural environment reflect a critical and justified impetus for action. Therefore, what is to be addressed here are the means instead of the ends. It is very likely that an approach based upon a narrow understanding of ecology may inspire extensive state interventions based partly

155

upon ignorance and good intentions, rather than by a hidden authoritarian or socialist agenda. With ample evidence of the failure of socialism in East and Central Europe, it is almost certain that this model will not intentionally be chosen again. However, warnings to safeguard human rights are not misplaced if they help to avoid unintended and unforeseen institutional arrangements that result in de-humanizing outcomes similar to those under authoritarian socialist regimes. In fact, the German National Socialists under Hitler implemented many policies would have warmed the hearts of some of the most extreme ecologists. One expression of the guiding philosophy of the Nazi Party (*gemeinnutz vor Eigennutz*) suggests that the good of the whole comes before the good of the individual.[10] This view was translated into a mandate to insure racial hygiene or purity by attacking alcohol and tobacco consumption. Thus, the Nazis would likely find agreement with those in the ecological movement who reject the classical liberal ideal that promotes the division between public and private life and which seeks to protect the rights and freedoms of the individual.

Potential flaws in environmentalist reasoning

In response to enhanced public awareness of environmental issues, economists have increasingly turned their attention to an evaluation of the relationship between economic growth and exploitation of the environment. In this regard, one of the most critical tasks for economists is to clarify some of the conceptual flaws in common approaches to solving problems with pollution and waste. In the first instance, the costs of government-imposed regulation of the economy are not generally well understood. When governments issue mandates to curb pollution, this is too often undertaken without due consideration for the costs of compliance. The costs arising from such mandates are not merely borne by the targeted polluter. They are shifted onto workers and consumers, and they will also affect the costs of goods in competing or complementary industries. Because these costs do not appear in government budgets, there is a little incentive for regulators and legislators to take them into account. Consequently, the costs of compliance for all of America's regulations have risen from 40 percent of the federal budget in 1980 to 47 percent in 1995.

One of the most controversial explanations for environmental degradation offered by economists is that pollution is something that members of all communities 'desire.' This is because virtually every productive activity has some negative side effects. Therefore, the only way to have zero pollution would be to have zero production. Since almost no one wants zero production, we collectively express a willingness to accept a certain amount of pollution. In any case, a clean environment is only one item in a complex basket of things that people seek to have. If one is suffering from AIDS or is in need of an organ transplant, advanced medical research and a modern transportation system necessary to deliver the necessary medical supplies may be of a higher priority than clean air.

Most environmentalists tend to view economic growth with an unbalanced view of the benefits and costs associated with it. Those costs are usually identified as either the depletion of energy or other natural resources, or the creation of waste as a byproduct of production and consumption.[11] At the same time, there is a 'materialist' bias in the consideration of the benefits. Rising per capita income is most often cited as the main benefit. This simplistic approach ignores the enhanced possibilities of human achievement, increased literacy, decreased mortality and increased interdependency, the latter fostering increased prospects of peace due to its importance for economic growth. Critics who ignore these non-material aspects of growth provide a negatively biased view of the overall environmental impact of economic activities.

Growth and development can lead to an improved capacity to pay for environmental damage or to avoid future damage related to economic activity. Benefits will accrue to the environment through technological advancement, improved efficiency, and increased productivity in the use of scarce resources. An important point almost always ignored by non-economists is the consequence of increasing (relative) scarcity of resources. As something that is useful becomes less available in relation to how much of it people demand, there will nearly always be a subsequent rise in relative prices that induces greater economizing and a deeper sense of a need to conserve. Conservation may thus be accordingly viewed as a special form of investment, it is recognized that it should be subjected to the same rational evaluation. However, a recent study suggests that the problem of increased scarcity is much exaggerated. In reviewing the price behavior of 38 resources, there were in most cases, substantial decreases in their real costs and declines in the real price of most foods.[12]

Distributional effects of environmentalism

It is often (always?) claimed that regulations and policies that protect the environment benefit everyone, especially future generations. Such a claim is likely to be misleading. Claims for the existence of such benefits should not overlook disparities in distribution, nor the magnitude and impact of offsetting costs arising from such actions. Many of these costs and their distributional consequences are often unintended and unanticipated. However, in a world of finite resources, this is an inadequate apology. Good intentions, unfortunately, do not compensate for bad results.

In terms of distribution, demands for protection of wilderness areas will probably result in a concentration of direct benefits to some, while costs tend to be dispersed to a large group of others. The primary beneficiaries are those who

157

fish and hike in or otherwise use these areas. In a broad sense, their 'income' will therefore be higher. Those who pay the direct costs of preserving these areas will be the general taxpayer and those who consume products, such as lumber for housing, which will necessarily be more expensive. The former have a strong motivation to promote such policies due to the relatively large individual benefits they receive. Their cohesion will be likely to lead to their exerting a disproportionately large political influence. Those who incur the costs have a weak motivation to oppose even a costly project because the costs will be dispersed over a larger group that is more difficult to identify. Thus, even under well-functioning representative democracy, the majority may be overwhelmed by the political interests of a minority.

In this particular example, a perverse income redistribution effect may also arise. Assume that those who derive pleasure from use of the wilderness areas are likely to be in a relatively high income group. A (perverse?) net transfer then will be directed to the rich from the poor who tend to spend a higher proportion of their total income on housing. Due to the presence of such distributional consequences, environmental policies should be closely examined to see who bears the costs and receives the benefits of alternative programs.

Demands for a new environmental ethic pose another problem. It is a common claim of spokespersons for interest groups and politicians to speak glibly about collective goals as though they are known, objective functions that can be solved like a mathematical puzzle. It is virtually impossible to gather, much less assimilate, the required data to make correct decisions for a (large) community due to continual change, and because the information is available only from the community's widely dispersed and disparate members. This problem proves intractable even in culturally homogeneous communities like those in many of the East Asian countries. Authoritarian regimes create an illusion that they are able to do this. Nonetheless, their successes will be limited by the passage of time that allows their citizens to absorb new information and to develop new understandings about the world. Despite cultural differences, community preferences will be chosen individually and subjectively. However, government interpretations of community preferences can be subjective and manipulated for political reasons.

Attempts to make collective decisions based upon 'fact' can often lead to unforeseen and undesirable expansions of power in the hands of governments. When democracy is treated as a vehicle for the acquisition of power to right a specific wrong, even enlightened leaders, despite their claims, will often be inclined to ignore or act against the wishes of the masses. History provides clear lessons that when citizens resist compulsion of strong interventionist measures by the state, leaders begin to disregard electoral signals. Warnings about the excesses associated with Stalinism and Maoism were not exaggerations, nor were Stalin's or Pol Pot's excesses a historical accident. They can be viewed as a symptomatic feature and the unpleasant outcome, of a dogma driven by rulers who would not allow their citizens to make choices for themselves.

On the one hand, paternalistic politicians who claim to speak for the entire community or the 'masses' are too often budding despots. On the other hand, spokespersons who assert that their group or ruling party is acting in the best interest of the overall community may simply be protecting or furthering a set of narrow, vested interests.

A clean environment and a free society

Environmentalism as it has developed in the 1990s may manifest itself in an intolerance for individual choice and a predisposition against private property. Eco-terrorism and the confiscation of private property are unfortunately viewed as acceptable tactics among a small but growing number of people. Their behavior exhibits an arrogance and a disregard for individual rights and property similar to authoritarian regimes in East Asia and elsewhere. The 'legitimacy' of their collectivistic ends is expressed in the sort of language used by autocratic regimes.

The approach of the millennium provides the world community with some mixed omens of hope for the future. While the decline of authoritarian socialism (communism) merits three cheers, the outcomes from the belated awareness of environmental issues might deserve only two. In the absence of a critical assessment of the means which some environmentalist groups would apply, a real and present danger exists that the rise of the environmental movement may prompt authoritarian intervention and a disregard for individual rights and freedom of action, as in the failed socialist experiments in Burma-Myanmar, Cambodia, China, Laos, North Korea, and Vietnam. Unless care is taken in the implementation of environmental policy, citizens of these countries may be jumping out of the fire into the frying pan. In all events, an approach that views government intervention and regulation as the appropriate vehicle for resolving environmental problems overlooks a large body of literature that argues for reliance upon market mechanisms. Examples of these mechanisms include the marketing of pollution rights, privatization of wilderness areas and of wildlife, and innovative techniques of 'tagging' that can be used to allow for the identification of ownership of dispersed resources or to trace the source of pollution.[13] Each of these proposals relies upon strong individual incentives as revealed by market-generated prices, and the opportunity to benefit directly from the enhancement of value that arises from privately owned property.

One approach to avoiding damage to both the social and natural environments in the future is through the guarantee of individual rights and freedoms. Most economists accept that the most perplexing problems of environmental decay arise from the absence of the assignment and/or enforcement of private property rights. But these rights will not be adequately enforced by a regime that denies political freedoms. Private property ownership and the adherence to the rule of law are the best chance for encouraging long-term husbandry of resources and respect for the environment. Only under extensive private property rights can pricing mechanisms discover the value a community places upon a clean environment or exploitable resources. Assignment of property rights would also allow for the emergence of a price that producers would be willing to pay for the right to pollute.

In sum, the impact of the proposed corrective mechanisms upon the rights and freedoms of individuals should not be ignored. Zero-sum games should be avoided where gains in the natural environment are offset by losses in the social environment. For almost 70 years the Soviets deluded their supporters into believing that economic and political rights were separable. Perhaps it will require another miracle before authoritarian Asian governments see that repression is part of the problem, not the solution.

Of equal importance is that all governments in East Asia must learn the difference between being 'pro-business' versus being 'pro-market.' Policies that are pro-business favor special business or industrial interests by granting them subsidies and monopoly concessions. Too often this largess is doled out to serve narrow political ends. Thus, in order to avoid worsening a bad situation, there should be a minimum of state ownership. Similarly, the regulatory behavior of politicians and bureaucrats should be transparent enough in order to limit their influence so that it is not worth buying. Widespread corruption of the natural and social environment is one of the important costs of government intervention in the process of exchange.

In contrast, pro-market policies tend to serve the broader public by allowing free access to commercial activities that, after all, are nothing more than the aggregate expressions of citizens as consumers and producers. The purpose of politics is often about closing off access to free markets and allowing groups of producers or workers to advance their own purposes against the interests of consumers and suppliers. Free markets without these politically-imposed obstructions tend to reward according to merit and offer greater class mobility. Clearly, neither free market nor political decisions will lead to a pristine environment or a use of resources that pleases everyone. However, there is a temptation to use the power of governments to make matters worse on both counts. The policies of corporations that offend can be subjected to boycotts of their products or shunning of their stock offerings. Unfortunately, refusing to pay taxes in response to offensive government policies is almost certain to land protesters in court or in jail.

Protecting people and preserving the environment

Although the debate remains unsettled, there is strong evidence that market-oriented strategies for dealing with environmental concerns have much to commend them. The general policy framework in much of East Asia, with its emphasis on collective or communitarian goals, may be based upon good intentions. However, many of the goals are selected and enforced by a political or economic clique rather than by the general public. The absence of political accountability allows these rulers to ignore the impacts of their actions upon individuals or relatively powerless groups in the community, such as indigenous peoples. One flaw in relying upon governments for solving environmental problems is that there are reasons to expect that public policy errors will occur more frequently, and will also be corrected more slowly, than errors made in the private sector.

Whenever a policy is implemented under any form of government, there are relatively few mechanisms for correcting errors of judgment. Since the costs of errors are seldom borne directly by the decision maker (bureaucrats or politicians), they may be less likely to take prompt remedial action. If public policies are implemented that incur costs that exceed the intended benefits, the harm to the community is more likely to be greater since more lives are affected. However, the fact that these impacts are widely dispersed means that there are weak incentives for individual policy makers to repair flawed programs. Normally there would have to be an open and public admission of fault that might include pointing fingers at their superiors. Clearly, either of these steps is unlikely in the hierarchical or authoritarian regimes that are dominant in East Asia.

The private sector tends to provide stronger inducements for the avoidance and correction of errors in judgment. Generally, the errors will affect a smaller number of persons since market transactions require unanimous approval of the participants (buyers or sellers) in the exchange process. Private sector arrangements seldom have the sort of nationwide impact that public sector decisions involve. These effects are also likely to be concentrated upon the decision maker, their (extended) family, or their company. As a result, private sector decision makers have a stronger incentive to avoid making mistakes. For example, the choice by a firm to use one form of energy over another in its production process is likely to have limited impact on the environment. However, it may have a significant impact on its shareholders.

Market-based environmental strategies offer an opportunity to resolve some pollution problems unique to Asia. An appropriate scheme of marketing rainforest products can reduce deforestation. In addition, the assignment of property rights over the forests to indigenous peoples will provide them with the legal means to protect their habitat. The bargaining process between timber users (e.g., builders and home owners) and their 'owners' (e.g., forest dwellers in Java or Borneo) will better reveal the value of timber products relative to the value of unexploded rain forests. Instead of governments or western environmentalist choosing for them, forest dwellers could choose the extent to which they would trade off their lifestyles for modern conveniences.

On balance, it would appear that environmental problems in developing countries in East Asia and elsewhere could be addressed through granting expanded rights to individuals. Most important, there must be mechanisms for defining and enforcing private property rights so that markets can be harnessed to resolve environmental issues.

Doubtless, this sort of shift in political paradigms will be a difficult one. It would require a massive change in many of the underlying values and institutions in Asian cultures. However, this transition is a necessary one for Asians to undertake. Most likely the question is *when* the changes will occur, not *whether* they will occur. Pressures imposed by economic and political realities can be expected to induce both leaders and citizens to seek more effective mechanisms for resource management. In the end, the resulting governmental and market forms must involve some innovative combination of Asian and Western thinking.

There is no reason why the transition of East Asian economies toward a more liberal trading order cannot be compatible with sustainable development. Indeed, it is through high rates of economic growth that these countries can develop the resources and abilities to cope with environmental problems. As in the case of poverty, it is the lack of appropriate institutional structures or physical infrastructure that impedes the implementation of sound policies.

Ironically, aggressive expressions of environmentalism that have surfaced in some Western industrialized countries share an intolerance for individual choice and a predisposition against private property that are evident in East Asian authoritarian regimes. Eco-terrorist acts, the destruction of private property by obsessed individuals, and the confiscation by governments to serve environmental causes have gained credibility among some environmentalists in America and elsewhere. Those who would support collectivist actions that serve their narrow purposes may overlook the wider impacts. By introducing policies or validating actions that disregard property rights, a dangerous precedent has been set that might lead to broader encroachments on individual freedoms.

Behind the notion of an 'Asian Century' is a presumption that collectivism lies behind the economic success in East Asia and provides an alternative path for modernization. By contrast, economic and political institutions associated with the 'American Century' are generally understood to have emerged out of the expansion of individual rights and freedoms. The examination of these two notions in the next chapter will provide some insights into what the future holds.

Notes

1   G. Hardin, 'The Tragedy of the Commons', *Science* (1968, Vol. 162) pp. 1243-48.
2   V. Smil, *Environmental Problems in China: Estimates of Economic Costs,* Honolulu: East-West Center Special Report, No. 5, April 1996.
3   R. Broad and J. Cavanaugh, *Plundering Paradise: The Struggle for the Environment in the Philippines,* Berkeley: University of California Press, 1993.
4   J. S. Hammer and S. Shetty, *East Asia's Environment: Principles and Priorities for Action,* Washington, DC: World Bank, Discussion Paper Number 287, 1995.
5   Singapore represents a rather extreme case. Whereas forests take up 3 percent of the land area, golf courses take up 2 percent. There are plans for 30 golf courses to be in operation by the year 2000 to serve its projected population of 4 million.
6   G. McCormack, *The Emptiness of Japanese Affluence,* Armonk, NY: M. E. Sharpe, 1996.
7   T. Ito, *The Japanese Economy,* Cambridge, Mass.: The MIT Press, 1992, p. 411.
8   The prospects of the failure of government action in an attempt to correct 'market failure' raise several issues. Once the problems are identified and clear goals are set, there must be some convincing argument that these goals are met. Also, it should be certain that other unexpected effects do not offset the expected benefits. Finally, there need to be protections that access to these appointed powers will not lead to predatory behavior.
9   Government policy-induced environmental damage occurs in ways other than the large-scale agricultural mono-culture that it encourages. In the US, the Army Corps of Engineers has radically altered the course of many naturally flowing waterways. The political and economic environments have suffered under centralized economic and social planning.
10 See R. N. Proctor, *Racial Hygiene: Medicine Under the Nazis,* Harvard University Press, 1988.
11 These claims have been disputed on grounds that they either involve exaggerations of catastrophic consequences or relied upon spurious statistical methods. See, for example, R. Gillette, 'The Limits to Growth: Hard Sell for a Computer View of Doomsday', *Science* (10 March 1972) and J. Maddox, *The Limits to Growth: The Case Against,* Council of Europe Document (Number 3233), 1973.

12   S. Moore, 'So Much for "Scarce Resources"', *The Public Interest* (Winter 1992, No. 106), pp. 97-107.

13   T. Anderson and D. Leal, *Free Market Environmentalism*, Boulder: Westview Press, 1991.

9 The end of the 'American Century': Is there decline in the West?

The notion of an 'Asian Century' is usually based upon some fairly simplistic assumptions about a post-millennium shift away from American economic and strategic dominance. The changes that are emerging are not merely a reflection of an apparent decline in America's global reach. Instead, the underlying reality is that the internationalization of commerce and the globalization of human relations have speeded up the modernization process and narrowed the gap between the US and emerging economies. Consequently, the power and position of the US no longer inspire awe. However, changing the relative positions of the players in the competitive global economy is not a zero-sum game where the rise of one region or country displaces others. Just as free trade provides an opportunity for all partners to gain, the fruits of the next century will be more widely shared.

In addition to the impact of modernization and internationalization, there are other influences at work that are changing the perception of the role of the American and other Western industrialized powers (including Japan) in East Asia. The local and regional media in East Asia provide fairly uncritical views on development in that region. As suggested in Chapters Five and Seven, the international media have been extremely subdued in their criticisms. At the same time, they have been less than reserved in their disparagement of the West.

It is troubling that this distorted media reporting provides an important basis of public policy formation. Perhaps worse, there is evidence that the considerable amount of money spent on lobbying by foreign interests can subvert the democratic process. To complicate matters further, funds are provided by foreign governments or commercial interests in order to influence otherwise independent American institutions that provide 'objective' studies in support of public policy initiatives.

Another factor fostering the perception that America is in decline with respect to East Asia is the impression that the American military is retreating from that region. However, it would be wrong to suppose that American policy makers lack either the resolve or the interest in remaining solidly engaged in East Asia. While there has been some rationalization of the number and location of armed forces, there has been no diminution in the depth or the breadth of America's military and economic presence in East Asia. The closures of bases at Clark Air Base in the Philippines and of Subic Bay and , as well as the highly publicized reduction of forces in Okinawa, have been offset by other arrangements. In any event, most of these changes are consistent with the changing mission and capability of American forces, whereby more sophisticated weaponry is substituted for military personnel.

Taken together, all of the above have created the popular perception that Asian institutions have followed a superior development model while the US and other Western industrialized countries have languished. Optimism about East Asia's growth prospects is such that one might conclude that the region is now immune to the business cycle. The conventional wisdom had been that the adoption of the efficient production techniques associated with the Japanese model accounted for the vibrant economic performance of the 'miracle' economies in the region. Now with Japan mired in a stagnating recession, it remains to be seen how its East Asian disciples can expect to escape the same spiral of over-extended growth.

The media enthralled

The widespread impression that Western institutions are declining while Asian institutions are ascending may be attributed to a systematic bias in media reporting, coupled with some journalists' exaggerated optimism for Asia's prospects. Unlike their Asian counterparts, Western institutions are subject to open and unlimited criticism by critics from within and without. While multicultural skirmishes have created a perception of decay and disarray, political correctness has engendered a sense of disaffection with Western culture. Similarly, the often painful adjustments necessitated by changing global economic realities have fostered an impression of economic decline in the West. At the same time, the stellar growth rates of the emerging Asian economies are highly publicized, with little regard for whether or not the underlying fundamentals provide a permanent basis for prosperity.

More importantly, while there are numerous East Asian commentators ready to join the chorus against the West, few are willing or able to criticize developments in the East. In many Asian countries, censorship and restrictions on information flows relegate the domestic media to cheerleading for the views of the incumbent parties. In addition, 'sound byte' media coverage lends itself to deft manipulation by Asian authoritarian leaders, whose grand pronouncements make good headlines, but which cannot withstand in-depth scrutiny.

This unbalanced portrayal of East and West is used by authoritarian leaders to justify the 'Asian Model' of development, which offers to purge the unsavory influences of the West from the modernizing experience of East Asians. Among these insidious influences are Western concepts of individual freedom and rights, multiparty democracy, and a free press.

The perceived 'success' of the East Asian economies may be the result of a misplaced emphasis on the specific outcomes observed over a relatively limited time period. While it is true that some economies in the region have recorded rapid growth with an equitable distribution of income for thirty years or more, history is replete with numerous examples of institutional arrangements with fundamental and ultimately fatal defects which are able to generate favorable results for an extended period of time. In addition to the Spanish economy under Generalissimo Franco, the economies under South Africa's apartheid regime and the Soviet Union exhibited high growth rates before internal contradictions caused their collapse. Similarly, the economies of Cambodia, Laos, North Korea, and Vietnam were able to chug along for several decades.

More important than these temporary results is whether the underlying institutions can provide a permanent basis for growth that withstands business cycles and external shocks. Despite its flaws, Western capitalism features supporting institutions that have allowed it to be resilient, adaptable, and durable enough to survive all the stresses and ideological challenges that have emerged over the past several centuries. Unfortunately, the institutions that are credited with having been the basis for the rise of East Asia may lack such flexibility and resiliency, thereby making it difficult for them to respond to the hazards of a globalized economy.

Buying of the western mind

In order to further the distorted image of Asian superiority emanating from the regional and international media, a variety of East Asian interests have applied considerable pressure to influence public opinion in foreign capitals. Lobbying efforts by Japanese firms and government agencies to gain influence in Washington have been well documented.[1] This issue achieved prominence during the 1996 American presidential campaign when it was revealed that some of President Clinton's political appointees had received large financial payments from influential Indonesian interests. It also became known that the

Democratic National Committee was forced to return illegal contributions from an American subsidiary of a South Korean conglomerate. Apparently, some individuals and parties interpret international financial support for their domestic political activities as a benign act of public relations on the part of the donor. Others view these measures as part of a dangerous trend that subverts the democratic process by providing a voice to non-citizens. Certainly the issue of conflict of national interests arises in connection with such activities.

From a technical standpoint, the illegality of these actions does not depend upon the degree of involvement of foreign agents in the decision-making apparatus of the government. The inherently corruptive nature of such activity makes it illegal, per se.

Unfortunately, foreign influences over American government policy go beyond direct lobbying efforts. By funding domestic foundations, universities, and think tanks, foreign interests are able to legitimize beneficial policies by gaining the support of ostensibly independent institutions. One study estimates that, up to 1991, Japanese interests have placed over $4.5 billion into American scientific, educational, and economic policy endeavors.[2] These contributions allow foreign donors to sway the direction of university research and possibly gain access to sensitive projects. Also, this harnessing of US brainpower provides cost-effective access to R&D and technological innovations. It is reasonable to assume that the availability of foreign funding is determined by donors' perception of the influence wielded by prospective recipients. By funding the research of sympathetic university professors, foreign organizations gain powerful allies in promoting their causes to students and the general public.

Financial support with strings attached is not limited to Japanese donors. Studies that have examined the funding pattern of the South Korean government have detected a tendency to provide financial support to those American scholars and politicians who lobby on their behalf.[3] A similar problem recently arose in connection with an offer by the Chiang Ching-kuo Foundation of Taiwan to fund a new center for Chinese studies. This offer of $3 million over a ten year period represents a significant addition to the $20 million provided by the foundation since 1989. Although various universities expressed interest in receiving the funds, there was concern that the political strings attached might compromise the academic integrity and independence of their scholars. For example, one of the conditions of funding was that the center be named after the son of anti-communist leader and former Taiwanese president, Chaing Kai-shek. The Taiwanese government provided about one-half of the foundation's $98 million endowment.

In these situations, the most visible experts on foreign relations issues may lose the independence necessary to formulate objective analyses. This being the case, citizens and policy makers can be misled by their conclusions, which may conflict with America's national interest. Equally disturbing are attempts by foreign governments and corporations either to buy or steal the fruits of technological advance from American universities and public or private research institutions.

Retreat of the US military from the region

With the elimination of Cold War tensions, East and Southeast Asian nations feel that there is less of a need for the American military to underpin security interests in the region. Perhaps this sentiment also reflects a residual resentment of the presence of foreign troops on Asian soil, whether invited or not. At the same time, a variety of domestic pressures in the US have raised questions about the willingness of America to continue serving as the world's policeman. Whatever the reasons, there has been a definite reduction in US armed forces strength in Asia, bespeaking a trend that is likely to continue.

Reductions in the physical presence America's military are offset by its ability to generate and apply advanced technologies. Obviously, the capacity to project its military prowess across the globe is a function of the dominance of US industries in advanced fields like microelectronics or even genetic engineering. Likewise, the professional status of American military forces provides disciplined soldiers and officers that are trained to answer many different assignments from their civilian overseers.

Nonetheless, serious commitments remain through joint defense agreements throughout Asia. US forces continue to hold joint military exercises with their counterparts from many East Asian countries. In mid-1996, Australia offered access to a vast area in the Northern Territory near Darwin to be used as a permanent training facility. Base access accords have also been reached with smaller countries like Singapore, and even the Sultanate of Brunei.

Presumed superiority of Asian models of management

A variety of circumstances have conspired to create the impression that Asians have discovered a superior model of economic development. In large measure, this impression was driven by erroneous perceptions of extravagant wealth in Japan. This illusion was partly based upon the sky-high property values associated with Japan's 'bubble economy,' and the subsequent rise in the value of the Japanese yen. At the same time, Japanese firms have built an impressive record of vanquishing their competitors in markets around the world, despite having the burden of 'lifetime employment' and while maintaining a deep

169

commitment to production quality. Adding to the myth in the 1980s was a wave of high-profile acquisitions of US real estate and corporate interests by Asian investors, and most especially the Japanese.

The Japanese management approach is characterized by an emphasis upon gaining or holding market share even if profits suffer in the short term.[4] This is accomplished in large measure by a commitment to 'total quality management,' itself an innovation of an American management guru.[5] Like their Soviet counterparts, Japanese corporations were thought capable of focusing upon the very long term.

In-reality, the Japanese 'miracle' was based upon three key factors that actually heightened the vulnerability of the economy to the business cycle's inevitable downturn. First, the Japanese manufacturing powerhouses are technological 'parasites.' Although they are unquestionably adept at applying mass-production techniques to processes developed elsewhere, they are unable to generate the true invention that would allow them to mitigate or overcome business downturns.

Second, Japanese companies were able to make significant incursions into Western markets through the affirmative interventions of MITI, which promoted protectionist policies aimed at insulating domestic companies from true global competition. As long as foreigners were kept out of the Japanese domestic market, Japanese companies were able to pass along to Japanese consumers the costs of 'lifetime employment.'

Third, the heavily regulated nature of the Japanese economy discouraged true performance measurement in key sectors, especially banking. The deliberate lack of transparency allowed mediocrity and unsound business judgment to go undetected and undisciplined until reaching crisis proportions.

All of the above combined to prevent Japan from responding to the challenges posed by the stubborn recession of the 1990s. Ironically, even the previously reciprocal relationship between MITI and Japanese corporations has broken down, owing to the now multinational profile of powerhouses like Sony and Matsushita. These entities are no longer sufficiently 'Japanese' to have interests that coincide with the protectionist bent of MITI.

Conventional wisdom attributes the vibrant economic performance of East Asian newly industrialized economies (NICs) to the ruthless application of efficient production techniques associated with the Japanese model. This simplistic impression is seemingly supported by an annual growth rate over the past 25 years that has averaged between 6 and 8 percent for the NICs. However, there is compelling evidence that the NICs have lagged in terms of productive efficiency in comparison to the major industrialized countries. Although these mature economies have only averaged about 3.1 percent annual growth over the same period, they have registered significant productivity gains.[6]

Capital accumulation accounted for about 65 percent of the reported economic growth for the NICs for most of their high-growth period. At the same time, their expenditures on education and health care account for 15 percent of their economic growth. Interestingly, technical progress accounted for none of the economic growth of the NICs, while it accounted for 50 percent of economic growth in industrialized countries. Part of the difference is due to the fact that the development and application of 'managerial software' in the NICs lagged considerably behind the developed economies.

There is substantial evidence to support the contention that economic growth in the NICs has been based primarily upon mobilizing the substantial savings from the region and reinvesting profits. Since this strategy neglects internal R&D and technological innovation, it can only be expected to work in the early stages of development. Thus, it is only a matter of time before the NICs begin to experience the pangs of overextended growth similar to their mentor country, Japan.

In order to correct some of the weaknesses of the Japanese system, MITI has introduced a new industrial policy that is designed to encourage nascent firms. A new stock market that will operate along the lines of the US-based NASDAQ will be a source of capital for startup businesses. Legislation is also being considered to allow for the introduction of an American-style incentive-compensation plan involving the provision of stock options to managers.[7] This approach reflects an attempt to encourage entrepreneurship by breaking the mold of conservative business practices in Japan that thrive on order and predictability. A new breed of performance-oriented Japanese entrepreneurs is finding a niche by adhering to free market discipline. This sort of unconventional risk-taking is a necessary step toward allowing Japan to develop the sufficiently diversified and responsive economic base that it needs to remain a competitor in the global economy.

Contrary to popular perception, many American firms actually do take the long-term view, as evident in the dominance of America's pharmaceutical industry in the world market. Despite being arguably the most heavily regulated industry in the world, this sector accounted for ten percent of all American companies' profits for the first six years of the 1990s. Similarly, Intel and Microsoft respectively dominate the 'heart' and 'soul' of the electronics industry. R&D investments by these firms have certainly been guided by the long view, and have resulted in American dominance of these strategically critical industries.

From the Information Age to the age of productivity

Much has been made of the impending 'Information Age' as post-industrial rising tide that will inevitably raise all ships. All the observed electronic advances in information distribution are really nothing more than a means to enhance economic production and therefore improve living standards. This can be accomplished only if this newly accessible information can be translated into gains in productivity. With this goal in mind, technical improvements are often combined with changes in managerial strategy, such as out-sourcing and restructuring. The resulting gains in efficiency and productivity of individuals, firms, and industries are eventually reflected in gains in the aggregate measures recorded for their respective countries. Higher productivity leads to rising profitability that in turn allows firms to hire additional workers and to pay higher salaries. It is only in the early stages of development that firms can afford to 'earn ugly,' i.e., by exploiting a competitive advantage of cheap labor with little regard for efficiency. Once markets mature or are opened up to global competition, commensurate gains in productivity become the *sine qua non* for sustainable growth.

Some of the pessimism surrounding the state of the American economy stems from a productivity growth rate that is slower than that of its principal trading partners. For example, US productivity growth declined from 2.7 percent in the 1960s to about 1 percent in the early 1980s.[8] At the same time, comparable measures of productivity gains in Germany and Japan have been markedly higher. However, what is lost in this analysis is a comparison of overall productivity levels. When this is considered, Japanese workers are only about 55 percent as productive, with German workers only about 90 percent as productive as their American counterparts. Measures of capital productivity reveal a similar disparity, with Japanese and German measures at about two-thirds of US levels. From 1985 to 1993, productivity of American industry rose by 35 percent while Japanese productivity rose only about 4 percent.

American productivity gains in recent years have been grounded in an ability to offer innovative and flexible responses to a changing world economic order. These gains were motivated by the loss of the protective cocoon of interventionist legislation, coupled with the sobering effect of competition from foreign producers. US industry rapidly implemented new technology, introduced innovative marketing techniques, increased capital spending, and undertook aggressive restructuring.[9] Between 1983 and 1993, US corporations in the Fortune 500 reduced their payrolls by more than 18 percent (from about 14 million to just over 11 million employees). Over the same period, inflation-adjusted profits increased by more than 57 percent.

It was this increase in profitability that allowed US corporations to invest more, and thereby create more jobs than their principal competitors in Japan and Europe. Over the past decade, 18 million net new jobs for Americans were created. The Japanese economy added 8 million workers to the payrolls, while in Europe only 6.9 million new jobs were created.

Political risks in East Asian emerging markets

Because of their rapidly changing nature, most emerging markets exhibit relatively high political risks. In this context, 'political risk' refers to the negative economic repercussions associated with deliberate government actions in particular, or with government instability in general.

It is likely that most investors in reform-minded Asian economies have been pleased with the economic policies of those governments. Although the willingness to pay will always remain a fundamental question of sovereign analysis, investors can take some comfort in the fact that Asian governments have only twice repudiated their debts: Japan in 1941 and communist China in 1949. Similarly, instances of other commercially disruptive government actions have been rare. For example, although the independence of the central banks in some Asian countries is suspect, investors have generally not had to contend with things like hyperinflation or the unexpected imposition of exchange controls. Even China is making real progress toward the unrestricted convertibility of its currency, the renminbi.

The economic risk posed by government instability is usually associated with disruption to commercial activity caused by internal conflicts like civil war or power struggles. Certainly, this brand of political risk exists in Asia, as evidenced by the questions of political succession in China, and the insecurity of the ruling military junta in Burma-Myanmar. However, a number of countries in the region are perceived as politically stable, thanks to strong authoritarian regimes. Many of these countries, like Malaysia and Singapore, have been able to attract investors because of their ostensible commitment to economic progress, coupled with their ability to control domestic social elements deemed disruptive to business activity.

Unfortunately, the authoritarian nature of many East Asian regimes actually raises the political risks associated with investing in these economies. Because the various one-party or one-family regimes have been in power long enough to perfect political repression, they are able to convey a misleading impression of stability. Such stability is likely to prove illusory and short-lived, however. If authoritarian rulers are too severe, they invite *coup d'etats* or assassination. If they are not strong enough, then the political opposition may sweep them out of office. The riots in Indonesia in July 1996 debunked the myth that the

173

strong control exercised for so long by the Suharto regime was a guarantee of stability.[10] Political risk is exacerbated in despotic situations because there is no legitimate political process for the orderly transition of power. Uncertainty over the succession is taking its toll in China, Indonesia, and Singapore.

As suggested above, secular dynasties have been established in many East Asian countries, even those which claim to be 'democracies.' Such unilateral transfer of political control to one family often occurred in situations where anti-colonial movements were led by charismatic nationalists who became autocrats. By keeping the citizenry ill-informed through the heavy-handed repression of political dissent, Asian autocrats are free to make decisions that are in the best interest of their family, regardless of the impact on the country or foreign investors.

Dynastic succession, a common feature in East Asian politics, is often mistakenly associated with stability. Like other forms of nepotism, intra-family political succession is consistent with the culturally imbedded commitment to family that is said to define social relations in much of Asia. From the standpoint of international investors, however, these Asian 'family values' are just another form of corruption associated with leaders whose authority is seldom challenged.

Where nepotism is prevalent, the community at large is saddled with a variety of tangible and intangible costs. Political costs arise as losses or lessening of civil rights. Nepotism invites economic inefficiency by diverting resources toward a single family or to the cronies of a dominant political party. By interfering with market-based asset allocation mechanisms, nepotism imposes real economic costs upon the greater community and upon investors because returns on gross investment are significantly reduced.

Before inheriting political power, the offspring of authoritarian rulers often develop their own power base, usually as government grants of national monopolies over certain economic sectors. As mentioned previously, Transparency International's 'Corruption Perception Index' identified Indonesia as the world's most corrupt regime in 1995, while in 1996, only nine other countries were more corrupt. Not surprisingly, Indonesia is also the country where relatives of the head of state are the most deeply involved in commercial activities, both national and international in scope. Thus, in most of the more corrupt economies in East Asia, the market-distorting influences of nepotism and special privilege adversely affect native, as well as foreign, business ventures.

In order to conceal their insider dealings, many of the regimes in the region obstruct the sort of transparency in economic affairs that is demanded by responsible international investors. For example, China's tight controls on domestic news reporting have been combined with new restrictions upon the flow of financial and commercial information from international news services, as well as access to the Internet. China's obsession for control over economic data is mirrored by a near-paranoid control of data in Singapore. This behavior makes it impossible for potential long-term investors to obtain all the data they need, and to corroborate independently the data the government eventually does release. Similarly, repression of a free press chokes off an independent source of information about events in these countries that is essential to foreign investors who are unable or unwilling to maintain an actual presence in the debtor countries. This lack of transparency is aggravated by the fact that most Asian countries lack domestic rating agencies to provide an independent assessment of the creditworthiness of local state or private enterprises.[11]

Information controls and capital flows

Asian governments seeking long-term debt capital have been disappointed in, and puzzled by, the relatively small degree to which US long-term investors have participated in financing the Asian 'miracle.'[12] Contrary to conventional wisdom, the reluctance of American pension funds and insurance companies does not reflect a predisposition against investing in exotic lands. Instead, it is the result of a combination of institutional arrangements in East Asian countries that discourage long-term lending. The protracted inability of East Asia to attract long-term debt capital will seriously impede infrastructure development in the region, thereby damaging continued growth prospects. According to the World Bank, as Asia enters the new millennium, it will seek about $1.5 trillion in financing for the development of their telecommunications, power, and transportation systems.

An international comparison of China's highway mileage per million people might be instructive. China's figure of about 540 miles (914 kilometers) is not significantly greater than that of India that has just over 1000 miles (1,784 kilometers) per million inhabitants. The measure in the US is over 15,000 miles (25,326 kilometers) of roads per million people, and in Japan it is about 5,400 miles (9,096 kilometers) per million. China plans to build 120,000 miles (200,000 kilometers) of highways over the next few decades at an estimated cost up to $52 billion.

The recent collapse of Malaysia's Perwaja Terengganu steelworks provides a painful example of investment risk when transparency is sacrificed to serve domestic politics and local patronage. Perwaja was forced to declare bankruptcy in May 1996 due to 'financial irregularities' and mismanagement by Eric Chia, a political appointee of Prime Minister Mahathir Mohamad. At the time of insolvency, Perwaja had accumulated losses amounting to $3 billion, or about twice its paid-in capital, and had about $2.5 billion in long-term debt.

While the government insisted that the company's poor performance was due to market-based factors beyond the control of Perwaja's managers, an audit by Price Waterhouse suggests otherwise. It appears that there was mismanagement of accounts, poor assessment of performance, and questionable procedures for tendering supply contracts and capital expenditures. It also appears that the board of directors took no active role in oversight of the firm's operation during the time when the huge losses were accumulated.

To stem recriminations and to avoid liquidation, the government maintained a minority share (19 percent) while the rest of the steel maker was taken over by a consortium of private investors. Although debt holders were not impaired, the Perwaja episode teaches prospective foreign investors two cautionary lessons. First, the optimistic pronouncements of government officials should not replace objective and verifiable financial reporting. As late as 1994, Prime Minister Mahathir publicly praised the now-discredited efforts of his appointee, Eric Chia. Second, long-term debt investments should only be made in those Asian corporations with a Western-style system of corporate governance to insure that fraud cannot go undetected by the company's board of directors.

With such high-level high jinks, the reluctance of American institutional investors to get heavily involved in Asia is not surprising. It is ironic that while explicit barriers to international capital flows have fallen generally, many Asian governments have policies that obstruct or impede the flow of information demanded by responsible investors demand. Interfering with information flows not only goes against a global trend, but is also antithetical to those country's long-run economic interests.

The essence of the problem is that political restrictions on data frustrate attempts by American institutional investors to exercise 'due diligence' in assessing the risk/reward profile of long-term Asian investments. 'Due diligence' is not simply based upon analysis of financial or economic data available at the moment of the investment decision. These long-term institutional investors follow a more 'organic' approach when considering foreign placements. This holistic method involves three basic elements. First, the relevant economic and financial data at hand must be timely, informative, reliable and amenable to independent verification. Second, the investor must be reasonably well-informed about the social and political situation of the government in question. Third, the fiduciary must be assured that reliable information channels are in place so that economic and political developments may be adequately monitored on an ongoing basis.

Government manipulation of investors' perceptions through the selective release and distortion of economic data is disturbingly common in parts of Asia. Making matters worse, the financial and political infrastructure of most Asian sovereigns precludes the pursuance of due diligence as outlined above.

For example, even Hong Kong does not publish capital flows. China's economic data are exceptionally problematic. The regime's obsession for control and frequent manipulation of its numbers preclude meaningful analysis.

Even an ostensible economic powerhouse like Singapore has disclosure problems. Based on data derived from the IMF and Singapore national government sources, a Goldman Sachs report has noted that in the balance of payments, three-quarters of the 1994 current account surplus and all of the surplus for the first three quarters of 1995 were exceeded by unexplained capital outflows, by errors and omissions.[13] In turn, it appears that the bulk of GDP expansion was explained by the statistical discrepancy.

Because the record of high economic growth is a major attraction for investors to East Asia, the integrity and verifiability of these data are crucially important. Attempts by investors to obtain relevant information are often met with reticence on the part of Asian government officials, especially those representing authoritarian regimes. Accustomed to a deferential citizenry, such officials often expect foreign investors to refrain from questioning in accordance with 'Asian values' that are an implicit part of their paternalistic social order. The conduct of due diligence is therefore sometimes mistakenly viewed as a sign of disrespect.

In the end, the opaqueness created by authoritarian regimes will be self-defeating. Transparency of contracts within a judicial system that offers protections to individual contractual parties is certain to become an increasingly important determinant of competitive advantage in a globalized economy. Western contract law is grounded in protections of individual interests in economic, as well as political, arrangements. For the most part, such a value system is incompatible with the priority placed by most Asian authoritarian regimes on community welfare versus individual rights. In the absence of individualist-based economic institutions, it is likely that outsiders will be obliged to consort with commercial elites, whose economic influence contributes to an inefficient oligopolistic market structure.

Stifling domestic political discourse by suppressing contrary views will also hamper investors and financial sleuths in their quest for reliable intelligence. For example, tight controls on domestic news reporting are evident in the twelve-year prison sentence given to a Hong Kong based journalist who reported on the Chinese central bank's interest rate and gold reserve policies. It was asserted by prosecutors that this data was a state secret. China has also announced its intention to restrict the flow of financial and commercial information from international news services. While the limits placed upon political debate in Singapore are well known, the ruling party went has also gone to great lengths to punish individuals for leaking economic data. In 1994, several journalists, a private investment adviser, and a civil servant were prosecuted for publishing quarterly GDP estimates before these data were officially released.

Such obsessive control of data thwarts the sort of independent corroboration that long-term investors will demand. The absence of committed, long-term investors partially explains the wide and wild swings in the stock markets of Asia's emerging economies. In this regard, the *Economist* reported that Americans kept more than 90 percent of their assets at home, even though the American securities markets accounted for less than half of the world's market capitalization.

An argument for increased freedom of information is supported by 'efficient markets theory.' This theory suggests that all consequential information is factored into debt prices. As such, the relatively high prices of Asian government bonds should provide evidence of their good and fair value. One problem with this reasoning, however, is that large proportion of these bonds is usually placed with Asian investors. As is the case of less sophisticated traders in other emerging markets, Asian investors do not conduct as comprehensive a due diligence investigation as their Western counterparts. Therefore, a notion of market efficiency in such settings is misleading, at least in the short run.

It might be argued that the due diligence responsibility of US institutional investors can be fulfilled by relying upon investment bank research and Moody's or Standard & Poors ratings. However, a conflict of interest arises when investment banks provide data on the quality of the government issues that they are selling. Similarly, investment bankers vying for debt origination mandates in a highly competitive setting are reluctant to publish brutally honest research reports for fear of offending current and prospective clients. With respect to rating agencies, they do not have superior access to non-public information. (If they did, this would raise questions over insider trading.) In any case, the rating agencies were clearly no more prescient about the Mexican meltdown than anyone else. At best, the rating agencies tend to be a lagging indicator of sovereign integrity.

Although economic analysis is the bedrock of any investment decision, an evaluation of the social and political conditions of the host country constitutes an integral component of long-term lending. For those financial institutions unwilling or unable to maintain a physical presence in the debtor nation, a reasonably free indigenous press serves as an indispensable tool for gauging and monitoring political risk. Unfortunately, press freedoms tend to be severely circumscribed throughout much of East Asia. A 1996 survey by Freedom House indicates that the print and broadcast media of China, Indonesia, Malaysia, and Singapore are among the least free in the world. This problem is compounded by the demonstrated willingness of the international media to censor itself to avoid sanctions from authoritarian governments. Besides diminishing their utility to investors, media self-censorship also undermines the development and survival of reliable information channels that enable fiduciaries to monitor their investments on an ongoing basis.

In asserting that 'Asian values' serve as the basis of their impressive record of growth, some East Asian regimes insist that freedom of information is not consistent with the traditions that served their economies so well. However, the imposition of control over information is one area where cultural values may impose more costs than benefits. Many East Asian countries are ruled by one party or one family. These autocratic leaders are unaccustomed to answering questions, and they have a serious problem understanding outsiders' insistence upon independent verification of their government's data.

The considerable evidence of self-censorship among the international media operating in Asia is especially disappointing. Part of this can be explained as a balancing act between principles of journalism and the bottom line. However, attempts to avoid stepping on the toes of authoritarian governments will prove to be shortsighted. On the one hand, self-censorship diminishes the value of media channels as an information source to investors who seek background on foreign countries. On the other hand, it undermines the survival of the independent media by undercutting the safety and integrity of the institutions of the Fourth Estate.

Economic pragmatism provides support for greater freedom in the flow of all information that rivals any arguments based upon an ideological commitment. Unimpeded information flows are the lifeblood of the global economy. Consequently, speech and press freedoms can no longer be considered 'Western peculiarities' because they are evolving into universal values. Governments in East Asia and elsewhere that would block these essential freedoms jeopardize the economic well being of their citizens and their own political survival.

The future of Asian trade deficits?

As is the case with most emerging markets, the much-vaunted growth of the Asian Tigers was led by exports of relatively low value-added goods to mature economies like Europe and America. However, by the mid-1990s, a variety of circumstances have culminated in a widespread slowdown in the capacity of Asian economies to export, especially in the area of consumer electronics. On the demand side, prices predictably began to decline for electronics goods in the mature markets of North America and Europe due to global overcapacity. On the supply side, the strengthening of the dollar *vis a vis* the yen and other Asian currencies actually weakened exports from the region since most output is priced in dollars. At the same time, production costs in East Asia have risen as wages, interest rates, and land prices continued their upward climb. In sum, excess global capacity and inventory buildup have taken their toll as East Asia's relatively low value-added export markets have become saturated.

Declining fortunes in the US semiconductor business are no longer limited to sagging values in the Dow Jones Average. These setbacks sent shock waves into most East Asian economies. A major factor contributing to the rise in Asian trade deficits is the over-concentration of many regional economies in a few industries. This has become problematic because many of these industries are acutely vulnerable to pricing pressures stemming from excess production capacity worldwide. For example, Singapore's government revised its GDP growth forecast downward twice during 1996 due to a downturn in the electronics industry. Third quarter growth was reported to be only 3.2 percent, the lowest rate in over a decade. This poor performance of Singapore's economy can be explained by the fact that electronics production generates about 15 percent of Singapore's GDP and accounts for about 52 percent of all manufacturing output.

Consequently, trade deficits for many of the countries in the region are beginning to grow at the high pace formerly associated with GDP growth. For example, 1995 GDP growth for Indonesia, Malaysia, and Thailand were 7.3 percent, 9.6 percent, and 8.5 percent, respectively. At the same time, their current account deficits as a proportion of GDP were 4 percent, 9 percent, and 7 percent, respectively.

These statistics seem to follow the typical life cycle progression of emerging economies from trade surpluses to trade deficits. To meet growing infrastructure requirements and to maintain growth, most of these countries had to attract substantial foreign direct investment and loans, leading to upward pressure on the exchange rates of their respective currencies. As a result, exports become more 'expensive,' and therefore less attractive to those countries with relatively weaker currencies. At the same time, imports become 'cheaper' and more attractive to domestic consumers. On balance, the current account begins to move toward a deficit, or trade surpluses begin to shrink. Since most of the emerging economies pursue export-oriented growth strategies, this development will seem unwelcome.

Indeed, export growth has slowed for many East Asian high-growth economies, with several now running significant current account deficits. For example, Thailand's exports rose only seven percent in value in the first half of 1996, compared with a 27 percent rise in the previous year. China's exports have actually fallen. Malaysia and Thailand seem to be running current account deficits of about 10 percent and 8 percent of GDP respectively for 1996. This figures are alarmingly familiar to Mexico's situation in 1994. Even South Korea is not immune, with a current account deficit of about two percent of GDP for the first half of 1996.

Of greater concern, however, are the economic consequences of the expedient solutions offered by the region's policy makers. Prime Minister Mahathir of Malaysia has hinted at import controls on 'non-essential' goods. South Korea and Thailand have begun official campaigns to discourage luxury imports. Alternatively, many of these countries may resort to intervention on the world currency markets by their central banks in an attempt to restore a more favorable balance in their trade accounts. This would involve pushing the value of their currencies down and so improve the international competitiveness of their country's products and services.

However, all these remedial measures are fraught with peril. Import restrictions can have dangerous implications for economies that depend heavily on free trade. An exchange rate policy aimed at maintaining an under-valued currency can often undermine monetary control by making it hard to raise interest rates. In addition, the heavy inflows of capital in recent years have caused rapid expansion in the growth rate of the money supply, which in turn triggers inflation or higher imports. Easier money has also facilitated unwise investment in projects that do not enhance these countries' long-term export potential. While constructing the world's tallest building in Kuala Lumpur may provide Malaysia with a prestigious status symbol, it contributes little to the country's long-run current account position.

As mentioned earlier, Asia's emerging economies have been a magnet for foreign capital inflows. These funds arrive as direct investment in factories and equipment, loans, and as bond purchases or equity purchases. While these inflows are attractive and help provide the basis for continued growth, this process may result in some unwanted side-effects.

The most immediate consequence is that countries that are recipients of large inflows of foreign capital will see the international value of their currencies tend to rise. Under these circumstances, a deficit in the trade accounts is nearly unavoidable as their competitive position worsens. However, the instinctive reaction of policy makers to these developments may worsen the situation.

Thus, emerging economy policy makers can find themselves between a political rock and an economic hard place. Economic growth and rising living standards supported by exports have provided legitimization for political leadership. As exchange rates appreciate, it will mean that those enterprises engaged in international trade will lose their competitive edge. However, rising domestic inflation will have the same effect and will impact more generally upon the citizenry. Both of these outcomes will be politically unpopular, but they differ in terms of the timing of their impacts.

Political survival considerations generally induce policy makers to avoid short-term costs by shifting them to the long run. This way, someone else might be blamed for the future ills since the remote relationship between cause

181

and effect may not be well understood. Inflation tomorrow will almost certainly appear to be preferable to lower growth today for all but the most disciplined policy makers. Since equity markets suffer when inflation raises its ugly head, the East Asian high-growth economies seem poised for another round in the boom-and-bust cycle of Asia's stock markets.

Slowdown in East Asian economic growth: Structural or cyclical?

The decline in growth rates and the appearance of either current-account deficits or shrinking surpluses in most of the East Asian economies beginning in 1996 has prompted an important debate. There are differing views over whether these declines are part of a temporary, cyclical downturn or whether this is the beginning of a long-term structural slowdown for the region. Whatever the outcome of the debate, there is one consensus. There is little confidence that the East Asian economies will be able to rebound to the average rate of nearly eight percent recorded in 1995.

Regardless of the nature of the decline in economic growth in East Asia, the region is undergoing interesting changes and faces formidable challenges. Initially, the growing dependency upon intra-regional trade was viewed as a strength that would lend stability to the economies in the region. However, as economic growth has slowed for most regional trading partners, this increased economic interdependency has begun to look like a weakness. The economic slowdown in neighboring countries has amplified the problems of decreased exports to developed economies in Europe and North America. Unfortunately, the slump in East Asian exports has continued despite recoveries in many major markets, such as the US and Europe.

The most apparent problem is the excess capacity in East Asia's electronics industry due to a slump in global demand. This has been combined with unwelcome currency realignments due to the rapid rise and decline of the Japanese yen. In particular, South Korea and Thailand have developed large current account deficits. If these imbalances persist, they will have to be financed through short-term foreign exchange inflows. However, the normal policy to accomplish this, raising domestic interest rates, might cause growth to slow further. Obviously, these effects would reverberate across the region as government central banks attempted to stabilize the values of their own currencies. Due to their heavy dependence upon imported machinery or other inputs, devaluation is not a viable option for most East Asian economies.

In order to boost profits many industries in the region are trying to climb up the value-added ladder to offer higher quality products. These attempts are fraught with difficulty. On the one hand, the family-oriented businesses common to much of East Asia seem unsuited to high-tech industries. Their inher-

182

ent conservatism makes them slow to change policy, a curse in the face of high-paced technological change. Another problem relates to their reluctance to hire skilled managers from outside the family. On the other hand, as more capital-intensive production techniques are introduced, skilled labor shortages will push wages higher. Many multinationals operating in East Asia have already found that high and rising wages are undermining the competitive advantage of operating there.

It appears that there is considerable evidence supporting the notion that East Asia's economic problems are structural and long-term. Most obvious is the problem of bottlenecks arising from inadequate infrastructure that will plague most of these economies for decades to come.

Notably, the impact of Japan upon the economic fortunes of the region provides the most convincing evidence that the economic growth slowdown is a long-term phenomenon. Most of East Asia's high-growth economies have followed Japan's development model of export-oriented growth overseen by interventionist technocrats. The cycle of this development approach now finds Japan's economy mired in a long-term slump that began in the early 1990s.

As the other economies in the region begin to mature, they will begin to experience some of the same sorts of problems evident in Japan. Domestic industries are finding themselves hamstrung by rules and regulation that once served to protect them from outside competition. With the development of a global economy, capital, technology, information, and management skills have become increasingly mobile. The dead hand of ever-vigilant bureaucrats and technocrats will slow the capacity of the economies to respond to the demands of global competition.

East Asian infrastructure and long-term international capital

There will be numerous opportunities to invest in East Asia over the next decade. In order to accommodate expanding markets, countries in the region must undertake massive infrastructural development. Of the total of $1.5 trillion in expenditures expected by the World Bank, $600 billion needs to be directed toward improving port facilities, roads and other transportation systems. About $500 billion will be spent for expanded power capacity, $250 billion on telecommunication, and about $150 billion for water and sanitation facilities. Although this sum is large, it would only constitute about seven percent of average GDP for the region's economies. Even so, this represents an increase from four percent in 1994.

Unfortunately, the underdeveloped capital markets of the emerging economies of East Asia are likely to impose limits upon their capacity to grow due to a shortage of long-term capital lending. Despite high rates of household savings, the region's capital markets remain inefficient and far more underdeveloped than their trading systems. Emerging Asia-Pacific economies must develop a more efficient means to channel domestic savings and to attract international capital to provide funding for infrastructural investments in telecommunications as well as power and transport systems.

Several problems loom large in the provision of domestic or even regional funds for development projects in East Asia. On the one hand, a large proportion of the business assets in the region is held by family-owned companies that tend to be narrowly concentrated on trade or property development. On the other hand, widespread government ownership requires that a substantial amount of funding for business expansion will involve the issuance of public debt. Eventually, widespread privatization will allow capital to be raised through the sale of stocks and equities. However, firms based in East Asia will have to shed their preference for secrecy. Potential investors from outside the region will demand greater transparency before lending. Similarly, East Asian investments must offer a more attractive risk/return profile in order to attract funds away from emerging markets in other areas, like Latin America or Eastern Europe.

Another problem is the protracted payoff period from infrastructure investing. Most capital investments in plants, equipment or inventories by private enterprises can earn timely and visible returns to shareholders. However, large infrastructure projects may take decades before having a real impact on the economy. As domestic credit markets are tapped for these projects, funds that might have gone into productive activities that would expand the tax base are diverted into roads, bridges, rapid transit, ports, and power supplies whose beneficial impact will only be felt in the distant future.

In sum, despite having domestic saving rates of 30 percent and higher, East Asian economies do not mobilize their capital efficiently. Historical mistrust of financial institutions leads to high demands for liquidity by savers. In turn, the high stock of savings has not been transformed effectively into long-term investment. Governments and private borrowers in East Asia must develop more transparent and legally reliable investment frameworks. These include improved corporate governance, clearing and payment systems, acceptable accounting standards, and credit-rating systems.

Equity purchases in East Asian emerging markets

Inflows of long-term investment capital have also been discouraged by the wild swings in East Asia's equity markets. Like the equity securities of other emerging markets, East Asian stocks are characterized by a high degree of price volatility. Most recently, the collapse of the Mexican peso in 1994 sent reverberations through all emerging markets, including Asia.

Nonetheless, many investment advisers continue to promote portfolio holdings in emerging markets since the stock markets in most of them have out-performed the stock markets in the more developed economies. Indeed, some amount of price volatility provides opportunities for making lucrative buy/sell decisions. However, too much instability precludes the requisite predictability of return demanded by institutional investors.

There are numerous reasons underlying the volatility of stock markets in East Asia's emerging economies. With their low capitalization, they are susceptible to quick flights of 'hot capital.' These flows might represent movements away from bad news (e.g., *coup d'etats*, drought, strikes, doubts about succession of leaders, inflation, or structural fiscal deficits), or toward good news (e.g., deregulation, privatization, reduction of trade barriers, or structural reforms). Most of these countries provide little reassurance in terms of minimizing political risk, the constancy of real interest rates or stable prices, unimpeded capital movements, and the maintenance of overall economic freedoms. What can be expected is a vicious cycle where market volatility leads to a greater domination by 'hot capital,' which in turn produces greater volatility that frightens off more long-term investment.

In light of these concerns, it is almost certain that economic growth in the region will soon begin to slow. On the one hand, successful financing of public infrastructure will 'crowd out' other domestic investments by forcing up market rates of interest. On the other hand, if the infrastructural projects are not completed, then the capacity of these economies to accommodate high rates of growth will be severely limited. Therefore, it appears that a more sober look at investment opportunities in East Asia is in order.

Conclusion

The allusion to an 'Asian Century' is based upon several misleading images and some faulty logic. On the one hand, it relies upon the impression that the advance of East Asian economies is unquestionable and unstoppable, combined with the assumption of the decay and decline of those economies that rely upon a more Western development model. However, both of these observations are flawed. It seems likely that the rigidities of East Asian institutional political and economic structures will undermine long-term growth prospects in the region. There is also evidence to suggest that the greater flexibility of the industrialized economies will allow them to escape from the prolonged slump that began as the East Asian economies were beginning to enjoy their triumphs.

The requirements of the global economy will be defined by the need for open and efficient transfers of information and technology in the face of increasingly aggressive international competition. Those communities whose economies adjust rapidly will be the real winners in the 'Global Millennium,' as discussed in the next chapter.

Notes

1 P. Choate, *Agents of Influence: How Japan Manipulates America's Political and Economic System*, New York: Touchstone, 1990.

2 S. Epstein, *Buying the American Mind: Japan's Quest for U.S. Ideas in Science, Economic Policy and the Schools*, Washington, DC: The Center for Public Integrity, 1991.

3 See B. Cumings, *Korean Scandal, or American Scandal?*, JPRI Working Paper Number 20, Cardiff, Cal.: Japan Policy Research Institute, May 1996; and *South Korea's Academic Lobby*, JPRI Working Paper Number 7, Cardiff, Cal.: Japan Policy Research Institute, May 1996.

4 The European approach is generally considered to allow for the subordination of profits to high wages or welfare state benefits.

5 W. E. Deming, *The New Economics for Industry, Government, and Education*, Cambridge, MA: MIT Press, 1993.

6 Jong-Il Kim and Laurence Lau, 'The Role of Human Capital in the Economic Growth of the East Asian Newly Industrialized Countries.' Their study compares the growth of the NICs with the economies of France, Great Britain, Japan, the United States, and West Germany.

7 Due to stringent requirements for listing on exchanges in Japan, it took an average of nearly 17 years before companies would go public. Similarly, many of the established venture capital firms would shun companies if they had not been in operation for 10 years.

8 McKinsey Global Institute, 'Capital Productivity', Washington, DC: McKinsey & Company, June 1996.

9 Nike and Chrysler provide a good example of the decentralized corporate model. With all of its production contracted out, Nike owns no production facilities. Its primary assets are its brand loyalty and the image provided by its superstar promoters. Chrysler produces only about 30 percent of the parts it uses.

10 Indeed, it was a question about whether Suharto could withstand an electoral challenge from the daughter of the former ruler, Sukarno, whom he deposed in a power struggle.

11 Notable exceptions are the Rating Agency of Malaysia (RAM) founded in 1990 and the Thai Rating and Information Service (TRIS) founded in

1993. China, Indonesia, and the Philippines have begun to develop systems for rating domestic debt issues.

12 This section has drawn heavily from a jointly-authored paper with T. Wyszomierski, 'More Information, More Money', *Far Eastern Economic Review* (8 August 1996).

13 *Asia Economic Weekly*, 11 December 1995.

10 Summary: Economics and politics in the Global Millennium

The popular consensus of an impending 'Asian Century' is based on the hope that East Asia will realize the full economic potential promised by its impressive track record of material progress. This view has formed gradually over the past two decades since Nixon's seminal visit to China, and now occupies a firm place in Western consciousness. While the notion of the 'Asian Century' as currently understood reflects Western thinking, it has also been enthusiastically adopted by a few opportunistic Asian politicians in order to consolidate their own political standing.

The embrace of market economics by almost all governments in the region is generally considered the panacea that will liberate the region's vast human and natural resources. Thus, there is an expectation that East Asian economies will collectively equal and then surpass the economies of the West. First it was Japan that was expected to overtake the US as the premier economic superpower. Now China is expected to overtake both.

However, predictions about the sustainability of the high performance of East Asian economies are debatable. It is increasingly difficult to create and maintain a competitive advantage due to the globalization of economic activities. Cross-border shifts in capital, technology, information, and management skills are occurring with greater ease and frequency in the expanding, worldwide economy. Consequently, although recent gains in Asian economic competence have enhanced the influence of Asian institutions in world affairs, it does not follow that the West's role in the global order will be supplanted.

Many of the economies in East Asia might be said to have relied upon a form of 'Confucian corporatism' as the paradigm for economic development. This framework involves a close cooperative relationship between technocratic bureaucrats and the business elite. However, except for the overlay of Asian traditions upon economic and political structures, there are few differences between the institutional arrangements and consequences associated

188

with this 'Confucian corporatism' and with other forms of corporatism practiced elsewhere. For example, key elements of Confucianism like 'filial piety,' 'saving face,' and 'society above self' help reinforce the hegemony and hierarchical political structures of Asian corporatist arrangements. In Japan, this arrangement became know as an 'iron triangle' wherein bureaucrats, businesses, and politicians work together under conditions of close consultation.[1] However, this approach to business and government relations has many regional variations. For example, authoritarian regimes in Indonesia, Malaysia, and Singapore follow the close association between their governments and corporate interests as practiced in Japan, but they have relied more heavily upon political repression to maintain one-party rule.[2] While all these regimes tout their acceptance of market forces, they engage in a significant amount of intervention, generally at the urging of technocrats hired to referee the relationship between their governments and various corporate interests.

Unfortunately, most East Asian governments rely upon economic and political institutions that are plagued with internal contradictions and rigidities serving to retard continued development in the region. Ironically, the same institutional arrangements that have been identified as an important element of the East Asian winning formula may ultimately undermine the impressive gains of many of these high-growth economies.

Japan: From rubble to bubble economy to recession to hollowing out?

Japan provided the impetus for growth in Asia and also served as the institutional development model for many of the high-growth Asian economies. However, continued adherence to the Japanese formula will perpetuate the presence of those shared institutionalized rigidities that will in all likelihood lead to a premature end of the 'Asian Century.' Japan's earlier successes created the misleading impression that decisions made by technocrats, bureaucrats or politicians were superior to, and could replace, the decentralized decisions of entrepreneurs and other economic agents.

The myth of Japanese economic invincibility was exploded when, after several decades of spectacular achievement, Japan's economy became mired in a deep recession for the first half of the 1990s. A sign that the bureaucratic grip on Japan's economy has not lessened is found in the government's relentless attempts to boost growth rates by pump priming. Financial stimulus packages for 1994-95 amounted to 19 trillion yen ($170 billion) while 45 trillion yen was spent on similar schemes for the period 1992 to 1994. Consequently, Japan wound up with the worst deficit-to-GDP ratio of any OECD member country.

189

Meanwhile, the outlook for Japan's financial sector remains pessimistic because neither the highly regarded bureaucracy nor the politicians have exhibited sufficient will to undertake the reforms necessary to insure integrity in lending practices and performance measurement. There are expectations that a quarter of the $444 billion loan portfolio of Japan's financial system will be written off as non-recoverable loans, which could lead to the collapse of these lending institutions. Part of the strategy to avert bank failures has been to rely upon mergers. However, faced with restrictions that were designed to protect them from competition, members of Japan's insular banking industry now find themselves hobbled and unable to maneuver. Meanwhile, a face-saving conspiracy of silence between the Ministry of Finance and Japanese bankers has prevented the kind of market scrutiny needed to force resolution of the fundamental problems. This blurring of reality may allow Japan to avoid temporarily the necessary, albeit painful, adjustments. However, such deliberate obfuscation does little to shore up the tarnished reputation of Japan's banking sector.

The cozy institutional arrangements common in Japan have stalled the development of a truly independent and performance-oriented corporate governance function within Japanese firms. This structural lack of oversight and control contributed to massive trading losses at Daiwa Bank in New York and has greatly diminished the credibility of the private and public sectors. In this setting, accountability is directed toward protecting institutions, governments, or political figures, instead of customers, shareholders, or voters. The creation of a contrived sense of stability stifles the momentum necessary for restructuring or deregulation in the face of economic downturns.

Supporting the illusion of Japanese financial stability and economic strength are the continuing trade surpluses with most Western trading partners and, up until recently, an appreciating currency. In truth, Japanese citizens face dramatic rises in unemployment. It is estimated that about 3.5 percent of the people employed within the Japanese manufacturing sector are considered redundant as of the middle of 1996. Contributing to this situation of labor oversupply is the 'hollowing out' of the Japanese economy. This phenomenon continues to occur as Japanese corporations shift more of their production facilities overseas in an attempt to remain competitive. Rising production costs and the strong yen have eliminated the competitive edge on the prices of goods produced in Japan. Consequently, Japan's domestic industrial production has been slow or declining, while business inventories have been rising.

Ironically, while bureaucratization of its economic relations and activities appeared to be helpful in Japan's initial development stages, it has prevented the formulation of timely responses in reaction to changing economic conditions. In addition, the aggressive implementation of conventional policy tools to jump start the Japanese economy has not borne fruit. Neither the reduction

190

of interest rates by the Bank of Japan, nor spendthrift stimulus spending has been able to boost Japan's depressed economic growth rate. Despite the large public sector budget deficits, Japan's corporations are pushing for decreased corporate taxes to remain competitive, and to remain at home.

Given Japan's role as the region's engine of growth and developmental model, the uncertainty surrounding Japan's economic recovery does not bode well for the rest of East Asia. In the first instance, by failing to sustain its critical mass as a source of interregional support for capital investment, Japan's problems may short-circuit the growth path of Asian NICs or other emerging economies. In the second instance, those countries that follow Japanese 'Confucian corporatism' as a model for development are likely to face the same structural problems.

There are hints that Japan's bubble economy is being replicated in neighboring states, even if for different reasons. Inflated property prices and euphoric stock markets, especially in Hong Kong, Singapore and Taiwan, are poised for painful corrections similar to those now being experienced in Japan. Similarly, the oversight failures associated with the Monetary Authority of Singapore (in connection with the collapse of Barings Bank) as well as with the Board of Directors of Perwaja Steel of Malaysia (which required a government bailout from bankruptcy), cast real doubts on continued progress in the region. As suggested above, some analysts have pointed out dangers arising from the glut of real estate development projects in many of East Asia's most rapidly growing cities. These combined sources of volatility suggest that considerable caution is in order when it comes to long-term investment in East Asia.

China: Modernization and fragmentation?

As mentioned earlier, observers in the West experienced a dramatic shift from 'Sinophobia' to 'Sinophoria' during the 1980s. However, the assumptions underlying these expectations of China's future economic dominance are deeply flawed, and may lead to profound disappointment. In addition to its unique internal problems, China's economic and political institutions share many of the weaknesses exhibited by Japan and many other East Asian Tigers.

Even as China moves toward greater overall economic prosperity, it is beset with special problems arising out of growth differentials between urban and provincial areas, as well as the divisive and unsettling influence of fractious political forces. There is considerable evidence that the Beijing leadership is unable to exert centralized control over most of China's far-flung regions. The regime's inability to implement a national tax policy needed to shore up deficient government revenues is but one indication of centrifugal forces undermining central authority in China. Another is overt regional resistance to the various government-sponsored austerity campaigns. Of major concern is Beijing's inability to control corruption that has reached epidemic proportions, including even upper-echelon party cadres. Considering the long-term momentum of these developments, it is conceivable that China might succumb to the fragmenting pressures that are being brought to bear.[3] Put in this context, aggressive actions by the central government in Beijing against the 'rebel province' of Taiwan might be interpreted as a warning signal to other provincial leaders who might entertain the idea of expanding local autonomy too far.

After 1989, the interests of China's provinces have increasingly diverged and political power has undergone substantial *de facto* decentralization. First, existing regional disparities have been exacerbated by uneven development arising out of inefficiencies associated with Beijing's piecemeal approach to reform, as well as the residual effects of central planning. Second, the rulers in Beijing have been unable to muster the political will to eliminate subsidized loans to SOEs which, by increasing the cost of capital for legitimate private enterprise, causes national inflation targets to be missed. The citizens of the less-developed inland provinces have been hit hardest by inflation, because incomes there have not been rising as briskly as in the maritime provinces.

Indeed, the ambiguous nature of the growth targets in China's Ninth Five-Year Plan was widely interpreted as a signal from Beijing to the maritime provinces that they should not grow too fast. This implicitly reflects an admission that this uneven regional economic development is the unfortunate legacy of the former communist government's commitment to extensive state planning in economic and social affairs. Unfortunately, transition policies designed to correct these disparities are fraught with internal contradictions and have therefore have done little to correct this problem. Although agricultural reforms have produced absolute gains, unequal regional development in China or rural-urban income differentials has not been effectively addressed. Adding to these problems are delays in ownership reform, thereby perpetuating distortions in the allocation of resources between the private and public sectors.

It is not surprising that numerous alternative scenarios for the political reconfiguration of China have mushroomed with each stumble by the communist leadership on the road to modernization. Open piracy within China's coastal waterways, the inability to muster the political will to close factories producing pirated software and CDs, and the restiveness of provincial leaders who bridle at Beijing's attempts to restrain growth rates, all contribute to an unsettling trend of increasing political instability. In light of these developments, it will become increasingly difficult for China to maintain the current political and geographic status quo. In all events, modern political logic and modernization forces undermine the notion of stability for a large and disparate country with a highly centralized government.

Therefore, a more guarded optimism about the pace of China's economic advance is in order. In the first instance, there is evidence that the favorable reports on overall economic performance are greatly exaggerated. In the second instance, even if reported growth figures are correct, it is difficult to imagine political and social stability in a country with persistently high inflation and 100 to 200 million displaced workers crowding into the coastal provinces in search of jobs. One of the greatest ironies of China's economic reforms is that domestic credit policies have generated negative real interest rates, thereby encouraging investment in capital intensive production in a country with a vast labor surplus.

Asian economic development: Government policies or 'miracles'?

Obviously, the outlook for Asia's economic prospects has improved markedly from the post-World War II period, when many of the countries were merely teetering along at subsistence levels of income. That so many of these countries have come as far as they have is good news. That these countries will soon be in a position collectively to provide the military, moral, political, and economic leadership of the future after such a brief span of time strains credibility. The assertion that economic interests will be a sufficient glue to hold such a heterogeneous and unsettled region together is tantamount to fantasy.

A troubling feature behind the notion of the 'Asian Century' is the 'triumph of materialism' whereby non-economic considerations are scorned. Although there is no expectation of a major reversal of fortunes for East Asia in the near term, there are serious questions about long-term prospects for an uninterrupted economic growth path. Indeed, history is replete with numerous instances where a solid consensus based on bullish economic forecasts has proved to be wrong.

Conventional wisdom has it that the remarkably nimble transition and modernization of East Asian economies are the result of a proper alignment of government macroeconomic policies accommodating export-led growth. This notion was seemingly confirmed by the apparent success of Japan's highly bureaucratized approach to economic development.

Reactions to the World Bank's observation on the high-performing East Asian economies were varied, with all sides claiming victory for their respective paradigms.[4] Proponents of laissez faire economics tended to interpret the findings as vindication of their models espousing limited government. Proponents of industrial policy viewed the World Bank's observations as support for their models of judicious market intervention. At the same time, however, judicious non-intervention by East Asian governments was cited as a positive performance factor. Most significant was the ability of these countries to control inflation through a sensible approach to fiscal and monetary policies, while allowing

193

currency exchange rates to be competitively determined. The impact of government policies upon past economic growth in East Asia remains unsettled, however. As addressed here, analysis should instead be focused on the future implications of East Asian institutional arrangements and development strategies.

As discussed in Chapter Four, various researchers explained East Asia's high economic growth by examining the contributions of inputs in the context of technological change (as measured by total factor productivity or TFP). This analysis concluded that large increases in inputs of capital and labor accounted for about one-half of the recorded growth in East Asian income over the period studied. Another observation worth noting was the significant positive impact on growth that resulted from the reallocation of resources from the agricultural to the non-farm sector in those countries that began the period with relatively large agrarian economies, i.e., Indonesia, Japan, South Korea, and Taiwan. Subsequent surveys of the growth experience of Hong Kong, Singapore, South Korea, and Taiwan found quite mixed results across countries and over time. Although TFP was identified as a dominant source of growth, there is some indication that there has been a significant deceleration of TFP due to capital or labor market distortions. Government-directed incentives for production tend to interfere with resource allocation due to decision processes that are slow and based on imperfect information. Apparently, industrial policy by the governments in Singapore, South Korea, and Taiwan resulted in rigidities that interfered with efficient market signals.

An integral element of these countries' growth strategy is government-directed investment funded through taxes and forced savings. In addition, governments may be able to stimulate growth by offering subsidies and tax incentives to multinationals, but this can only be a short-run strategy. Just as in the early stages of development in the USSR, many of the East Asian economies have had to make large expenditures on physical and human capital. Although there may be notable differences in their development paths, there are signs that returns on investments in East and Southeast Asia are diminishing, and the volatility of their financial markets is relatively high.

In sum, these studies conclude that the impressive economic growth rates experienced by the East Asian economies cannot be expected to continue over the long run because they were the result of non-repeatable infusions of labor and capital into the economic system. Gains in output from this development strategy are restricted by the 'law of diminishing returns' unless offset by increases in overall productive efficiency. Growth in per-capita income can continue to rise only if there is also a rise in output per unit of inputs. It remains to be seen whether East Asian growth can be sustained by government policies that induce citizens to forgo current consumption in anticipation of future gains.

Some confirmation of the skepticism about the growth rates in East Asia is found in the response of businesses to the rapidly rising operating costs in the region. When rising costs exceed productivity gains, production facilities will migrate to areas where greater profit opportunities are available. Businesses are beginning to reposition themselves to escape rising costs in Japan, and even China, by moving to Malaysia and Indonesia. In early 1996, China's regime announced an intention to rescind tax breaks that had been offered as a lure for new foreign investments. Soaring costs of housing for expatriates in controlled property markets, continued interference and financial impositions from corrupt officials, a scarcity of skilled labor and management talent, and rising delivery costs due to regulations in the transport industry may soon place limits on the growth potential of East Asia's economies.

Comparisons between the economic growth experience of the East Asian economies and the failed communist experiments of Eastern Europe prompted numerous objections. Although this analogy may not hold in all respects, there are striking similarities when it comes to government control of information and repression of dissent. The stifling of free thinking and the open flow of ideas can be expected to have a similar effect upon arresting productive efficiency in East Asia's high-growth economies just as it did in the Soviet economies. Similarly, there is some question as to whether the high pace of growth in East Asia was merely a spurt of 'catch-up' growth as that experienced in the early stages of Soviet communism.

Those Asian countries with remarkably high-growth phases began them long after the Western economies approached maturity. As such, the East Asian economies easily acquired off-the-shelf technologies to apply to their export-oriented industries. This allowed economic modernization to move at a more brisk pace than had been observed in the comparably early phases of development of the more mature Western countries. In addition, the growth spurts of most East Asian economies were exaggerated because they were recorded from the relatively low bases of underdeveloped economies. Another element of the catch-up process can be found in examining the shift of labor and other resources from agrarian production toward industrial output. As the economies began to modernize, labor resources were released from farming and were combined with increasing numbers of women seeking employment. This massive mobilization of the overall labor force allowed a substantial boost in production when combined with new capital investment.

One estimate suggests that the 'miracle' component of East Asian economic growth is less than one percentage point of the annual increase in GDP. To a large extent, the relatively high economic growth rates in East Asia can be explained by technology transfer and factor accumulation. In addition to these economic explanations, this apparent catch-up growth phase was proba-

195

bly also facilitated by the absence of the growth-stunting impacts of competing interest groups evident in more mature political arrangements.

Another reason to question the sustainability of East Asian economic growth is the fact that many countries have depended upon the unchecked exploitation of non-renewable resources. Whereas these limits were experienced in the Philippines during the 1970s, they are now becoming apparent in Indonesia and Thailand. Not surprisingly, these political and commercial interests turn a blind eye to the repressive regime of Burma-Myanmar in hopes of being granted concessions to its untapped lumber and petroleum resources. While the depletion of natural resources robs future generations of their birthright, the obsessive drive for adding to material wealth in the short run is leading to a seriously deteriorating environment for living generations in many of the Asian countries.

The prospects for sustainable growth can be dramatically worsened if private property rights are not properly defined or enforced. Although these problems are not exclusive to Asia, economies where private property rights do not exist, are ambiguous, or are arbitrarily transferred by government officials, have experienced the most damaging exploitation of the natural environment. Many Asian regimes provide bureaucrats or ruling elites with privileged access to contracts or insider information, thereby leading to the depletion of natural resources based upon political rather than economic considerations. In both instances, the absence of civic structures or private initiatives to moderate these decisions has contributed to serious abuse of the environment.

It is to be hoped that many other countries in other regions will soon 'get their basics right,' thereby leading to an increased degree of international competition and a diffusion of comparative advantage. Economies in Latin America and Eastern Europe are now entering the catch-up phase of the growth cycle, while many Asian Tigers are approaching the early stages of maturation. Eventually, the Tiger economies will confront the same sort of restructuring pressures that their own rise forced upon the West. Their ability to adapt in a timely fashion will determine whether Asian economies will dominate the world stage in the next millennium. As discussed earlier, however, Asian economies will be constrained by the limits of economic logic, as well as by the inflexibility of some of their traditional institutions.

The 'miracle' of the East and Southeast Asian economies may be no different from, and no more lasting than, the high-growth record exhibited by the USSR or other countries during the early stages of development. Most East Asian economies have relied upon ready access to technology and markets in the West to fuel their growth. Without developing their own domestic entrepreneurial talent and self-generated technological advance, these countries are doomed to remain parasitic followers, instead of world class leaders. Like Germany and America prior to World War I, the East Asian economies have probably benefited as much from expanding product and resource markets as they have from their own choice of development strategies. Furthermore, the increasingly complicated political relationships that inevitably accompany economic modernization are certain to overwhelm the management and control capacity of authoritarian leadership.

Modernization and tradition in East Asian political economy

One of the most important and controversial debates relating to the political economy of development in East Asia concerns the functional necessity of political authoritarianism for sustained economic growth. Much of the discussion revolves around claims for an Asian version of democracy, a hybrid form of government that ostensibly combines only the 'positive' features of authoritarianism with popular rule. Unfortunately, 'Asian democracy' is, in most cases, merely a mask for reactionary neo-conservatism.

Seductively cloaked in the catch words of progress, 'Asian democracy' is actually often a tool for retarding the forces of modernization and change. These regimes attempt to project an 'open society' image by undertaking economic reforms that presumably set citizens free to seek their fortune in the global marketplace. In reality, although export-oriented policies are promoted at the macro level, these regimes encourage economic growth through a selective but extensive scope of market interventions at the micro level. In addition, many of these governments rationalize the close, and largely opaque, relationship between technocratic bureaucrats and big business on the basis of the apparent success of Japan's 'Confucian corporatism.' At the same time, authoritarian restrictions on political discourse contradict the (misleading) impression of wide-ranging economic freedoms. In most instances, political stability is deemed synonymous with the continued dominance of the ruling party.

Without the mediating influence of the institutions of a 'civil society,' political conversation is reduced to a monologue by rulers guided and supported by technocrats whose loyalty is as crucial to their career path as are their skills. Consistent with Asia's mythic drive toward self-determination, all the Tigers express a commitment to democracy. However, at the core of this Asian variant is an anti-democratic refusal to acknowledge or even allow the expression of their citizens' political preferences. Challenges to the political status quo are often stifled by the explicit and forceful subjugation of the individual to the collective. The justifications for autocratic rule are often based practical, moral, and cultural considerations, including an allusion to the traditional subservience to authority associated with the Asian value of filial piety. Predicating political passivity upon the presumed superiority of the values and visions of the 'virtuous' political leadership, Asian democracies place strict limits

197

upon citizens' opportunities to participate in politics. In turn, these authoritarian regimes insidiously create a cycle of dependency, political immaturity, and deep insecurity among the populace. It is therefore not surprising that the rank and file have little confidence in their own judgment.

Critical to the region's course of future development are the incentive systems established by such regimes. In this regard, a variety of institutional arrangements have been established that serve to politicize commerce. For example, business politics may involve market intervention motivated by interest group pressures, or preferential arrangements offered by the regime to specific individuals. This form of crony capitalism, (in)famous under the Marcos regime in the Philippines, occurs elsewhere in the region as a subtle form of corruption. These governments may therefore support uneconomic commercial endeavors solely to further their political agenda.

The ruling parties of Asian authoritarian regimes also protect their position by engaging in business transactions that benefit from insider information or political influence. This is observed in many countries with one-party regimes, including China, Indonesia, Malaysia, Singapore, South Korea, and Taiwan. By providing protected access to funds, such 'commercialization of politics' helps to perpetuate political domination by the ruling party. By contributing to corruption, crony capitalism, and money politics, these activities undermine domestic market efficiency and investor confidence.

In general, Asian institutions based upon collectivism are widely seen as a source of strength, and stability underlying the development of the 'miracle' economies. As such, these economies are nominally free enterprise but are largely guided by an authoritarian hand. Where competition is allowed, it is only on terms set by the relevant governments. As such, private sector economic success relies heavily upon a sheltered relationship with the ruling party.

At best, governments are only able to partially fulfill this role of economic arbitrator in the short run, given that an entrepreneur's function extends beyond merely buying low and selling high. In absence of market-driven economic institutions that encourage individual initiative, outsiders must deal with bureaucrats or commercial elites whose economic behavior is biased toward the inefficiency associated with oligopolistic market structures. It is unlikely that ersatz entrepreneurs will be able to provide the innovative spark of 'true' entrepreneurs who improve market efficiency by exploiting market share opportunities, or by instigating changes to the policy framework.

One serious side-effect of the institutionalized collectivism common in parts of East Asia is an 'entrepreneurial brain drain.' Discouragement of institutions that promote individualism will frustrate native entrepreneurs. Disillusioned entrepreneurial free thinkers are therefore likely to seek a more hospitable environment outside the region. The subsequent shortage of domestic entrepreneurial talent eviscerates one of the most important internal sources of innovation-based development. Consequently, these countries are likely to remain dependent upon foreigners for access to markets and creative invention. Although there are opposing views as to whether or not such a dependency is consistent with a high growth path, the fact remains that most East Asia economies depend upon North America and Europe for technological innovations. In addition, the Asian Tiger economies have lacked the creative capacity to solve their lagging productivity problem. The situation is doomed to worsen because those countries without their own source of domestic innovation will face a growing technological gap.

Governments that attempt to control and direct their economies will naturally develop structures that generate internal contradictions and unintended consequences. It is therefore not surprising that corruption is rampant in those East Asian regimes where economic decision-making authority is vested in political functionaries, as opposed to the free market. Most of these regimes rely upon a system built upon party patronage that generates contradictory signals and warped incentive structures. Even though financial corruption is worst among the emerging economies of Asia, South Korea and even Japan face formidable problems. Eventually, the political costs of corruption may culminate in the collapse of ruling coalitions, as experienced with alarming regularity in Japan and now more conspicuously in South Korea.

Motivated by the Asian tradition of 'saving face,' many Asian governments attempt to deceive voters as well as prospective investors by controlling perceptions about the extent of corruption. By promoting consensus and limiting dissent, they can more readily conceal their shortcomings and failures. However, the reality of rampant corruption in these countries inflicts severe economic damage by putting 'clean' businesses at a competitive disadvantage and reducing their profitability.

The loss of economic vitality arising out of the repression of individual-oriented institutions will eventually undermine the political base of these regimes. To make up for the absence of voluntary and spontaneous support derived from open democratic rule, authoritarian regimes will be forced to spend ever larger sums of money to buy the support of the middle class. For example, in Singapore, civil servants receive extravagant compensation to insure their loyalty. Unfortunately, this irresistible monetary lure diverts the educated elite from more productive activities that might better serve the economy. Thus, those government officials who would seek to follow the lead of either Japan's 'Confucian corporatism' or East Asian authoritarian regimes, ignore these problems at their own political peril.

The end of East Asian 'miracles'?

All the euphoria surrounding the spectacular pace of East Asian economic activity cannot change the lessons of history. Fundamentally, there is little reason to expect that the modernization process in East Asia will follow a course that is significantly different from other mature, developed economies.

A more worldly explanation for the 'miracle' of East Asia is that the growth in output experienced by most of the booming economies in the region is the simple and inevitable result of massive injections of inputs. As illustrated by the failure of Soviet-style economies, there are theoretical and practical limits to the rates of economic expansion achievable using this economic development formula. From a theoretical standpoint, this approach is subject to the law of diminishing returns, whereby the incremental output per unit of input steadily decreases, unless offset by improvements in overall productivity. Indeed, many East Asian economies, such as Singapore, have experienced lower growth because productivity gains have lagged far behind nominal output growth.

From a practical standpoint, the global supply of inputs in not infinite. Growth spurts associated with the depletion of non-renewable resources (e.g., long-growth timber and minerals) are not only unsustainable, but could cause long-term reversals for Burma-Myanmar, Cambodia, Laos, and Vietnam. By the beginning of the 1980s, the physical limits to growth based upon natural resource extraction brought an end to expansion in the Philippines. Thailand has begun to show signs of slowing for the same reason. Even Indonesia, with a larger stock of natural resources, will be stretched to extract enough to drive the economy at its heretofore brisk pace. As for human resources, these too are subject to the same law of diminishing returns, as well as obvious physical limits. This being the case, the benefits to economic growth from increases in labor force participation rates and higher educational levels have a logical end.

At the same time, an exaggerated sense of optimism has also prompted the formation of financial and property bubbles in many East Asian emerging economies, similar to Japan's experience during the 1980s. Hong Kong's experience with stratospheric property prices in the early 1990s has been replicated in Singapore, driven partly by the migration of companies and individuals seeking to escape the uncertainty associated with Hong Kong's change of leadership in 1997. In both city-states, soaring real estate prices have made private home ownership a privilege reserved for only the very wealthy. To make matters worse, domestic retail sales have sagged in both Hong Kong and Singapore, with only an anemic recovery visible in late 1996. The retail slump in Singapore caused the closure or operational downsizing of many deep-pocket foreign retailers, such as K-Mart of the US, Galeries Lafayette of France, and Lane Crawford of Hong Kong. However, unlike Hong Kong's real estate sector, Singapore has not yet undergone the inevitable wrenching 'correction' phase that will lower property values to a more realistic level.

Such downward adjustments should come as no surprise. Driven by an expansionary monetary policy, speculative activity in the late 1980s led to absurdly inflated real estate prices. At one point, the aggregate market value of real estate in the urbanized area of Tokyo was estimated to be greater than that for all of the property in the USA. With the appreciation of the yen, property prices plummeted to about 40 percent of their late 1980s peak. Unfortunately for Singaporeans, the price of housing is not the only cost of living factor that is inflated. For example, per capita GDP figures for Singapore are estimated to exceed Australia's. However, Australians have greater access to better quality, lower priced consumer durable goods such as housing or automobiles, than are generally available in Singapore.

For every highly publicized achievement of the East Asian economies, there is a disturbing parallel development associated with the unwillingness of their respective governments to disengage gradually from their economies. Believing their own propaganda or lacking the political will, some governments of East Asia's 'miracle' economies may find it psychologically more difficult to abstain from market interventions than their formerly socialist counterparts in East and Central Europe. Indeed, the acid test may be whether or not the Chinese government can maintain the ideological cognitive dissonance required by 'one country, two systems' to refrain from interfering in Hong Kong's future economic affairs.

Despite its potentially disruptive political implications, the high-growth Asian economies must acknowledge the need for increased flexibility and efficiency in information flows as a precondition for future production. Just as continued world economic growth depends upon a regime of expanding free trade in goods and services, the modern global economy requires access to, and production of, knowledge-based commodities. Social progress also depends upon open competition among political and cultural institutions regardless of their geographic origin. Unfortunately, many Asian authoritarian regimes have imposed a form of 'cultural protectionism' designed to inoculate their citizens against modernizing influences that might encourage the liberalization of individual rights and freedoms. However, impediments to cultural and intellectual exchanges are likely to be as self-defeating as politically-inspired trade protectionism.

As mentioned in Chapter One, Samuel Huntington portrays the post-Cold War future as a 'clash of civilizations.' More specifically, his view is that at least three (and as many as seven or eight) great civilizations are likely to become embroiled in a troubling and unstable struggle for dominance. Due to the increased economic and military power of non-Western civilizations, conflict in the future is seen as occurring along cultural faultlines rather than be-

201

ing based upon ideological or economic frictions. Western cultural dominance can expect to be countered by a globalized inter-cultural struggle. These conflicts are predicted to occur at both local and macro levels. Conflict may develop as localized struggles taking place along territorial fault lines or within transnational forums where newly developed countries seek to assert greater control over international institutions.

While Soviet communism has disappeared and Maoism is on its way out, despotic governments have subtly changed the ways in which they to continue to the challenge the 'liberal capitalism' of the West. However, a clash of civilizations is by no means a *fait accompli*, at least not in a violent sense. Perhaps a more realistic scenario can be defined by the facilitation and widening of more efficient communication flows. What would then emerge is a competitive process whereby citizens choose parts or entire aspects of various cultural arrangements from a global menu. There is no particular reason to expect that the clashes of civilizations will be played out along cultural rather than economic or political lines.

The flow of modern history might then be more accurately interpreted as a mutual exchange of ideas and an evolution of cross-cultural institutional development. By contrast, most of the prolonged, open disharmony in history can readily be identified as civil or intra-cultural wars. As such, these struggles were among peoples of similar cultures rather than antagonists across distinct cultural lines. Similarly, it is inappropriate to ascribe the interaction of cross-cultural institutions as arising solely out of the colonial sword or imperialist dictate.

If the past is not merely a sequence of uninterrupted, internecine clashes of civilizations, then it is probably incorrect to project the future in such a manner. An alternative interpretation of cultural interaction is that 'superior' institutions traverse the globe through a competitive process of adaptation, adoption and imitation. Those institutions that provide the best opportunity for individuals to attain their individual goals within a group setting, and provide the most admirable results are the most likely to be copied. Cultural differences do exist, but there is no evidence that these differences are immutable or result from an absence of a set of fundamental universal values. In an open setting, citizens can choose to graft new or modernized cultural arrangements onto traditional institutions.

In light of the above, the economic record of the Asian Tigers will soon be subjected to daunting challenges. This is especially problematic for the authoritarian regimes in the region, because successful resolution involves choices that are antithetical to one-party regimes. On the one hand, an inability or refusal to adapt to constantly changing realities arising out of the globalized economy may cause rates of economic growth to fall, thereby weakening the government's principal claim to popular support. On the other hand, relaxation of government economic controls will, per se, undermine the regime's political dominance. In the long run, East Asian authoritarian regimes must either adapt or die.

Ultimately, only those countries with flexible and efficient institutions and responsive economic arrangements will attract capital and retain their competitive edge. These conditions underlie innovation-driven growth, which is substantially different from the sort of catch-up growth experienced by many of the East Asian economies. Innovation-driven growth is long-lived, because it is constantly rejuvenated by creative problem-solving and invention. In contrast, although catch-up growth may appear to be meteoric, it is short-lived because it only represents the belated incorporation of technology or ideas that were developed elsewhere. Thus, those governments characterized by strict and inflexible hierarchical rule will inadvertently hinder high rates of economic growth by stunting innovation. In the context of global mega-competition, such a politically self-serving approach is fatally flawed. Unless these governments can create the intellectual environment conducive to technological innovation, the 'miracle' of Asia's stunning economic successes will be short-circuited. Even if East Asian economies are able to avoid some of the more catastrophic contradictions of the East European communist economies, prospects for the 'Asian Century' are no more likely than they might have been for a 'Soviet Century.'

The next millennium will be characterized by competition among institutions and cultures that is as vigorous as any competition in goods and services. Those regimes attempting to thwart this marketplace of ideas will do so at the risk of their long-term survival. Like economic protectionism, cultural isolationism will lead to the same measure of self-inflicted social and political costs. Neither wishful thinking, nor strong-armed authoritarian rule, will be able to hold back the forces behind the 'Global Century.'

The end of the East Asian 'model'?

There are good reasons to applaud the rising economic tide in East Asia. People in the region deserve credit for the initiative and hard work that is pulling them out of what for many decades had been a cycle of grinding poverty. In addition, case studies of the high-growth economies may provide insights for others who wish to boost their economic performance.

To this end, much analysis has been devoted to identifying those underlying factors responsible for the sudden and dramatic change in East Asia's fortunes after decades or even centuries of lackluster economic performance. One explanation points to the contribution of the allegedly distinctive cultural values observed in the region, and the institutions that emerge out of them. However, it is unlikely that these values were the catalyst sparking the Asian 'miracles,' given that they presumably existed alongside disastrous social experiments, such as Chairman Mao's Great Leap Forward or Pol Pot's barbaric socialism. If these values are only contingent factors in the equation, then the real causes of the material gains in East Asia must be found elsewhere.

Although it is not clear that there have been specifically 'Asian values' at work, it does seem possible that some sort of cultural or institutional 'competitive advantage' could exist. This would imply that a unique set of cultural characteristics allows one group of people to be more productive than others. However, there is scant evidence to suggest that Asian workers are more productive than their Western counterparts. Furthermore, there is even less reason to believe that 'hard work' is a long-run substitute for technological advance and invention.

A non-exhaustive list of the values that are supposed to be peculiar to the Asian economic 'miracle' includes unquestioning respect for authority as an extension of filial piety, a deep respect for education as a means for advancement, and a strong work ethic. It may be that these cultural mores constitute an important glue that binds their communities. However, identifying and promoting these values as though they were national treasures are just as likely to be a ruse by regional leaders to rationalize their autocratic regimes.

Secular and religious leaders are often able to influence the content and direction of the culture of their fellow citizens. However, those elements imposed through coercion will be the first to be challenged by the modernization process. The very fact that cultural institutions must be imposed or protected suggests that they are in conflict with the will of the people. It is likely that the most enduring components of culture arise naturally out of the behavior and choices of individuals while seeking to fulfill their life purposes. In this sense, culture and the institutions that it spawns are the result of a 'spontaneous order' whereby cultural conventions survive only if they serve the ends of the bulk of the community.

Clearly, culture and its associated values are the result of an evolutionary community process, not the dictates of an individual or an elite group. Rules and norms that define a given culture are not constructed through a rational act or decision. These rules reflect the actions and decentralized choices of individuals with diverse, even competing, purposes. Attempts by leaders to resist cultural change will eventually be ineffective due to the dynamics of the actions of the general population. Those cultural values that will survive are those that naturally emerge out of human actions, and which promote harmonious human interaction.

Numerous studies show that East and West share the same values, but differ in terms of their priority rankings. Thus, many of the values observed in East Asia are universal in that they can be 'rediscovered' by other countries that may have overlooked them. It may be that the current emphasis of certain values in Asia reflects the region's present stage in the life cycle of economic and political development. These 'Asian values' will endure, and institutional reform will be implemented, only if they facilitate the voluntary interaction of individuals in the pursuit of their private and collective goals. Similarly, they will eventually be abandoned in East Asia if they no longer serve as facilitating mechanisms.

In crediting 'Asian values' for their new prosperity, various Asian leaders and intellectuals have insisted upon protecting their cultural patrimony from the corrupting influence of outsiders. Even if there are regionally-specific values at work, attempts to preserve them will be needless at best, and futile at worst. First, if these cultural norms serve the interests of their communities, they will independently withstand the onslaught of foreign influences. Second, if they are inherently weak, the various protectionist tools of censorship or isolation will not only prove to be ineffective, but will be detrimental to continued economic growth.

One element that is distinctly associated with East Asian culture is the promotion of the community over the individual. It is questionable, however, as to whether a communitarian (community-oriented) approach that suppresses individualism is consistent with sustained growth as economies move along their life cycle. Those East Asian cultural norms dictating that 'the exposed nail is hammered down' or that promote 'society above self' clearly favor and reward gradual change achieved through consensus, rather than innovation achieved through individual initiatives. Enforced consensus is a costly brand of conservatism when it retards responsiveness to outside competition. Despite its apparent social appeal, the communitarian approach is a luxury that few can afford in the rapidly changing global economy.

In sum, the analysis offered here does not bode well for the conservative forces that insist upon promoting and protecting 'Asian values.' Even if the weak case for the existence of such values is accepted as a basis for East Asia's robust economic activity, these values are not likely to serve such ends in the long run. Attempts to preserve or instill these values by keeping out new ideas and stifling individualism are likely to suppress the sort of homegrown innovation that will be necessary for sustained growth in the highly competitive global economy.

The beginning of the Global Millennium

In today's world, economic relationships are increasingly being defined along global lines. Already, a new set of economic realities has rendered the concept of exclusively local or domestic markets virtually obsolete. Given the unprecedented scope of the impending globalization of capital markets along with the enhanced mobility of technology, information, and management skills, it is unclear what the full impact will be on heretofore relatively autonomous economies. As markets become increasingly internationalized, a dramatic change in politics will also occur. The impact of highly mobile managers along with capital and technology will demand that public policies affecting business decisions must take into account the fact that input and output prices are set on the world stage if they ignore global forces. Politicians or producers will eventually find their policies doomed to failure or contributing to the worsening of most citizens' standard of living. Specifically, protectionist policies will be more clearly seen to provide only economic benefits in the short or medium term to special interest groups. Similarly, related increases in employment shall be short-lived, because gains to one sector will be offset by losses to others. Ultimately, the real choices may be reduced to self-inflicted stagnation under autarky, or a momentum toward economic growth through ever-widening trade.

The trend toward globalization of capital markets began in earnest with the liberalization of London's financial markets in 1987, known as the 'Big Bang.' In order to remain competitive, those countries that allowed for the free flow of capital into and out of their countries were forced to deregulate their capital markets. Many of the countries that imposed restrictions on capital outflows found that the same policy impeded capital inflows. Today countries that seriously seek to be plugged into international financial flows have moved toward open capital and foreign exchange markets. Meanwhile, there were accompanying advances in communications technology that dramatically increased the volume and frequency of international capital movements. Consequently, global capital flows serve increasingly as a substitute for trade flows. The economic and political repercussions triggered by these events will be the hallmark of the Global Millennium.

One aspect of this new international trading regime is especially significant for most East Asian countries. Increased transparency and ease of capital flows effectively minimize the impact of interventionist and protectionist policies. By readily flowing around protectionist barriers, capital transfers allow 'foreign' producers to become 'domestic' producers. This relocation of productive activities through the movement of capital arises from both push and pull factors. On the push side, economically irrational domestic policies encourage capital migration. On the pull side, international capital will be attracted to countries whose policy mix generates increased profit opportunities and unrestricted repatriation of those earnings. Therefore, policy makers who wish to attract foreign capital or retain domestic investment, should encourage lower operating costs and reduce financial risks, while allowing greater flexibility in management decisions. Assuming no span of control problems, encouraging companies to develop themselves as multinational enterprises tends to reduce production costs through the rationalization of capacity management. Specifically, by calculating capacity on a global basis, excess capacity in one region can be readily utilized to cover production requirements in another.

Although the liberalizing influence of the Global Millennium will limit the impact of economically irrational decisions, there will continue to be some efficiency lost from interventionist-protectionist policies. However, increased market transparency will make it increasingly difficult for governments to delude their citizens into believing that protectionist policies can preserve or promote jobs in the domestic economy as a whole. Citizens will be better able to see through government intervention that harms them doubly. As consumers, they will recognize that protected markets lead to higher prices and fewer choices. As laborers, they will see that protected markets will lead to greater job insecurity instead of 'lifetime employment.' Most of these detriments will fall upon the least mobile resource, which of course is labor. Domestic job preservation requires government policies that are capital friendly, not protectionist.

Clearly, there is widespread confusion, fear and anger among citizens in low-growth, high-unemployment Western economies. With the discrediting of the welfare state and socialism, the real divisions of economic life have been brought into sharper focus. Economic life is no longer being viewed as a struggle between proletarian and capitalist classes, nor between the rich North and the poor South. The struggle is now more clearly cast as being between those whose fortune depends upon ever-expanding government programs and those who must pay for them. Bureaucrats, politicians and special interest groups exploit productive members of the community through rules, regulations and taxes that promote their own position. As voters come to understand the nature of this struggle they will shun politicians who make false promises of 'creating jobs' and 'growing the economy.' The functioning of representative democracies in the Global Millennium will therefore change in very real ways. One positive result is that less interventionist legislation will be put into place for the narrow gain of special interest groups with the costs borne by the wider community.

In the Global Millennium, interventionist government policies, at least in the long term, will be reduced to populist rhetoric. This outcome represents a step toward a form of international democracy where consumers express their (material and other) values through participation in an increasingly global marketplace. It might be argued that democracy works best when the values of all participants are taken into account. Market transactions result from mutual accord between buyer and seller, producer and consumer. The resulting consensus arising out of voluntary market transactions represents an improvement over majoritarian decision rules. It may be that market transactions impose some costs on individuals who are not directly involved in the deal. However, ill-conceived public policies and bureaucratic inertia impose costs on citizens that are more pervasive and long-lasting. Worse yet, such policies are often coercivics enforced by governments' monopoly on the use legal use of violence. Enhancement of the international flow of factors of production and commodities shall diminish the impact of policies that might otherwise have led to inefficiency and price distortions.

A further consequence of the Global Millennium will be a de-emphasis on formalized agreements for regional economic integration. Interestingly, free trade areas like ASEAN and NAFTA, common markets like the European Union or treaties and associations that broaden global trade like GATT and the WTO are becoming increasingly irrelevant. However, evaluation of these organizations requires a new perspective. In the first instance, a great deal of good will is lost in conflicts over reaching final agreements on these associations. International relations were placed under considerable stress in the negotiations over the Uruguay Round of GATT. Domestic political capital is often dissipated and nationalist divisions are often created, as was the case in Mexico, the US, and Canada concerning the implementation of NAFTA. Once politicians and diplomats comprehend the ramifications of the Global Millennium, however, they will be able to direct their attention to other issues where they might offer real contributions. In terms of election or reelection prospects, the adage that 'all politics are local' may still be true. However, continued economic growth and prosperity require that future policies recognize and adapt to the fact that 'all business is global.'

In the Global Millennium, those communities with the most flexible political institutions and economies will be most able to innovate, and will have the best chance of enjoying continued prosperity. Owing to their short-term outlook and heavy dependence upon technology transfers from other countries, it will be increasingly difficult for trade-based economies to thrive in the long run. Prosperity can be expected to come to those countries whose entrepreneurs can effectively challenge both the economic and the political status quo.

Notes

1   C. Johnson, *Japan, Who Governs? The Rise of the Developmental State*, New York: Norton, 1995.

2   Many of the socialist economies undergoing marketization while seeking to continue with one-party might be aiming toward such a political arrangement. These include Burma-Myanmar, China, Laos, Vietnam and perhaps eventually North Korea.

3   Different views on China's economic and political cohesion can be found in J. A. Goldstone, 'The Coming Collapse of China', *Foreign Policy*, Summer 1995, Vol. 99, pp. 35-53, and Yasheng Huang, 'Why

China Will not Collapse', *Foreign Policy*, Summer 1995, Vol. 99, pp. 54-68.

4   A. Amsden (ed.), 'The World Bank's *The East Asian Miracle: Economic Growth and Public Policy*', *World Development*, 1994, Vol. 22, No. 10, pp. 615-63.

Glossary

APEC is an acronym for Asian-Pacific Economic Cooperation forum. Participants in this forum agree broadly to enhance trade among themselves. APEC participants include Australia, Brunei, Canada, Chile, China, Hong Kong, Indonesia, Japan, Malaysia, Mexico, New Zealand, Papua New Guinea, the Philippines, Singapore, South Korea, Taiwan, Thailand, and the United States.

ARF, the ASEAN Regional Forum, is a security grouping of ASEAN members that also includes other countries with interests in East and Southeast Asia region.

ASEAN, the Association of Southeast Asian Nations, was formed in 1967 by Indonesia, Malaysia, the Philippines, Singapore, and Thailand with Brunei joining in 1984 and Vietnam joining in 1995. Membership for Burma-Myanmar, Cambodia, and Laos is currently under negotiation.

Authoritarian capitalism is a system with extensive freedom in market activities but extensive intrusions by government into citizens' social and political choices. A one-party or one-family state is common. Economic performance primarily depends upon international policies, particularly export-oriented growth policies.

Authoritarian socialism is the combination of extensive government controls over the economy that is matched by substantial political repression. This includes Soviet style, centrally planned economies that are associated with slow economic growth and underdevelopment with lagging social indicators and a one-party state.

Civil society reflects spontaneous emergence of voluntary organizations of citizens that oversee the exercise of power by (democratic) governments. These organizations are a source of the development of interactive skills whereby individuals integrate into the community and also assist in the transmission of cultural values across generations. Counted among these organizations might be religious associations, educational institutions, political parties, newspapers and the media, trade unions or professional associations, and similar groups.

Clash of Civilizations is a hypothesis associated with Samuel Huntington, who projected that future conflicts will be generated by cultural differences rather than by ideological struggles over political or economic interests.

Collective consumption goods have attributes such that if they are provided for one person, they can be enjoyed by an entire community. These attributes are that it is difficult or impossible to exclude anyone from using the good, and if the use of the good by one person does not interfere with its use by others. The most commonly used example is national defense.

Collectivism is an approach to social organization that can be contrasted with individualism. Institutions based upon collectivism promote the interests over the community at the expense of the individual constituents, whereby group rights may be elevated over individual rights.

Command economy is the imposition of a central plan of extensive government control over an economy that might include setting production targets, the socialization or nationalization of property and resources, or the imposition of controls over market prices.

Communitarian democracy is a political system whose supporters feel that setting limits upon individual choices is a necessary means to promote values and standards of the community. Aside from subjugating individual rights, there is a denial of transcultural standards.

Comparative advantage describes a situation where some set of attributes (e.g., superior access to technology or relative abundance of resources) generates a relatively higher level of efficiency to an economic resource of one country.

Constructive engagement describes the trade-based foreign policy approach of ASEAN members that is seen as an effective tool to encourage political liberalization with the transitional authoritarian regimes in the region.

Corporatism involves a system of governance wherein public policies interfere with market forces to benefit special interest groups. Corporatist policy making often leads to trade protectionism or government subsidies for the promotion of certain industries. While benefits accrue to large business concerns or organized labor organizations, the wider community is burdened by higher taxes, fewer choices, and higher prices arising out of restricted competition.

Confucian corporatism exhibits the attributes of conventional corporatism with justifications based upon certain East Asian traditions and cultural institutions.

Crony capitalism describes a dependency relationship wherein a political elite offers protection and special access to markets for business interests that provide political or financial support.

Cruel Choice hypothesis offers support for a pro-authoritarian argument whereby developing economies can most readily experience economic growth if civil and political freedoms are limited. It suggests that without authoritarian restrictions on the polity, demands for redistribution or elements of the welfare state might place a drag on the economic growth potential by undermining political stability.

Cultural protectionism involves a set of policies that attempt to protect a particular set of cultural institutions from dilution or debasement by outside influences.

EAEC, the East Asian Economic Caucus, refers to a grouping of Asian Pacific countries that would address issues relating to the region without providing a voice for outsiders like the US. This association was the suggestion of Prime Minister Mahathir of Malaysia.

East Asia includes Brunei, Burma-Myanmar, Cambodia, China, Hong Kong, Indonesia, Japan, Laos, Malaysia, the Philippines, Singapore, South Korea, Taiwan, Thailand, and Vietnam.

East Asia Co-Prosperity Sphere is the term the Japanese used to describe the area of its conquests from 1936 to the end of World War II.

Filial piety is one of the most common Confucian themes or topics wherein sons owe absolute duty and unquestioning obedience to fathers.

Free rider is a person (country) that seeks benefits from a 'collective consumption good' made available even to those members of community that do not contribute to its provision.

GATT, or the General Agreement on Tariffs and Trade, was a treaty agreement among most trading economies of the world. It has been replaced by the World Trade Organization (WTO).

GDP, or gross domestic product, is an accounting measure of the total value of final goods and services produced in an economy within a year.

Guanxi describes a set of informal arrangements that rely upon family ties or other inside contacts as a means to facilitate business or bureaucratic transactions. This practice is widely known among Chinese traders.

Hegemony in a political context reflects the outcome of attempts by a ruling party to insure its dominance and survival by consolidating or co-opting all bases of power.

Hollowing out occurs when companies maintain their corporate headquarters in their home countries but transfer their production abroad.

Law of diminishing returns describes how increases in the quantity of inputs impact upon the rate of increase in output. When the quantity of at least one input cannot be changed, additions of variable inputs will eventually generate diminishing additional increases in output.

Liberal capitalism is an encompassing system that combines the elements of liberal democracy and market-based capitalism. This involves a commitment to multiparty democracy with relatively few restrictions upon economic freedom.

Liberal democracy is a political system that places a high priority upon the assignment of rights and freedoms to individual citizens in order to protect them from the prospective tyranny of governments.

Lifetime employment describes the promise of permanent employment in Japan that is generally limited to male workers and to companies with 300 or more employees. It is a norm to which many companies aspire, but it has no legal basis.

Liberal Socialism involves a commitment to multiparty democracy but with restrictions upon economic freedom. These restrictions involve a high degree of regulation, heavy taxation for redistributive purposes, and/or protectionist policies. It may also be known as 'social democracy.'

'Miracle' or high-performing Asian economy, as identified by the World Bank. For the purpose of the World Bank study on East Asia's economies, the group includes China, Hong Kong, Indonesia, Japan, Malaysia, Singapore, South Korea, Taiwan, and Thailand.

MITI, the Ministry of International Trade and Industry, is the bureaucracy in Japan that has been credited with much of the industrial policy that has guided post-World War II economic development.

MNC, or multinational corporation, describes commercial enterprises that operate within more than one country.

NAFTA is the North American Free Trade Agreement consisting of Canada, Mexico, and the United States. This constitutes a 'free trade area' wherein barriers to international trade are substantially reduced.

Rent seeking involves the expenditure of resources to induce a government to implement policies that bestow benefits upon an individual or upon members of a special interest group. These actions divert resources from alternative uses that could improve the well-being of the entire community. Lobbying by businesses uses resources that might have gone into R&D or qualitative improvements in production.

Singapore School is represented by a variety of officials linked to the regime who allude to the existence of a unique set 'Asian values.' These values are presumed to contain elements of neo-Confucianism and other attributes that are claimed to be uniquely Asian.

Special interest groups are coalitions formed to apply political leverage in order to further the interests of some subset of the community. These 'distributional coalitions' include consumer groups or labor unions as well as producer cartels. Rent seeking by these groups represents an attempt to gain financial or social advantages for their members. These efforts usually lead to losses for the remainder of the citizens.

Tiger Economies, also know as 'miracle' economies, are the common reference to the Southeast Asian newly industrialized economies, Hong Kong, Singapore, South Korea, and Taiwan. More recently Indonesia, Malaysia, and Thailand have been added to the list of 'baby' tigers.

Total factor productivity (TFP) is a measure of overall changes in the efficiency of inputs (e.g., labor, land, and capital) derived from the adoption of new production technologies.

Tragedy of the commons describes a situation where ownership rights are in suspense or are shared by all. This leads to a distortion of incentives since individual gains from conservation tend to be relatively small. Similarly, the impact of the losses from waste is dispersed over the wider community and has a small impact upon any individual. Thus, there is a tendency for abuse or overuse of commonly held property such as the atmosphere or resources found in international waters.

WTO, the World Trade Organization, is an association of trading countries that have agreed to remove protectionist barriers to trade (e.g., tariffs or quotas). It is the successor organization to the General Agreement on Tariffs and Trade (GATT).

Index

Biggs, B. 20
Bowring, P. 117
brain drain 198
Breslan, J. 27
British Commonwealth 41
Brunei 9, 27, 169, 210, 212
'bubble economy' 68, 169
Burma-Myanmar 4, 9, 15, 19, 20,
   25, 31, 36, 43, 45, 105, 113, 130,
   131, 132, 133, 134, 135, 143,
   147, 152, 159, 173, 196, 200,
   208, 210, 212

Calder, K. 45, 143
Cambodia 4, 9, 19, 20, 25, 27, 35,
   43, 79, 142, 147, 149, 152, 159,
   167, 200, 210, 212
Canada 18, 27, 95, 111, 140, 208,
   210, 213
capital markets 9, 44, 48, 51, 75,
   139, 183, 184, 206
censorship 59, 89, 90, 114, 115,
   118, 121, 125, 152, 166, 179,
   205
Central Provident Fund (CPF) 66
Chen, E. 45, 71
China vii, 2, 4, 8, 9, 10, 12, 15, 16,
   17, 18, 19, 20, 21, 25, 27, 29, 31,
   34, 36, 41, 42, 43, 44, 45, 46, 50,
   51, 54, 56, 58, 59, 60, 65, 66, 67,
   68, 71, 74, 75, 76, 77, 78, 79, 80,
   81, 82, 83, 84, 85, 86, 87, 88, 89,
   90, 91, 92, 93, 94, 95, 96, 97, 98,
   99, 100, 101, 102, 105, 106, 110,
   111, 113, 118, 119, 120, 121,
   126, 128, 131, 135, 136, 137,
   138, 139, 140, 141, 142, 147,
   148, 153, 154, 159, 163, 173,
   174, 175, 177, 178, 180, 187,
   188, 191, 192, 193, 195, 198,
   208, 210, 212, 213
Choate, P. 186

civil society 141, 152, 197, 210
clash of civilizations 7, 201, 202
Cold War II 75, 96, 97, 98, 140
commercialization of politics 111,
   198
competitive advantage 7, 16, 43,
   51, 58, 61, 80, 92, 120, 172, 177,
   183, 188, 196, 204
competitive capitalism 78, 112
'Confucian corporatism' 188, 189,
   191, 197, 199, 211
Confucian values 14
corporatism 189, 211
corruption 5, 10, 33, 34, 35, 37, 50,
   51, 74, 75, 76, 83, 91, 93, 100,
   106, 107, 108, 109, 110, 112,
   132, 150, 154, 160, 174, 192,
   198, 199
crony capitalism 5, 111, 198
Cruel Choice hypothesis 212
'cultural protectionism' 7, 201, 212
Cumings, B. 28, 71, 186

Daiwa Bank 63, 190
Deng Xiaoping 18, 36, 78, 79, 137,
   140
Diaoyu Islands 136
   See also Senkaku Islands
due diligence 176
dynastic politics 117, 124

EAEC 24
   See also East Asian Economic
   Caucus
East Asian Economic Caucus 12,
   128, 212
   See also EAEC
East Asian high-growth economies
   21, 31, 37, 38, 39, 47, 54, 55, 56,
   57, 58, 65, 133, 180, 182, 195
   See also 'miracle' economies

'Tiger' economies 19, 26, 36, 38, 40, 43, 50, 67, 179, 191, 196, 197, 199, 202, 214
See also 'miracle' economies
total factor productivity 68
See also TFP
total quality management 170
'tragedy of the commons' 146, 152, 214
transparency viii, 5, 33, 64, 66, 87, 89, 109, 136, 170, 174, 175, 177, 184, 206, 207
Transparency International 34, 51, 71, 106, 174
Tung Chee-hwa 86

United States 2, 18, 27, 28, 123, 124, 186, 210, 213

Vietnam 4, 9, 10, 18, 19, 20, 25, 27, 36, 43, 45, 59, 66, 79, 105, 110, 120, 126, 127, 147, 152, 159, 167, 200, 208, 210, 212
Vittachi, N. 124
Vogel, E. 27

Wall Street Journal 95, 119
Wang Dan 87
Wei Jingsheng 87
Weidenbaum, M. 73
Wickman, K. 101
Wood, C. 72, 73
World Bank 6, 24, 28, 37, 38, 46, 52, 70, 100, 102, 103, 107, 163, 183, 193, 209, 213
World Trade Organization 92
See also WTO
WTO 60, 70, 91, 92, 93, 94, 128, 138, 208, 212, 214
See also World Trade Organization
Wyszomierski, T. vi, 187

xenophobia 44, 137, 140

Yahuda, M. 101
Young, A. 53, 54, 71

Zakaria, F. 123
zero-sum game viii, 109, 160, 165
Zhu Rongji 93

For Product Safety Concerns and Information please contact our EU
representative GPSR@taylorandfrancis.com Taylor & Francis Verlag GmbH,
Kaufingerstraße 24, 80331 München, Germany

Printed and bound by CPI Group (UK) Ltd, Croydon, CR0 4YY
08/05/2025
01864366-0007